CONTENTS

1 ARMS

frédéric delavier

STRENGTH TRAINING ANATOMY

SECOND EDITION

HUMAN KINETICS

For my father

Library of Congress Cataloging-in-Publication Data

Delavier, Frédéric.
  [Guide des mouvements de musculation. English]
  Strength training anatomy / Frédéric Delavier.-- 2nd ed.
    p. cm.
  ISBN 0-7360-6368-4 (soft cover)
  1. Muscles--Anatomy. 2. Weight training. 3. Muscle strength. I. Title.
  QM151.D454 2005
  612.7'6--dc22

                2005020894

ISBN-10 : 0-7360-6368-4
ISBN-13 : 978-0-7360-6368-5

This book is a revised edition of *Guide des Mouvements de Musculation*, published in 2006 by Éditions Vigot.

Acquisitions Editor: Martin Barnard; **Managing Editor:** Amanda M. Eastin; **Translator:** Robert H. Black R.M.T.; **Copyeditor:** Annette Pierce; **Graphic Designer:** Emma Brante; **Cover Designer:** Keith Blomberg; **Illustrator:** Frédéric Delavier; **Printer:** Pollina s.a., - n° L46864

Human Kinetics books are available at special discounts for bulk purchase. Special editions or book excerpts can also be created to specification. For details, contact the Special Sales Manager at Human Kinetics.

Printed in France   15   14   13   12

Human Kinetics
Web site: www.HumanKinetics.com

United States: Human Kinetics, P.O. Box 5076, Champaign, IL 61825-5076
800-747-4457
e-mail: humank@hkusa.com

Canada: Human Kinetics, 475 Devonshire Road, Unit 100, Windsor, ON N8Y 2L5
800-465-7301 (in Canada only)
e-mail: info@hkcanada.com

Europe: Human Kinetics, 107 Bradford Road, Stanningley
Leeds LS28 6AT, United Kingdom
+44 (0) 113 255 5665
e-mail: hk@hkeurope.com

Australia: Human Kinetics, 57A Price Avenue, Lower Mitcham, South Australia 5062
08 8372 0999
e-mail: info@hkaustralia.com

New Zealand: Human Kinetics, Division of Sports Distributors NZ Ltd.
P.O. Box 300 226 Albany, North Shore City, Auckland
0064 9 448 1207
e-mail: info@humankinetics.co.nz

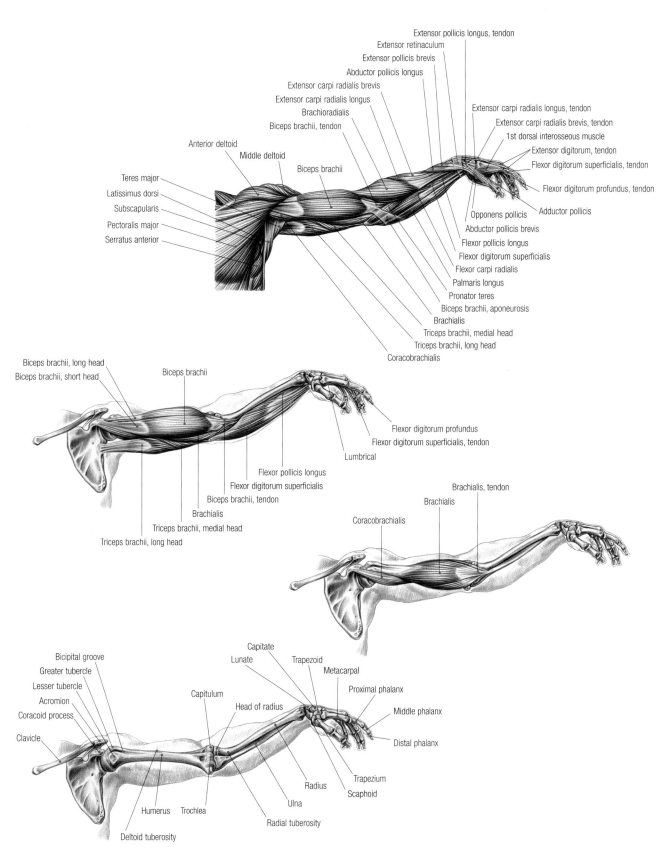

Extensor pollicis longus, tendon
Extensor retinaculum
Extensor pollicis brevis
Abductor pollicis longus
Extensor carpi radialis brevis
Extensor carpi radialis longus
Brachioradialis
Biceps brachii, tendon
Anterior deltoid
Middle deltoid
Biceps brachii
Teres major
Latissimus dorsi
Subscapularis
Pectoralis major
Serratus anterior

Extensor carpi radialis longus, tendon
Extensor carpi radialis brevis, tendon
1st dorsal interosseous muscle
Extensor digitorum, tendon
Flexor digitorum superficialis, tendon
Flexor digitorum profundus, tendon
Adductor pollicis
Opponens pollicis
Abductor pollicis brevis
Flexor pollicis longus
Flexor digitorum superficialis
Flexor carpi radialis
Palmaris longus
Pronator teres
Biceps brachii, aponeurosis
Brachialis
Triceps brachii, medial head
Triceps brachii, long head
Coracobrachialis

Biceps brachii, long head
Biceps brachii, short head
Biceps brachii

Flexor digitorum profundus
Flexor digitorum superficialis, tendon
Lumbrical

Flexor pollicis longus
Flexor digitorum superficialis
Biceps brachii, tendon
Brachialis
Triceps brachii, medial head
Triceps brachii, long head

Brachialis, tendon
Brachialis
Coracobrachialis

Capitate
Lunate
Trapezoid
Metacarpal
Proximal phalanx
Middle phalanx
Distal phalanx

Bicipital groove
Greater tubercle
Lesser tubercle
Acromion
Coracoid process
Clavicle
Capitulum
Head of radius

Trapezium
Scaphoid
Radius
Ulna
Radial tuberosity
Humerus
Trochlea
Deltoid tuberosity

1 CURLS

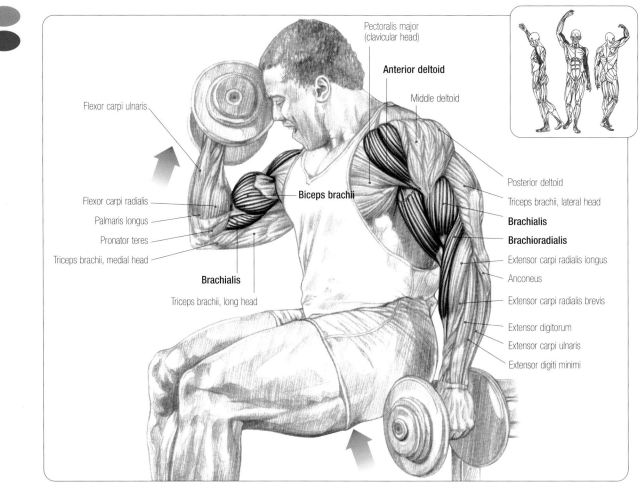

Pectoralis major
(clavicular head)

Anterior deltoid

Middle deltoid

Flexor carpi ulnaris

Posterior deltoid

Triceps brachii, lateral head

Brachialis

Brachioradialis

Biceps brachii

Flexor carpi radialis

Palmaris longus

Pronator teres

Triceps brachii, medial head

Extensor carpi radialis longus

Anconeus

Extensor carpi radialis brevis

Brachialis

Triceps brachii, long head

Extensor digitorum

Extensor carpi ulnaris

Extensor digiti minimi

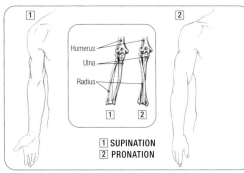

Humerus

Ulna

Radius

1 SUPINATION
2 PRONATION

Sit holding a dumbbell in each hand with arms hanging down and the palms of the hands facing the body:
- Inhale and bend the the elbow, rotating the palm up before the forearm reaches horizontal.
- Continue by raising the elbows at the end of the movement.

This exercise primarily uses the brachioradialis (long supinator), brachialis, biceps brachii, and anterior deltoid and, to a lesser extent, the coracobrachialis and clavicular head of the pectoralis major.

COMMENT: This exercise takes the biceps through its complete range of motion, which includes flexion, protraction, and supination.

THREE WAYS TO EXECUTE CURLS
1 EMPHASIZE BICEPS
2 WORK BRACHIORADIALIS INTENSELY
3 WORK MAINLY BICEPS AND BRACHIALIS

CONCENTRATION CURLS　2

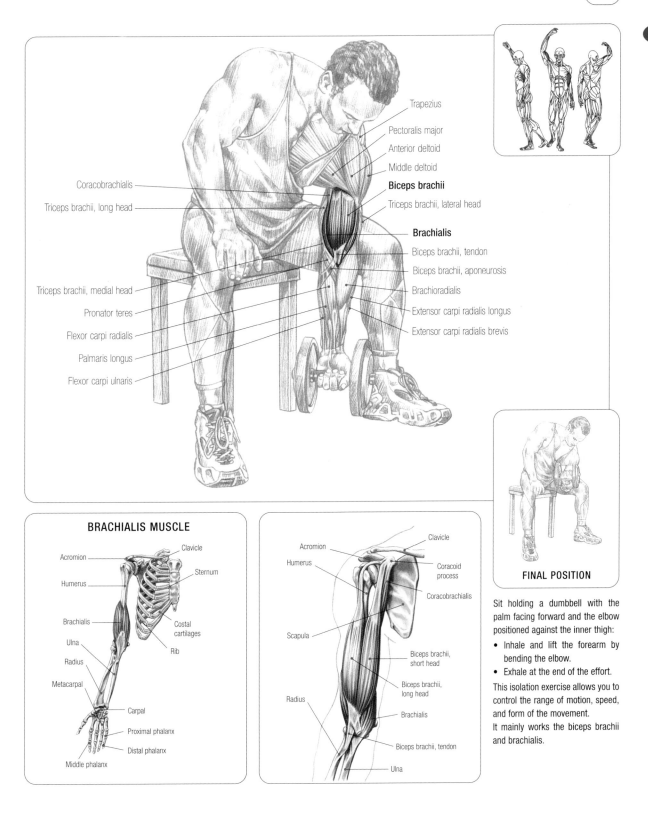

Coracobrachialis

Triceps brachii, long head

Triceps brachii, medial head

Pronator teres

Flexor carpi radialis

Palmaris longus

Flexor carpi ulnaris

Trapezius

Pectoralis major

Anterior deltoid

Middle deltoid

Biceps brachii

Triceps brachii, lateral head

Brachialis

Biceps brachii, tendon

Biceps brachii, aponeurosis

Brachioradialis

Extensor carpi radialis longus

Extensor carpi radialis brevis

BRACHIALIS MUSCLE

Acromion

Humerus

Brachialis

Ulna

Radius

Metacarpal

Clavicle

Sternum

Costal cartilages

Rib

Carpal

Proximal phalanx

Distal phalanx

Middle phalanx

Acromion

Humerus

Scapula

Radius

Clavicle

Coracoid process

Coracobrachialis

Biceps brachii, short head

Biceps brachii, long head

Brachialis

Biceps brachii, tendon

Ulna

FINAL POSITION

Sit holding a dumbbell with the palm facing forward and the elbow positioned against the inner thigh:

- Inhale and lift the forearm by bending the elbow.
- Exhale at the end of the effort.

This isolation exercise allows you to control the range of motion, speed, and form of the movement.

It mainly works the biceps brachii and brachialis.

3 | HAMMER CURLS

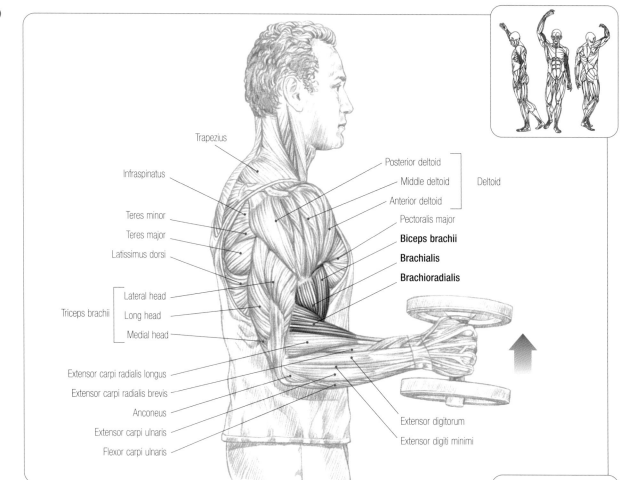

Trapezius

Infraspinatus

Teres minor

Teres major

Latissimus dorsi

Triceps brachii
- Lateral head
- Long head
- Medial head

Extensor carpi radialis longus

Extensor carpi radialis brevis

Anconeus

Extensor carpi ulnaris

Flexor carpi ulnaris

Posterior deltoid

Middle deltoid

Anterior deltoid

Deltoid

Pectoralis major

Biceps brachii

Brachialis

Brachioradialis

Extensor digitorum

Extensor digiti minimi

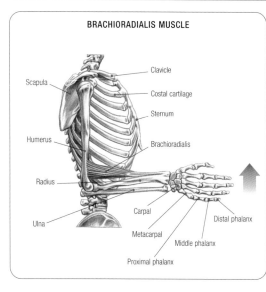

BRACHIORADIALIS MUSCLE

Clavicle

Scapula

Costal cartilage

Sternum

Humerus

Brachioradialis

Radius

Ulna

Carpal

Metacarpal

Distal phalanx

Middle phalanx

Proximal phalanx

Stand or sit gripping a dumbbell in each hand with the palms facing each other:

- Inhale and raise the forearms together or alternately.
- Exhale at the end of the movement.

This is the best exercise for developing the brachioradialis.

It also develops the biceps brachii, brachialis, and, to a lesser degree, the extensor carpi radialis brevis and longus.

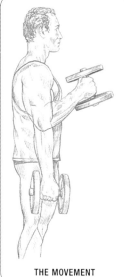

THE MOVEMENT

8

LOW-PULLEY CURLS $\boxed{4}$

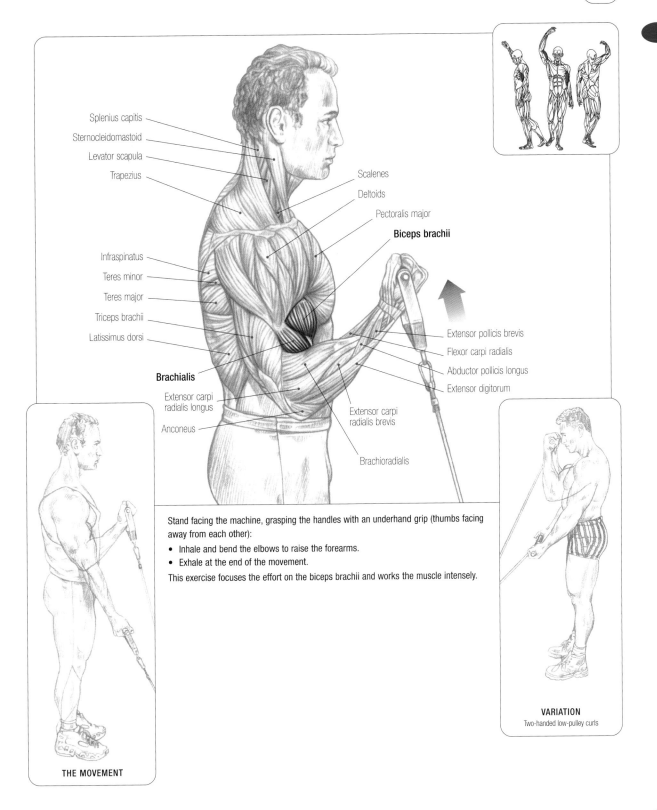

Splenius capitis
Sternocleidomastoid
Levator scapula
Trapezius
Scalenes
Deltoids
Pectoralis major
Biceps brachii
Infraspinatus
Teres minor
Teres major
Triceps brachii
Latissimus dorsi
Extensor pollicis brevis
Flexor carpi radialis
Abductor pollicis longus
Extensor digitorum
Brachialis
Extensor carpi radialis longus
Anconeus
Extensor carpi radialis brevis
Brachioradialis

Stand facing the machine, grasping the handles with an underhand grip (thumbs facing away from each other):

- Inhale and bend the elbows to raise the forearms.
- Exhale at the end of the movement.

This exercise focuses the effort on the biceps brachii and works the muscle intensely.

VARIATION
Two-handed low-pulley curls

THE MOVEMENT

5 HIGH-PULLEY CURLS

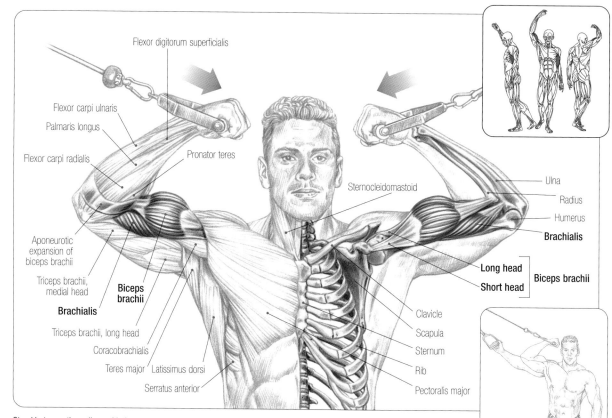

Stand between the pulleys with the arms outstretched in a "cross" and grasp the handles of the high pulleys with an underhand grip:

• Inhale and bend the elbows to bring the hands toward the body. Exhale at the end of the movement.

This exercise, which is most often performed as a cool-down at the end of an arm session, focuses the work on the short head of the biceps brachii, which has been stretched and put under tension in the "cross" start-up position.

This exercise also contracts the monoarticular brachialis elbow flexor.

Perform this exercise with light weights so that you can concentrate and feel the contraction at the inside of the biceps brachii. Sets of high reps provide the best results.

VARIATION
One-handed execution

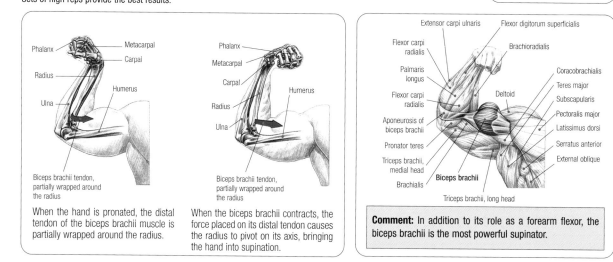

When the hand is pronated, the distal tendon of the biceps brachii muscle is partially wrapped around the radius.

When the biceps brachii contracts, the force placed on its distal tendon causes the radius to pivot on its axis, bringing the hand into supination.

Comment: In addition to its role as a forearm flexor, the biceps brachii is the most powerful supinator.

BARBELL CURLS 6

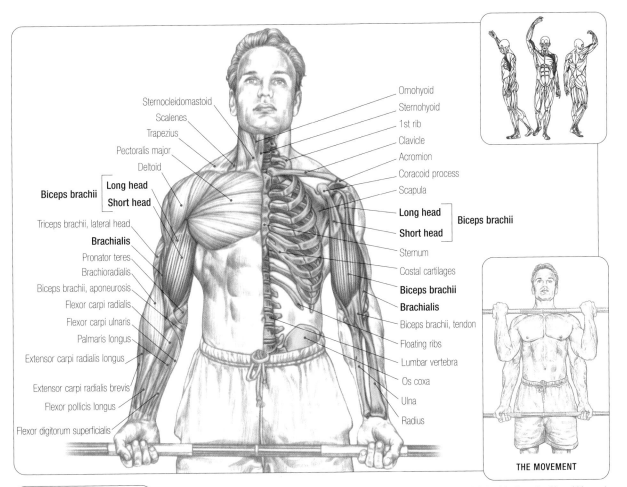

Sternocleidomastoid
Scalenes
Trapezius
Pectoralis major
Deltoid
Biceps brachii { Long head / Short head }
Triceps brachii, lateral head
Brachialis
Pronator teres
Brachioradialis
Biceps brachii, aponeurosis
Flexor carpi radialis
Flexor carpi ulnaris
Palmaris longus
Extensor carpi radialis longus
Extensor carpi radialis brevis
Flexor pollicis longus
Flexor digitorum superficialis

Omohyoid
Sternohyoid
1st rib
Clavicle
Acromion
Coracoid process
Scapula
Long head / **Short head** } Biceps brachii
Sternum
Costal cartilages
Biceps brachii
Brachialis
Biceps brachii, tendon
Floating ribs
Lumbar vertebra
Os coxa
Ulna
Radius

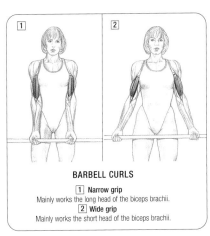

THE MOVEMENT

BRACHIALIS MUSCLE

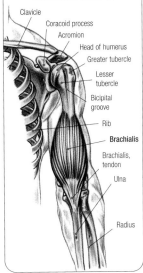

Clavicle
Coracoid process
Acromion
Head of humerus
Greater tubercle
Lesser tubercle
Bicipital groove
Rib
Brachialis
Brachialis, tendon
Ulna
Radius

Stand with the back straight, grasping the barbell with an underhand grip and hands slightly wider than shoulder-width apart:

- Inhale and raise the barbell by bending the elbows, taking care to stabilize the torso and spine by isometrically contracting the gluteal muscles, abdominal muscles, and spinal muscles.
- Exhale at the end of the movement.

This exercise mainly contracts the biceps brachii, brachialis, and, to a lesser degree, the brachioradialis, pronator teres, and the wrist flexor group.

Variations: Vary the width of the grip to work different parts of the muscle more intensely:

- Placing the hands farther apart isolates the short head of the biceps brachii.
- Placing the hands closer together isolates the long head of the biceps brachii.

Raising both elbows after they are flexed increases the contraction of the biceps brachii and contracts the anterior deltoid.

To make the exercise more difficult, perform the movement with the back against a wall so that the shoulder blades don't move.

You can lift more weight and gain strength by leaning the torso back while lifting the bar; however, to prevent injury, this requires good technique and well-developed abdominal and lumbar muscles.

BARBELL CURLS
1 Narrow grip
Mainly works the long head of the biceps brachii.
2 Wide grip
Mainly works the short head of the biceps brachii.

ELBOW STRUCTURE AND ITS EFFECT ON TRAINING

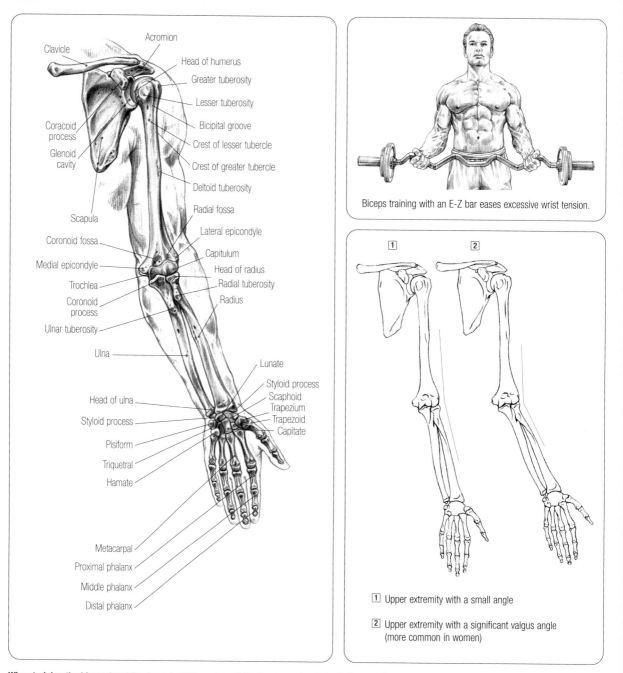

Clavicle
Acromion
Head of humerus
Greater tuberosity
Lesser tuberosity
Bicipital groove
Crest of lesser tubercle
Crest of greater tubercle
Deltoid tuberosity
Radial fossa
Lateral epicondyle
Capitulum
Head of radius
Radial tuberosity
Radius
Coracoid process
Glenoid cavity
Scapula
Coronoid fossa
Medial epicondyle
Trochlea
Coronoid process
Ulnar tuberosity
Ulna
Lunate
Styloid process
Scaphoid
Trapezium
Trapezoid
Capitate
Head of ulna
Styloid process
Pisiform
Triquetral
Hamate
Metacarpal
Proximal phalanx
Middle phalanx
Distal phalanx

Biceps training with an E-Z bar eases excessive wrist tension.

1   2

1 Upper extremity with a small angle

2 Upper extremity with a significant valgus angle (more common in women)

When training the biceps brachii using a barbell, take into account variations in each person's physical structure.

In the anatomical position (arms hanging alongside the body, palms facing forward, and thumbs pointing laterally), the angle at the elbow between the upper arm and the forearm varies from person to person. Someone whose forearm hangs distinctly away from the body in a valgus position must break excessively at the wrist when performing a curl with a straight bar, which is painful. Therefore, these people should work with an E-Z bar to spare their wrists.

Comment: Valgus of the elbow is usually more pronounced in women.

MACHINE CURLS 7

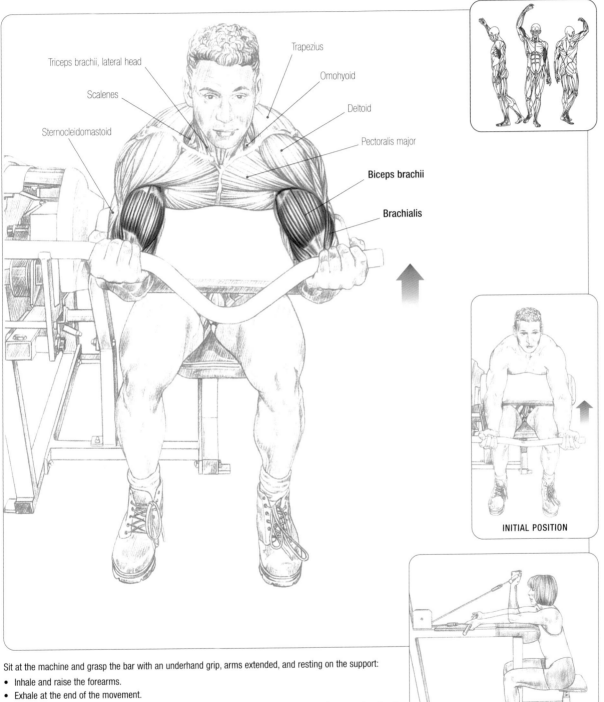

Triceps brachii, lateral head

Trapezius

Scalenes

Omohyoid

Sternocleidomastoid

Deltoid

Pectoralis major

Biceps brachii

Brachialis

INITIAL POSITION

Performing the curl with an Atlas pulley
is a great way to pump up the muscle.

Sit at the machine and grasp the bar with an underhand grip, arms extended, and resting on the support:

- Inhale and raise the forearms.
- Exhale at the end of the movement.

This is one of the best exercises for working the biceps brachii. Fixing the arms against the support makes it impossible to "cheat."

At the beginning, the muscle tension is intense, so be sure to warm up properly using light weights. To avoid the risk of tendonitis, do not completely extend the arm.

This movement also works the brachialis and, to a lesser extent, the brachioradialis and pronator teres.

8 PREACHER CURLS

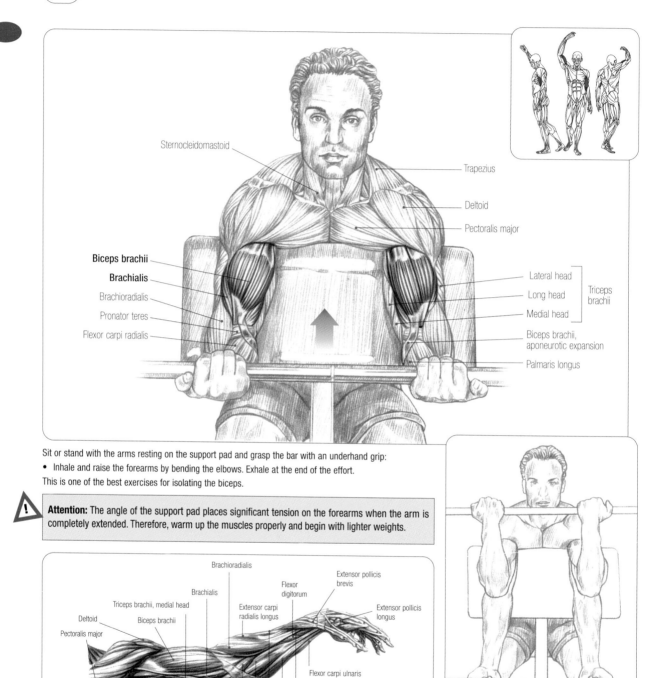

Sit or stand with the arms resting on the support pad and grasp the bar with an underhand grip:

- Inhale and raise the forearms by bending the elbows. Exhale at the end of the effort.

This is one of the best exercises for isolating the biceps.

Attention: The angle of the support pad places significant tension on the forearms when the arm is completely extended. Therefore, warm up the muscles properly and begin with lighter weights.

THE MOVEMENT

REVERSE CURLS 9

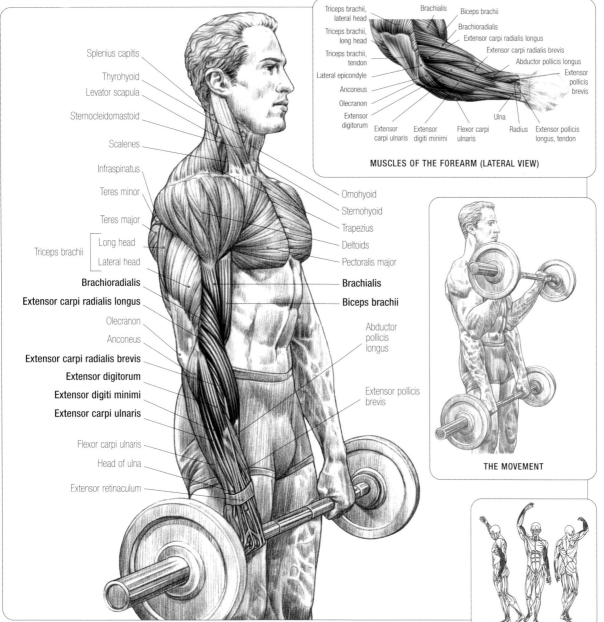

Triceps brachii, lateral head
Triceps brachii, long head
Triceps brachii, tendon
Lateral epicondyle
Anconeus
Olecranon
Extensor digitorum
Extensor carpi ulnaris
Extensor digiti minimi
Flexor carpi ulnaris
Ulna
Radius
Brachialis
Biceps brachii
Brachioradialis
Extensor carpi radialis longus
Extensor carpi radialis brevis
Abductor pollicis longus
Extensor pollicis brevis
Extensor pollicis longus, tendon

MUSCLES OF THE FOREARM (LATERAL VIEW)

Splenius capitis
Thyrohyoid
Levator scapula
Sternocleidomastoid
Scalenes
Infraspinatus
Teres minor
Teres major
Triceps brachii
Long head
Lateral head
Brachioradialis
Extensor carpi radialis longus
Olecranon
Anconeus
Extensor carpi radialis brevis
Extensor digitorum
Extensor digiti minimi
Extensor carpi ulnaris
Flexor carpi ulnaris
Head of ulna
Extensor retinaculum

Omohyoid
Sternohyoid
Trapezius
Deltoids
Pectoralis major
Brachialis
Biceps brachii
Abductor pollicis longus
Extensor pollicis brevis

THE MOVEMENT

Stand with the legs slightly apart and arms extended and grasp the bar with an overhand grip (with the thumbs facing each other):

• Inhale and raise the forearms by bending the elbows.

• Exhale at the end of the movement.

This exercise works the extensor muscles of the wrist: extensor carpi radialis longus, extensor carpi radialis brevis, extensor digitorum, extensor digiti minimi, and extensor carpi ulnaris.

It also acts on the brachioradialis, brachialis, and, to a lesser degree, the biceps brachii.

Comment: This is an excellent exercise for strengthening the wrist, which is often weak because of an imbalance caused by using the wrist flexors rather than the wrist extensors. For this reason, many boxers include it in their training. Many bench press champions use it to keep their wrists from trembling under extreme weights.

10 REVERSE WRIST CURLS

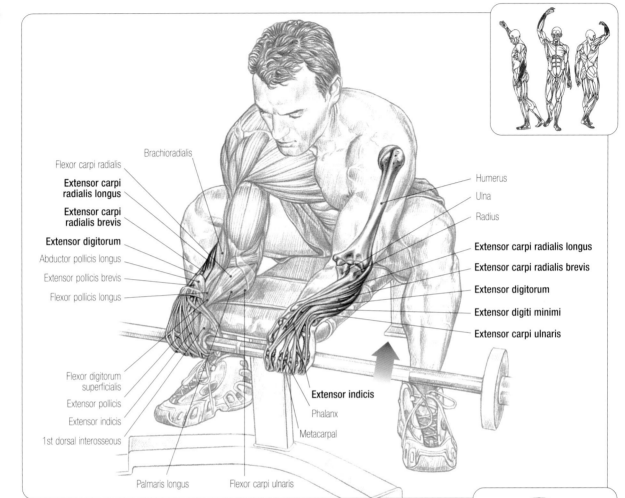

Brachioradialis
Flexor carpi radialis
Extensor carpi radialis longus
Extensor carpi radialis brevis
Extensor digitorum
Abductor pollicis longus
Extensor pollicis brevis
Flexor pollicis longus

Flexor digitorum superficialis
Extensor pollicis
Extensor indicis
1st dorsal interosseous

Palmaris longus
Flexor carpi ulnaris

Humerus
Ulna
Radius
Extensor carpi radialis longus
Extensor carpi radialis brevis
Extensor digitorum
Extensor digiti minimi
Extensor carpi ulnaris

Extensor indicis
Phalanx
Metacarpal

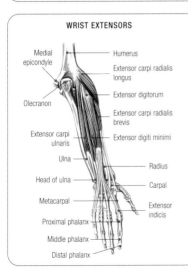

WRIST EXTENSORS

Medial epicondyle
Humerus
Extensor carpi radialis longus
Extensor digitorum
Olecranon
Extensor carpi radialis brevis
Extensor carpi ulnaris
Extensor digiti minimi
Ulna
Radius
Head of ulna
Carpal
Metacarpal
Extensor indicis
Proximal phalanx
Middle phalanx
Distal phalanx

Sit with the forearms resting on the thighs or on a bench and grasp the bar with an overhand grip and keep the wrists relaxed:

• Raise the hands by extending at the wrists.

This exercise contracts the extensor carpi radialis longus and brevis, extensor digitorum, extensor digiti minimi, as well as the extensor carpi ulnaris.

Comment: This exercise strengthens the wrists, which are often vulnerable because of weak wrist extensors.

FINAL POSITION

WRIST CURLS 11

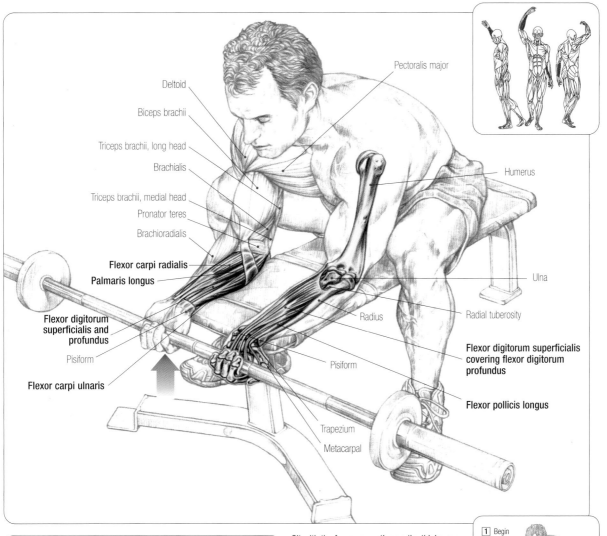

- Pectoralis major
- Deltoid
- Biceps brachii
- Triceps brachii, long head
- Brachialis
- Triceps brachii, medial head
- Pronator teres
- Brachioradialis
- **Flexor carpi radialis**
- **Palmaris longus**
- **Flexor digitorum superficialis and profundus**
- Pisiform
- **Flexor carpi ulnaris**
- Humerus
- Ulna
- Radial tuberosity
- Radius
- Pisiform
- Flexor digitorum superficialis covering flexor digitorum profundus
- Flexor pollicis longus
- Trapezium
- Metacarpal

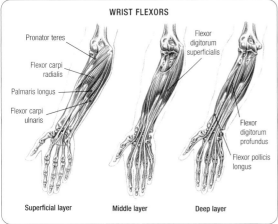

WRIST FLEXORS

- Pronator teres
- Flexor carpi radialis
- Palmaris longus
- Flexor carpi ulnaris
- Flexor digitorum superficialis
- Flexor digitorum profundus
- Flexor pollicis longus

Superficial layer   Middle layer   Deep layer

Sit with the forearms resting on the thighs or on a bench and grasp the bar with an underhand grip with wrists relaxed:

- Inhale and raise the hands by flexing at the wrists.

This exercise contracts the flexor carpi radialis, palmaris longus, flexor carpi ulnaris, and the flexors digitorum superficialis and profundus.

The latter two muscles, although located deep in the wrist, make up most of the muscle mass of the wrist flexors.

1 Begin

2 End

THE MOVEMENT

12 PUSH-DOWNS

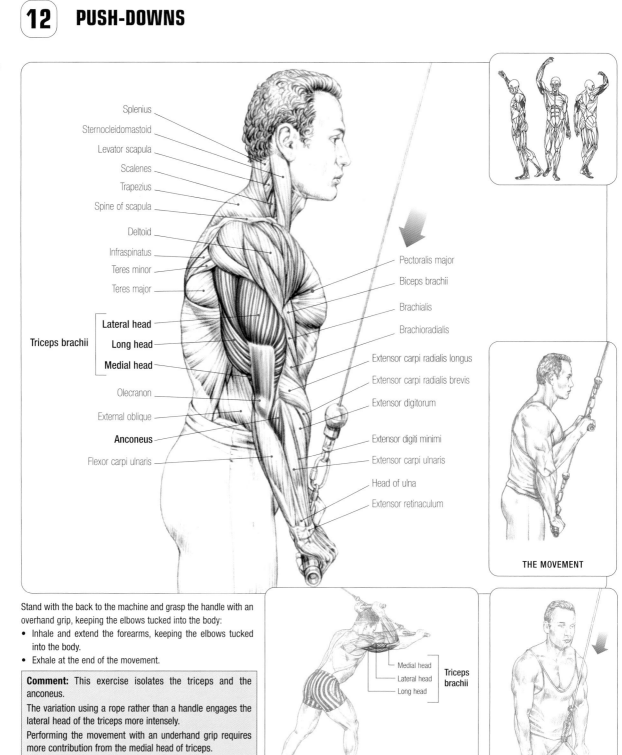

Splenius
Sternocleidomastoid
Levator scapula
Scalenes
Trapezius
Spine of scapula
Deltoid
Infraspinatus
Teres minor
Teres major

Triceps brachii
Lateral head
Long head
Medial head

Olecranon
External oblique
Anconeus
Flexor carpi ulnaris

Pectoralis major
Biceps brachii
Brachialis
Brachioradialis
Extensor carpi radialis longus
Extensor carpi radialis brevis
Extensor digitorum
Extensor digiti minimi
Extensor carpi ulnaris
Head of ulna
Extensor retinaculum

THE MOVEMENT

Stand with the back to the machine and grasp the handle with an overhand grip, keeping the elbows tucked into the body:

• Inhale and extend the forearms, keeping the elbows tucked into the body.

• Exhale at the end of the movement.

Comment: This exercise isolates the triceps and the anconeus.

The variation using a rope rather than a handle engages the lateral head of the triceps more intensely.

Performing the movement with an underhand grip requires more contribution from the medial head of triceps.

Hold an isometric contraction for one or two seconds at the end of the movement to feel the effort more intensely.

When using heavy weights, lean forward with the torso.

Beginners can use this exercise to develop enough strength to move on to more difficult exercises.

Medial head
Lateral head
Long head
Triceps brachii

VARIATION WITH BACK TO THE MACHINE
To isolate of the long head of the triceps.

VARIATION WITH A ROPE
To isolate the lateral head of the triceps

REVERSE PUSH-DOWNS 13

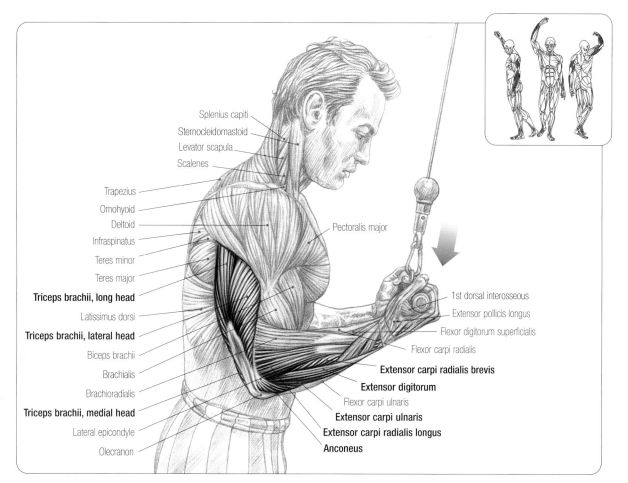

- Splenius capiti
- Sternocleidomastoid
- Levator scapula
- Scalenes
- Trapezius
- Omohyoid
- Deltoid
- Infraspinatus
- Teres minor
- Teres major
- **Triceps brachii, long head**
- Latissimus dorsi
- **Triceps brachii, lateral head**
- Biceps brachii
- Brachialis
- Brachioradialis
- **Triceps brachii, medial head**
- Lateral epicondyle
- Olecranon

- Pectoralis major
- 1st dorsal interosseous
- Extensor pollicis longus
- Flexor digitorum superficialis
- Flexor carpi radialis
- **Extensor carpi radialis brevis**
- **Extensor digitorum**
- Flexor carpi ulnaris
- **Extensor carpi ulnaris**
- **Extensor carpi radialis longus**
- **Anconeus**

Stand facing the machine with the arms next the body and elbows bent and grasp the handle with an underhand grip:

- Inhale and extend the forearms by straightening the elbows, keeping them tucked into the body.
- Exhale at the end of the movement.

The underhand grip isolates the medial head of the triceps brachii and precludes working with heavy weights.

When extending the forearms, the anconeus and wrist extensors also contract.

The extensor carpi ulnaris, extensor digitorum, extensor digiti minimi, and extensors carpi radialis longus and brevis keep the wrist straight with isometric contraction during the exercise.

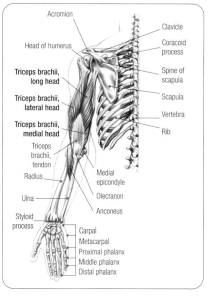

- Acromion
- Clavicle
- Coracoid process
- Head of humerus
- Spine of scapula
- **Triceps brachii, long head**
- Scapula
- **Triceps brachii, lateral head**
- Vertebra
- **Triceps brachii, medial head**
- Rib
- Triceps brachii, tendon
- Medial epicondyle
- Radius
- Olecranon
- Ulna
- Anconeus
- Styloid process
- Carpal
- Metacarpal
- Proximal phalanx
- Middle phalanx
- Distal phalanx

14 ONE-ARM REVERSE PUSH-DOWNS

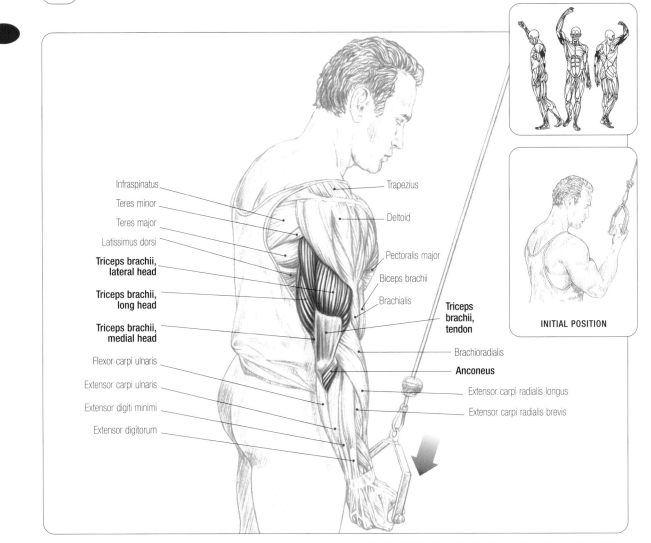

Infraspinatus

Teres minor

Teres major

Latissimus dorsi

Triceps brachii, lateral head

Triceps brachii, long head

Triceps brachii, medial head

Flexor carpi ulnaris

Extensor carpi ulnaris

Extensor digiti minimi

Extensor digitorum

Trapezius

Deltoid

Pectoralis major

Biceps brachii

Brachialis

Triceps brachii, tendon

Brachioradialis

Anconeus

Extensor carpi radialis longus

Extensor carpi radialis brevis

INITIAL POSITION

Stand facing the machine and grasp the handle with an underhand grip:

- Inhale and extend the forearm.
- Exhale at the end of the movement.

This exercise mainly works the lateral head of the triceps.

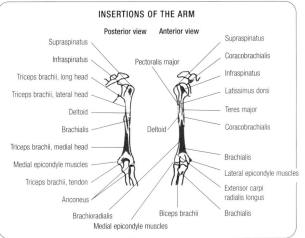

INSERTIONS OF THE ARM

Posterior view | Anterior view

Supraspinatus

Infraspinatus

Triceps brachii, long head

Triceps brachii, lateral head

Deltoid

Brachialis

Triceps brachii, medial head

Medial epicondyle muscles

Triceps brachii, tendon

Anconeus

Brachioradialis

Pectoralis major

Deltoid

Medial epicondyle muscles

Biceps brachii

Supraspinatus

Coracobrachialis

Infraspinatus

Latissimus dorsi

Teres major

Coracobrachialis

Brachialis

Lateral epicondyle muscles

Extensor carpi radialis longus

Brachialis

TRICEPS EXTENSIONS

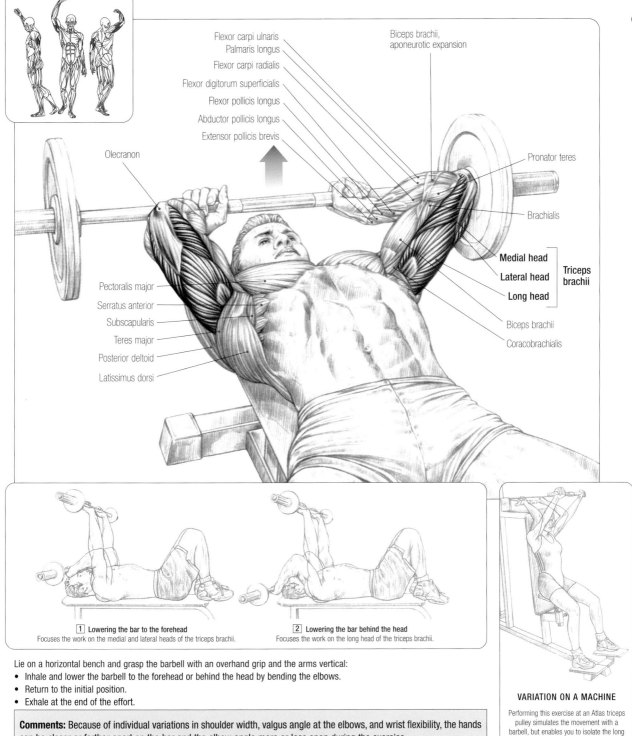

Flexor carpi ulnaris
Palmaris longus
Flexor carpi radialis
Flexor digitorum superficialis
Flexor pollicis longus
Abductor pollicis longus
Extensor pollicis brevis

Biceps brachii, aponeurotic expansion

Olecranon

Pronator teres

Brachialis

Medial head
Lateral head   Triceps brachii
Long head

Biceps brachii
Coracobrachialis

Pectoralis major
Serratus anterior
Subscapularis
Teres major
Posterior deltoid
Latissimus dorsi

1 Lowering the bar to the forehead
Focuses the work on the medial and lateral heads of the triceps brachii.

2 Lowering the bar behind the head
Focuses the work on the long head of the triceps brachii.

Lie on a horizontal bench and grasp the barbell with an overhand grip and the arms vertical:
- Inhale and lower the barbell to the forehead or behind the head by bending the elbows.
- Return to the initial position.
- Exhale at the end of the effort.

VARIATION ON A MACHINE

Performing this exercise at an Atlas triceps pulley simulates the movement with a barbell, but enables you to isolate the long head of the triceps brachii.

Comments: Because of individual variations in shoulder width, valgus angle at the elbows, and wrist flexibility, the hands can be closer or farther apart on the bar and the elbow angle more or less open during the exercise.
Using an E-Z bar helps prevent excessive strain at the wrists.

16 DUMBBELL TRICEPS EXTENSIONS

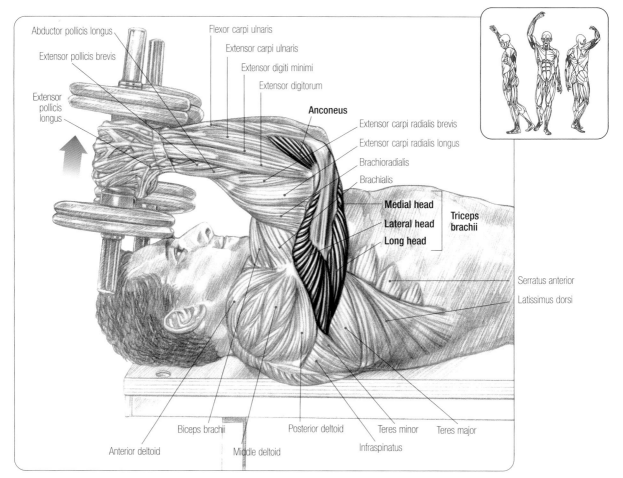

Abductor pollicis longus

Extensor pollicis brevis

Extensor pollicis longus

Flexor carpi ulnaris

Extensor carpi ulnaris

Extensor digiti minimi

Extensor digitorum

Anconeus

Extensor carpi radialis brevis

Extensor carpi radialis longus

Brachioradialis

Brachialis

Medial head

Lateral head   Triceps brachii

Long head

Serratus anterior

Latissimus dorsi

Biceps brachii

Anterior deltoid

Middle deltoid

Posterior deltoid

Infraspinatus

Teres minor

Teres major

Lie on a flat bench and grasp a dumbbell in each hand with the arms vertical:

- Inhale and lower the forearms by bending the elbow with a controlled movement.
- Return to the initial position.
- Exhale at the end of the effort.

This exercise works all three heads of the triceps brachii equally.

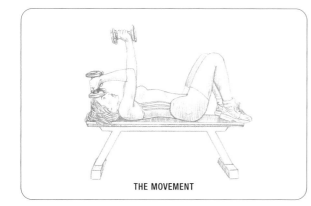

THE MOVEMENT

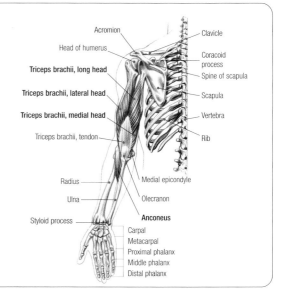

Acromion

Head of humerus

Triceps brachii, long head

Triceps brachii, lateral head

Triceps brachii, medial head

Triceps brachii, tendon

Radius

Ulna

Styloid process

Clavicle

Coracoid process

Spine of scapula

Scapula

Vertebra

Rib

Medial epicondyle

Olecranon

Anconeus

Carpal
Metacarpal
Proximal phalanx
Middle phalanx
Distal phalanx

ONE-ARM DUMBBELL TRICEPS EXTENSIONS 17

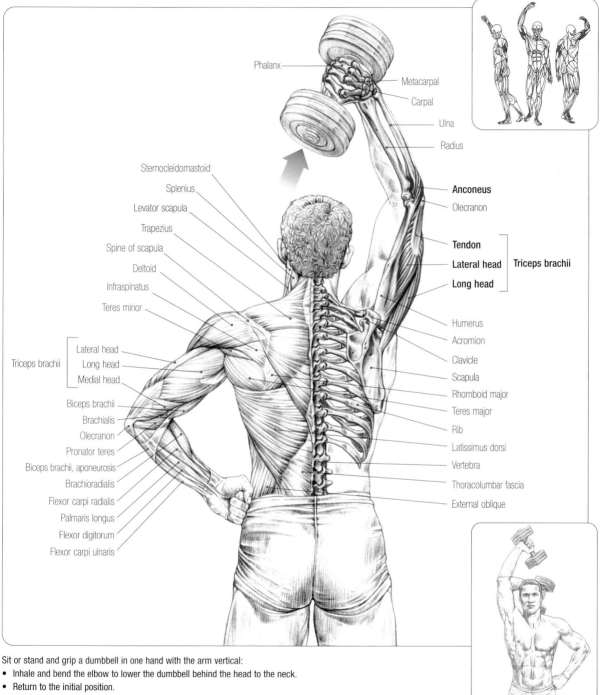

Phalanx
Metacarpal
Carpal
Ulna
Radius

Sternocleidomastoid
Splenius
Levator scapula
Trapezius
Spine of scapula
Deltoid
Infraspinatus
Teres minor

Anconeus
Olecranon

Tendon
Lateral head } Triceps brachii
Long head

Humerus
Acromion
Clavicle
Scapula
Rhomboid major
Teres major
Rib
Latissimus dorsi
Vertebra
Thoracolumbar fascia
External oblique

Triceps brachii {
Lateral head
Long head
Medial head

Biceps brachii
Brachialis
Olecranon
Pronator teres
Biceps brachii, aponeurosis
Brachioradialis
Flexor carpi radialis
Palmaris longus
Flexor digitorum
Flexor carpi ulnaris

Sit or stand and grip a dumbbell in one hand with the arm vertical:
- Inhale and bend the elbow to lower the dumbbell behind the head to the neck.
- Return to the initial position.
- Exhale at the end of the movement.

The vertical position of the arm stretches the long head of the triceps brachii, emphasizing its contraction while working.

Comment: Contract the abdominal core to prevent arching the low back. If possible use a bench with support for the low back.

THE MOVEMENT

18 SEATED DUMBBELL TRICEPS EXTENSIONS

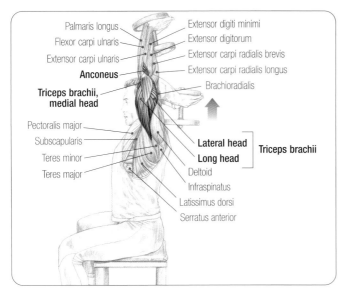

Palmaris longus
Flexor carpi ulnaris
Extensor carpi ulnaris
Anconeus
Triceps brachii, medial head
Pectoralis major
Subscapularis
Teres minor
Teres major

Extensor digiti minimi
Extensor digitorum
Extensor carpi radialis brevis
Extensor carpi radialis longus
Brachioradialis

Lateral head
Long head
Deltoid
Infraspinatus
Latissimus dorsi
Serratus anterior

} **Triceps brachii**

Sit and grasp a dumbbell, holding it behind the neck:

- Inhale, and extend the forearm.
- Exhale at the end of the movement.

The vertical position of the arm strongly stretches the long head of the triceps brachii, emphasizing its contraction while working.

Contract the abdominal core to prevent arching the low back. If possible use a bench with support for the low back.

19 SEATED E-Z BAR TRICEPS EXTENSIONS

Sit or stand and grasp an E-Z bar with an overhand grip and arms vertical:

- Inhale and bend the elbows to lower the bar behind the head.
- Return to the initial position.
- Exhale at the end of the extension.

The vertical position of the arms strongly stretches the long head of the triceps brachii, emphasizing its contraction while working.

An overhand grip isolates the lateral head of the triceps brachii.

Contract the abdominal muscles and avoid arching the low back. If possible use a bench with support for the low back.

THE MOVEMENT

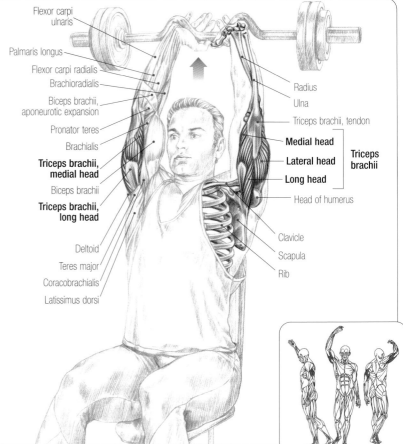

Flexor carpi ulnaris
Palmaris longus
Flexor carpi radialis
Brachioradialis
Biceps brachii, aponeurotic expansion
Pronator teres
Brachialis
Triceps brachii, medial head
Biceps brachii
Triceps brachii, long head
Deltoid
Teres major
Coracobrachialis
Latissimus dorsi

Radius
Ulna
Triceps brachii, tendon
Medial head
Lateral head
Long head
Head of humerus
Clavicle
Scapula
Rib

} **Triceps brachii**

TRICEPS KICKBACKS 20

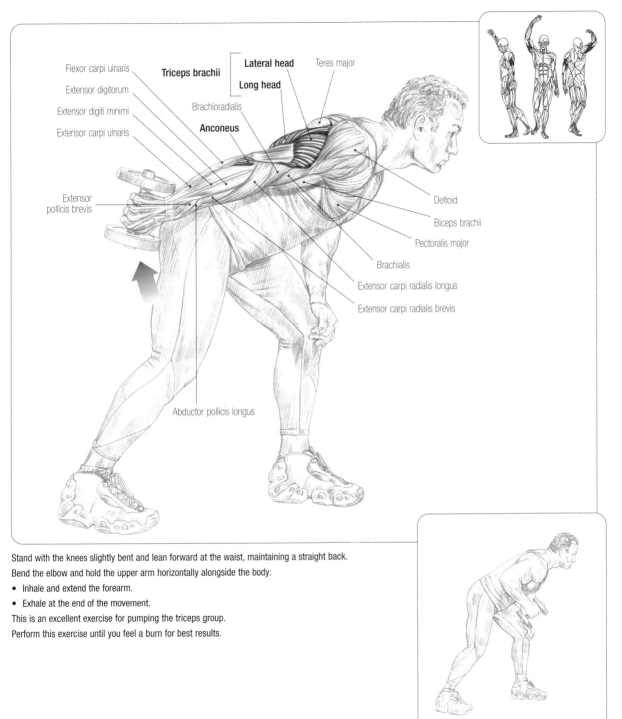

Flexor carpi ulnaris

Extensor digitorum

Extensor digiti minimi

Extensor carpi ulnaris

Triceps brachii

Brachioradialis

Anconeus

Lateral head

Long head

Teres major

Extensor
pollicis brevis

Deltoid

Biceps brachii

Pectoralis major

Brachialis

Extensor carpi radialis longus

Extensor carpi radialis brevis

Abductor pollicis longus

Stand with the knees slightly bent and lean forward at the waist, maintaining a straight back.

Bend the elbow and hold the upper arm horizontally alongside the body:

- Inhale and extend the forearm.
- Exhale at the end of the movement.

This is an excellent exercise for pumping the triceps group.

Perform this exercise until you feel a burn for best results.

INITIAL POSITION

21 TRICEPS DIPS

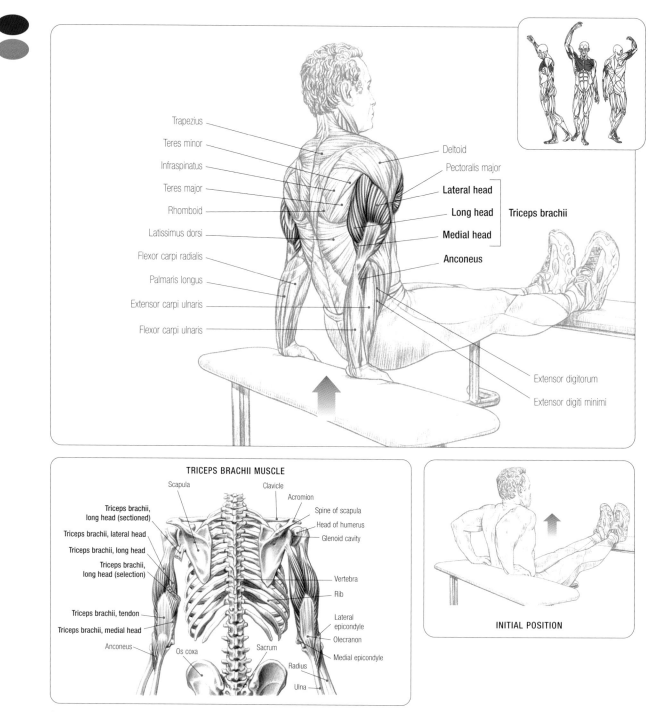

Trapezius
Teres minor
Infraspinatus
Teres major
Rhomboid
Latissimus dorsi
Flexor carpi radialis
Palmaris longus
Extensor carpi ulnaris
Flexor carpi ulnaris

Deltoid
Pectoralis major
Lateral head
Long head — Triceps brachii
Medial head
Anconeus
Extensor digitorum
Extensor digiti minimi

TRICEPS BRACHII MUSCLE

Scapula
Clavicle
Acromion
Triceps brachii, long head (sectioned)
Spine of scapula
Triceps brachii, lateral head
Head of humerus
Triceps brachii, long head
Glenoid cavity
Triceps brachii, long head (selection)
Vertebra
Rib
Triceps brachii, tendon
Lateral epicondyle
Triceps brachii, medial head
Olecranon
Anconeus
Os coxa
Sacrum
Medial epicondyle
Radius
Ulna

INITIAL POSITION

Suspend the body between two benches by placing the hands on the edge of one bench and the feet on the edge of the other bench:

- Inhale, then dip by bending the elbows and rise by extending the forearms.
- Exhale at the end of the movement.

This exercise works the triceps and pectorals as well as the anterior deltoid.

Resting weights on top of the thighs increases the difficulty and intensity of the dip.

2 SHOULDERS

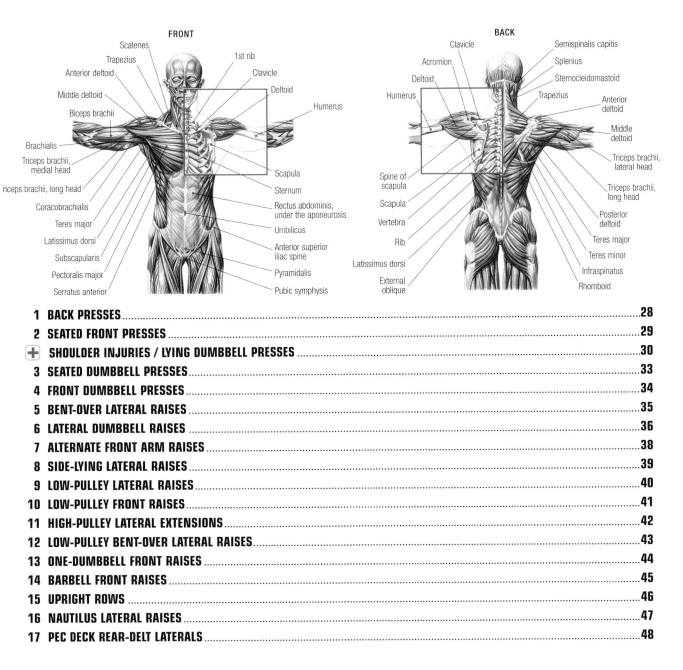

FRONT

Scalenes
Trapezius
Anterior deltoid
Middle deltoid
Biceps brachii
Brachialis
Triceps brachii, medial head
Triceps brachii, long head
Coracobrachialis
Teres major
Latissimus dorsi
Subscapularis
Pectoralis major
Serratus anterior

1st rib
Clavicle
Deltoid
Humerus
Scapula
Sternum
Rectus abdominis, under the aponeurosis
Umbilicus
Anterior superior iliac spine
Pyramidalis
Pubic symphysis

BACK

Clavicle
Acromion
Deltoid
Humerus
Spine of scapula
Scapula
Vertebra
Rib
Latissimus dorsi
External oblique

Semispinalis capitis
Splenius
Sternocleidomastoid
Trapezius
Anterior deltoid
Middle deltoid
Triceps brachii, lateral head
Triceps brachii, long head
Posterior deltoid
Teres major
Teres minor
Infraspinatus
Rhomboid

1 BACK PRESSES

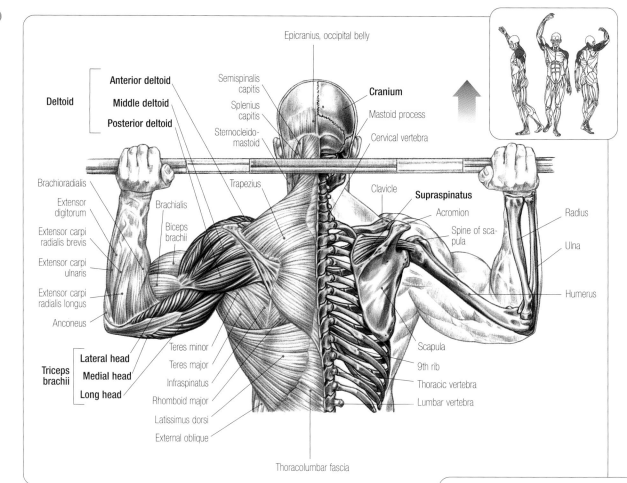

Epicranius, occipital belly

Deltoid
Anterior deltoid
Middle deltoid
Posterior deltoid

Semispinalis capitis
Splenius capitis
Sternocleido-mastoid

Cranium
Mastoid process
Cervical vertebra

Brachioradialis
Extensor digitorum
Extensor carpi radialis brevis
Extensor carpi ulnaris
Extensor carpi radialis longus
Anconeus

Brachialis
Biceps brachii

Trapezius

Clavicle
Supraspinatus
Acromion
Spine of scapula

Radius
Ulna

Humerus

Triceps brachii
Lateral head
Medial head
Long head

Teres minor
Teres major
Infraspinatus
Rhomboid major
Latissimus dorsi
External oblique

Scapula
9th rib
Thoracic vertebra
Lumbar vertebra

Thoracolumbar fascia

Sit with the back straight, holding the bar across the back of the neck with an overhand grip:

• Inhale and extend the bar straight up, keeping the low back as straight as possible.
• Exhale at the end of the effort.

This exercise uses the deltoid, mainly the middle and posterior fibers, as well as the trapezius, triceps brachii, and serratus anterior. Although not worked as intensely, the rhomboids, infraspinatus, teres minor, and, deeper in, the supraspinatus also contract. You can also perform this exercise while standing at a frame that guides the barbell. Various specific machines can help with the performance of this exercise.

⚠ **To prevent injury to the shoulder joint, which is vulnerable, lower the bar only as far as your unique shoulder structure and flexibility allow you to do comfortably.**

THE MOVEMENT

SEATED FRONT PRESSES | 2

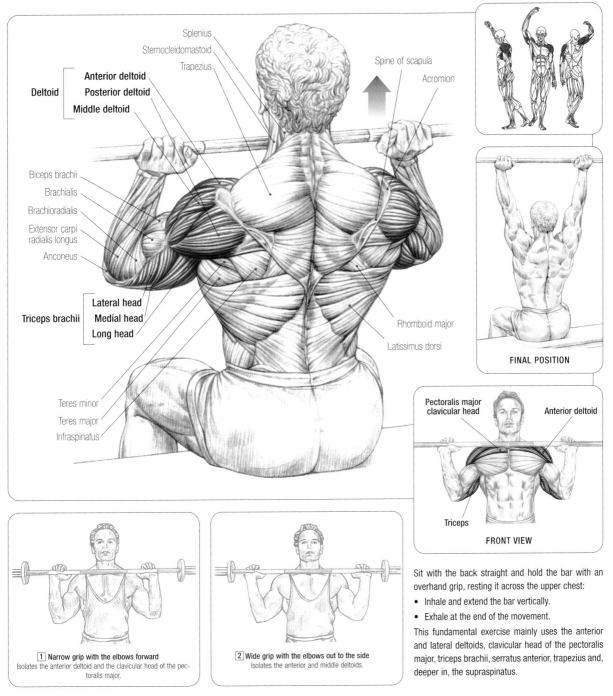

Deltoid
- **Anterior deltoid**
- **Posterior deltoid**
- **Middle deltoid**

Splenius
Sternocleidomastoid
Trapezius

Spine of scapula
Acromion

Biceps brachii
Brachialis
Brachioradialis
Extensor carpi radialis longus
Anconeus

Triceps brachii
- **Lateral head**
- **Medial head**
- **Long head**

Rhomboid major
Latissimus dorsi

Teres minor
Teres major
Infraspinatus

FINAL POSITION

Pectoralis major clavicular head
Anterior deltoid
Triceps

FRONT VIEW

Sit with the back straight and hold the bar with an overhand grip, resting it across the upper chest:

- Inhale and extend the bar vertically.
- Exhale at the end of the movement.

This fundamental exercise mainly uses the anterior and lateral deltoids, clavicular head of the pectoralis major, triceps brachii, serratus anterior, trapezius and, deeper in, the supraspinatus.

1 **Narrow grip with the elbows forward**
Isolates the anterior deltoid and the clavicular head of the pectoralis major.

2 **Wide grip with the elbows out to the side**
Isolates the anterior and middle deltoids.

You can also perform this exercise standing, as long as you keep the back straight, avoiding excessive curvature of the lumbar spine. Extending the barbell with the elbows forward isolates the anterior deltoid.

Extending the bar with the elbows spread apart isolates the middle deltoid.

You can use various machines for this exercise.

SHOULDER INJURIES

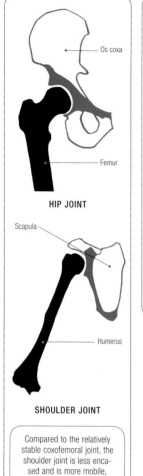

Os coxa

Femur

HIP JOINT

Scapula

Humerus

SHOULDER JOINT

> Compared to the relatively stable coxofemoral joint, the shoulder joint is less encased and is more mobile, which makes it more vulnerable to injury.

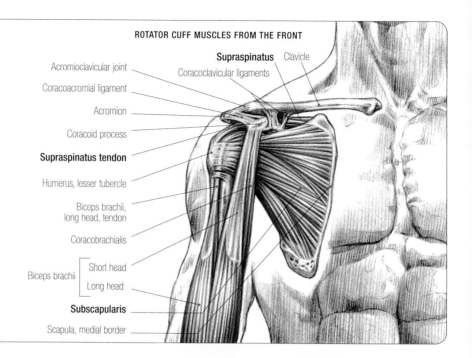

ROTATOR CUFF MUSCLES FROM THE FRONT

Acromioclavicular joint

Coracoacromial ligament

Acromion

Coracoid process

Supraspinatus tendon

Humerus, lesser tubercle

Biceps brachii, long head, tendon

Coracobrachialis

Biceps brachii — Short head / Long head

Subscapularis

Scapula, medial border

Supraspinatus — Clavicle

Coracoclavicular ligaments

Shoulder injuries occur frequently in weightlifting and especially in bodybuilding where developing the entire deltoid group requires the athlete to perform a significant number of repetitions and variations in exercises, which multiplies the risk of injury.

Compared to the stability of the hip joint, where the head of the femur sits deep in the glenoid cavity of the pelvis, the shoulder joint, which is very mobile and allows the arm to move through a wide range of motion, is in fact much less contained and protected.

The shoulder is defined as a ball-and-socket joint because the head of the humerus is mainly held within the glenoid cavity of the scapula by a complex musculotendinous group.

Most weightlifting injuries occur when training the deltoids, and they rarely result in muscle pulls or tears. They are usually caused by poor technique or overuse of the tendons reinforcing the articular capsule.

In contrast to contact sports, such as football, where sudden arm movements can create serious injuries involving dislocation or even torn tendons, the most serious injury in weightlifting involves entrapment.

When some people perform exercises in which they raise the arms, such as extensions from the neck or lateral raises, the supraspinatus tendon is rubbed and compressed between the head of the humerus and the osteoligamentous ceiling created by the inferior surface of the acromion and the coracoacromial ligament.

Inflammation follows. This generally begins with the serous bursa, which normally protects the supraspinatus from excessive friction, and extends to the supraspinatus tendon itself, which, without treatment, ends up affecting the adjacent infraspinatus tendon posteriorly and the long head of the biceps bra-

chii anteriorly. Raising the arm becomes extremely painful and eventually can cause irreversible deterioration of the supraspinatus tendon through calcification and even tearing; however, this usually happens to people 40 years of age or older.

The space between the humerus and the osteoligamentous acromiocoracoid ceiling varies from person to person. Some athletes cannot raise their arms laterally without excessive friction. These people should avoid all extensions from the neck, lateral raises that go too high, and back presses.

All barbell extensions for the shoulders must be performed to the front with the elbows slightly forward. When doing lateral dumbbell raises, you'll need to determine the proper height to raise the arms to. The correct movement is the one you can perform without causing pain.

Not everyone responds the same way to the same shoulder injury. Some people may perform all sorts of arm raises that compress the tendon, sometimes even causing tendon degeneration, without initiating a painful inflammatory process. This is how a torn supraspinatus tendon can be discovered during assessment without that person ever having complained of pain.

Another cause of shoulder pain may an imbalance in muscle tension around the articular capsule. Remember that the head of the humerus is solidly fixed against the glenoid fossa of the scapula by a group of muscle tendons adhering to or crossing over the articular capsule: In front, this is the subscapularis; a little more anterior is the long head of the biceps; superiorly, is the supraspinatus; and finally posteriorly, the infraspinatus and teres minor. Spasm, hypertonicity, or hypotonicity in one or more of these muscles can pull the shoulder joint into an incorrect position. This position can cause friction during arm movements, resulting in inflammation.

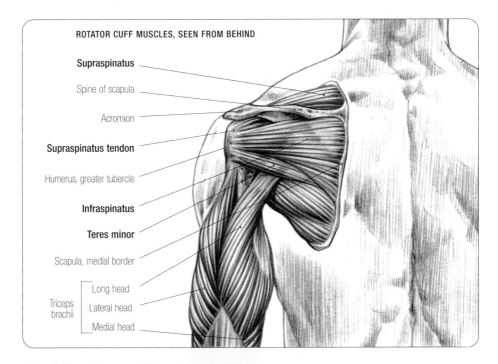

ROTATOR CUFF MUSCLES, SEEN FROM BEHIND

Supraspinatus

Spine of scapula

Acromion

Supraspinatus tendon

Humerus, greater tubercle

Infraspinatus

Teres minor

Scapula, medial border

Triceps brachii — Long head / Lateral head / Medial head

Example: Shortening or spasm of the teres minor and the infraspinatus will pull the head of the humerus in external rotation, which will cause rubbing at the anterior shoulder joint during arm movement. Over time, this will injure the long head of the biceps brachii.

Balance the training of the shoulder muscles and avoid exercises that feel awkward or painful.

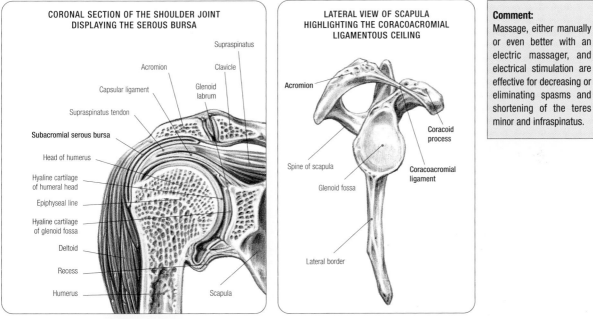

CORONAL SECTION OF THE SHOULDER JOINT
DISPLAYING THE SEROUS BURSA

Supraspinatus

Acromion

Clavicle

Capsular ligament

Glenoid labrum

Supraspinatus tendon

Subacromial serous bursa

Head of humerus

Hyaline cartilage of humeral head

Epiphyseal line

Hyaline cartilage of glenoid fossa

Deltoid

Recess

Humerus

Scapula

LATERAL VIEW OF SCAPULA
HIGHLIGHTING THE CORACOACROMIAL
LIGAMENTOUS CEILING

Acromion

Coracoid process

Spine of scapula

Coracoacromial ligament

Glenoid fossa

Lateral border

Comment:
Massage, either manually or even better with an electric massager, and electrical stimulation are effective for decreasing or eliminating spasms and shortening of the teres minor and infraspinatus.

LYING DUMBBELL PRESSES

This is one of the rare exercises that may be performed by people suffering from the all-too-common entrapment syndrome.

Performing arm extensions with dumbbells while lying on a bench and keeping the elbows next to the body works the anterior deltoid and, to a lesser degree, the middle deltoid intensely while preventing excessive rubbing at the anterior shoulder.

When performed regularly, this maintains size and tone of deltoids despite the existence of injury. You can also use this exercise to reeducate the pectoralis major following tearing. Extending while keeping the elbows against the body reduces its stretch, thus reducing the risk of tearing the scarred area.

Performing the exercise:

Lie on a bench with the chest expanded, back slightly arched, feet flat on the ground, and the elbows bent next to the body, holding a dumbbell in each hand.

- Inhale and extend the arms vertically.
- Exhale at the end of the movement.
- Return to the initial position with a controlled movement.

SEATED DUMBBELL PRESSES $\boxed{3}$

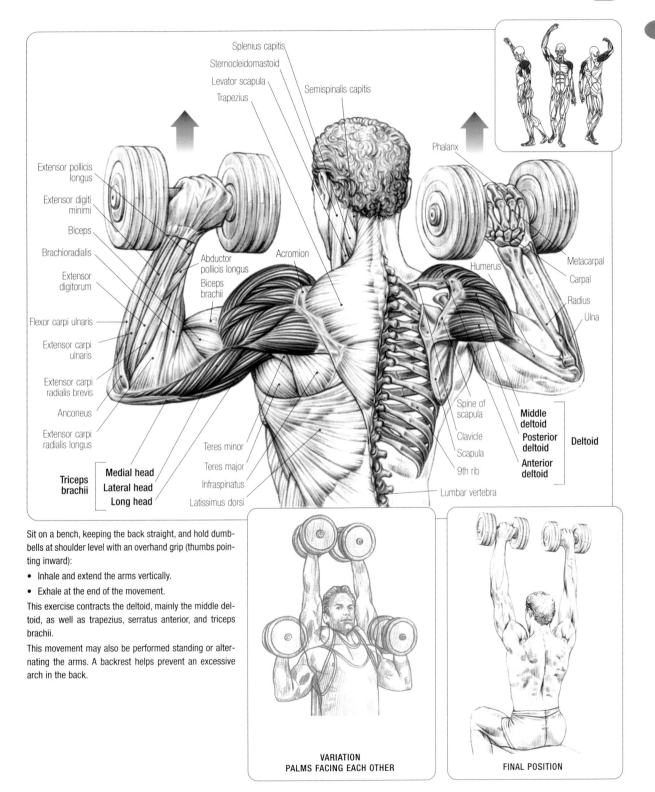

Splenius capitis
Sternocleidomastoid
Levator scapula
Semispinalis capitis
Trapezius

Extensor pollicis longus
Extensor digiti minimi
Biceps
Brachioradialis
Extensor digitorum
Flexor carpi ulnaris
Extensor carpi ulnaris
Extensor carpi radialis brevis
Anconeus
Extensor carpi radialis longus

Abductor pollicis longus
Biceps brachii
Acromion

Triceps brachii
Medial head
Lateral head
Long head

Teres minor
Teres major
Infraspinatus
Latissimus dorsi

Phalanx
Metacarpal
Carpal
Radius
Ulna
Humerus

Spine of scapula
Clavicle
Scapula
9th rib
Lumbar vertebra

Middle deltoid
Posterior deltoid
Anterior deltoid
Deltoid

Sit on a bench, keeping the back straight, and hold dumbbells at shoulder level with an overhand grip (thumbs pointing inward):

- Inhale and extend the arms vertically.
- Exhale at the end of the movement.

This exercise contracts the deltoid, mainly the middle deltoid, as well as trapezius, serratus anterior, and triceps brachii.

This movement may also be performed standing or alternating the arms. A backrest helps prevent an excessive arch in the back.

**VARIATION
PALMS FACING EACH OTHER**

FINAL POSITION

4 FRONT DUMBBELL PRESSES

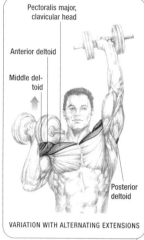

Pectoralis major, clavicular head

Anterior deltoid

Middle deltoid

Posterior deltoid

VARIATION WITH ALTERNATING EXTENSIONS

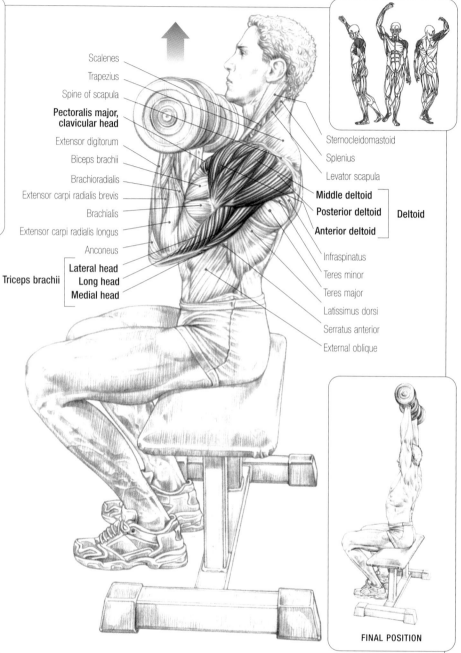

Scalenes
Trapezius
Spine of scapula
Pectoralis major, clavicular head
Extensor digitorum
Biceps brachii
Brachioradialis
Extensor carpi radialis brevis
Brachialis
Extensor carpi radialis longus
Anconeus
Triceps brachii
Lateral head
Long head
Medial head

Sternocleidomastoid
Splenius
Levator scapula
Middle deltoid
Posterior deltoid } Deltoid
Anterior deltoid
Infraspinatus
Teres minor
Teres major
Latissimus dorsi
Serratus anterior
External oblique

FINAL POSITION

Sit on a bench, keeping the back straight. With elbows bent and pointing forward, hold the dumbbells at shoulder level with an underhand grip (thumbs pointing away from each other):

- Inhale and extend the arms vertically while rotating 180 degrees at the wrists, bringing them into an overhand grip (thumbs pointing toward each other).
- Exhale at the end of the movement.

This exercise solicits the deltoid, mainly the anterior deltoid, as well as the clavicular head of the pectoralis major, triceps brachii, trapezius, and serratus anterior.

Variations:

This exercise may be performed seated against a backrest to help prevent an excessive arch in the back, standing, and alternating arms.

Comment: Working with the elbows pointing forward prevents excessive friction, which triggers inflammation in the shoulder that can eventually develop into a more serious injury.
This movement is recommended for people with weak shoulders and is meant to replace more intense exercises, such as classic dumbbell extensions with the elbows pointing to the sides or extensions from behind the neck.

BENT-OVER LATERAL RAISES | 5

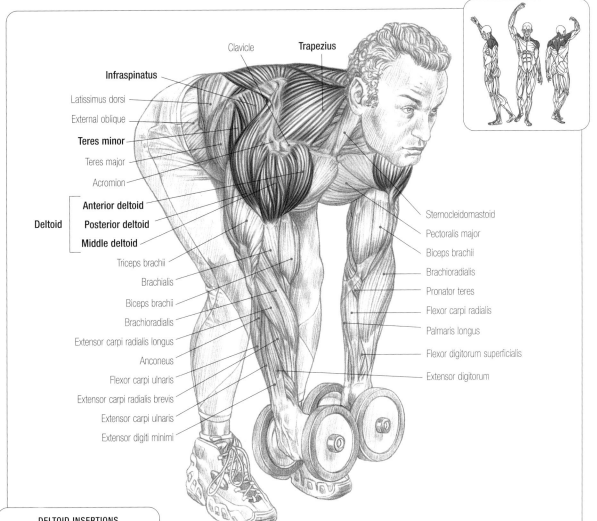

Clavicle
Trapezius
Infraspinatus
Latissimus dorsi
External oblique
Teres minor
Teres major
Acromion
Anterior deltoid
Deltoid **Posterior deltoid**
Middle deltoid
Triceps brachii
Brachialis
Biceps brachii
Brachioradialis
Extensor carpi radialis longus
Anconeus
Flexor carpi ulnaris
Extensor carpi radialis brevis
Extensor carpi ulnaris
Extensor digiti minimi

Sternocleidomastoid
Pectoralis major
Biceps brachii
Brachioradialis
Pronator teres
Flexor carpi radialis
Palmaris longus
Flexor digitorum superficialis
Extensor digitorum

DELTOID INSERTIONS

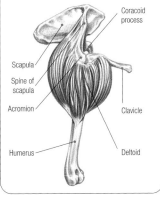

Coracoid process
Scapula
Spine of scapula
Acromion
Humerus
Clavicle
Deltoid

Stand with legs slightly apart and knees slightly bent and lean forward at the waist while keeping the back straight. With arms hanging down, grasp the dumbbells with the elbows slightly bent:
- Inhale and raise the arms to horizontal.
- Exhale at the end of the effort.

This exercise works the shoulder group, accenting the work of the posterior deltoid. Squeeze the shoulder blades together at the end of the movement to contract the middle and lower portions of the trapezius, rhomboids, teres minor, and infraspinatus.

Variation: The exercise may be performed facedown on an incline bench.

FINAL POSITION

6 LATERAL DUMBBELL RAISES

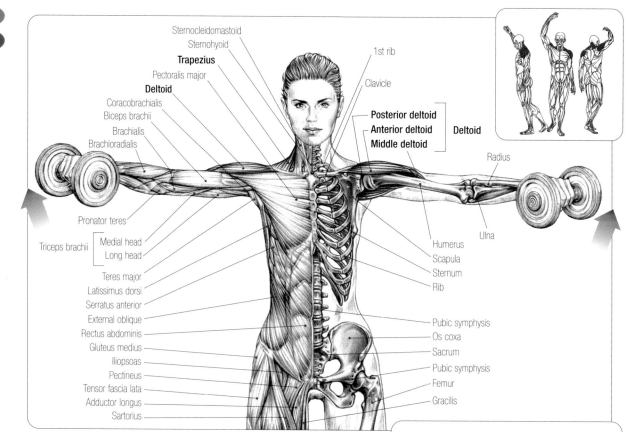

Sternocleidomastoid
Sternohyoid
Trapezius
Pectoralis major
Deltoid
Coracobrachialis
Biceps brachii
Brachialis
Brachioradialis

1st rib
Clavicle

Posterior deltoid
Anterior deltoid   Deltoid
Middle deltoid

Radius

Pronator teres

Triceps brachii [Medial head
                  Long head

Teres major
Latissimus dorsi
Serratus anterior
External oblique
Rectus abdominis
Gluteus medius
Iliopsoas
Pectineus
Tensor fascia lata
Adductor longus
Sartorius

Humerus
Scapula
Sternum
Rib

Ulna

Pubic symphysis
Os coxa
Sacrum
Pubic symphysis
Femur
Gracilis

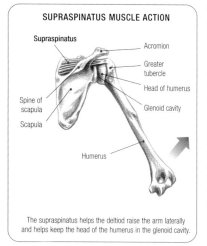

SUPRASPINATUS MUSCLE ACTION

Supraspinatus

Acromion
Greater tubercle
Head of humerus
Glenoid cavity

Spine of scapula

Scapula

Humerus

The supraspinatus helps the deltoid raise the arm laterally and helps keep the head of the humerus in the glenoid cavity.

Stand with a straight back, with legs slightly apart, arms hanging next to the body, holding a barbell in each hand:

- Raise the arms to horizontal with the elbows slightly bent.
- Return to the initial position.

This exercise mainly uses the middle deltoid.

The three divisions of the deltoids create a multipennate muscle whose different fiber directions converge on the humerus. Their function is to support relatively heavy weight and to move the arm through its full

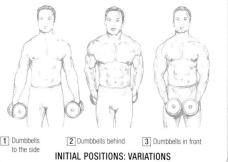

1 Dumbbells to the side   2 Dumbbells behind   3 Dumbbells in front

INITIAL POSITIONS: VARIATIONS

range of motion with precision. Therefore, it is important to adapt training to the specifics of this muscle by varying the initial position of the movement (hands behind, to the side, or in front). This thoroughly works all the fibers of the middle deltoid. Because everyone's physical structure is different (length of the clavicle, shape of the acromion, and height of the insertion at the humerus), you must find the angle of the initial position that is best for you. Lateral raises contract the supraspinatus, although you can't see this because it is located deep in the supraspinatus fossa of the scapula (shoulder blade), where it attaches to the lesser tubercle of the humerus.

Raising the arm above horizontal contracts the upper part of the trapezius; however, many bodybuilders don't work above horizontal so that they isolate the the lateral deltoid. This exercise should not be performed with heavy weights, but instead in sets of 10 to 25 reps, while varying the working angle without much recuperation time until you feel a burn. To increase the intensity, maintain an isometric contraction for a few seconds with the arm at horizontal between each repetition.

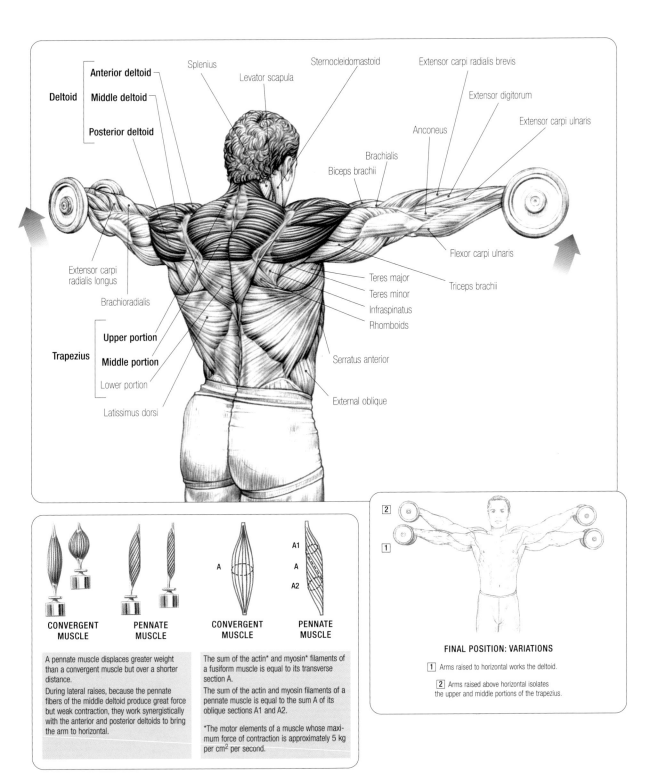

Deltoid
- **Anterior deltoid**
- **Middle deltoid**
- **Posterior deltoid**

Splenius

Levator scapula

Sternocleidomastoid

Extensor carpi radialis brevis

Extensor digitorum

Extensor carpi ulnaris

Anconeus

Brachialis

Biceps brachii

Flexor carpi ulnaris

Triceps brachii

Teres major

Teres minor

Infraspinatus

Rhomboids

Serratus anterior

External oblique

Extensor carpi radialis longus

Brachioradialis

Trapezius
- **Upper portion**
- **Middle portion**
- Lower portion

Latissimus dorsi

CONVERGENT MUSCLE

PENNATE MUSCLE

A

CONVERGENT MUSCLE

A1

A

A2

PENNATE MUSCLE

A pennate muscle displaces greater weight than a convergent muscle but over a shorter distance.

During lateral raises, because the pennate fibers of the middle deltoid produce great force but weak contraction, they work synergistically with the anterior and posterior deltoids to bring the arm to horizontal.

The sum of the actin* and myosin* filaments of a fusiform muscle is equal to its transverse section A.

The sum of the actin and myosin filaments of a pennate muscle is equal to the sum A of its oblique sections A1 and A2.

*The motor elements of a muscle whose maximum force of contraction is approximately 5 kg per cm^2 per second.

FINAL POSITION: VARIATIONS

1. Arms raised to horizontal works the deltoid.

2. Arms raised above horizontal isolates the upper and middle portions of the trapezius.

7 ALTERNATE FRONT ARM RAISES

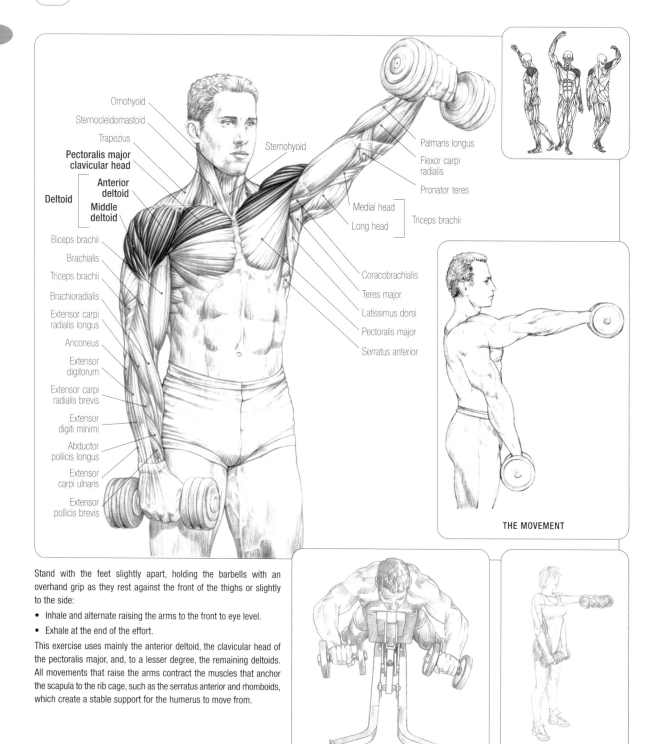

Omohyoid
Sternocleidomastoid
Trapezius
Pectoralis major clavicular head
Deltoid
Anterior deltoid
Middle deltoid
Biceps brachii
Brachialis
Triceps brachii
Brachioradialis
Extensor carpi radialis longus
Anconeus
Extensor digitorum
Extensor carpi radialis brevis
Extensor digiti minimi
Abductor pollicis longus
Extensor carpi ulnaris
Extensor pollicis brevis

Sternohyoid
Palmaris longus
Flexor carpi radialis
Pronator teres
Medial head
Long head
Triceps brachii
Coracobrachialis
Teres major
Latissimus dorsi
Pectoralis major
Serratus anterior

THE MOVEMENT

Stand with the feet slightly apart, holding the barbells with an overhand grip as they rest against the front of the thighs or slightly to the side:

• Inhale and alternate raising the arms to the front to eye level.
• Exhale at the end of the effort.

This exercise uses mainly the anterior deltoid, the clavicular head of the pectoralis major, and, to a lesser degree, the remaining deltoids. All movements that raise the arms contract the muscles that anchor the scapula to the rib cage, such as the serratus anterior and rhomboids, which create a stable support for the humerus to move from.

VARIATION
Lying facedown on an incline bench.

VARIATION
Raising to the front using both hands.

SIDE-LYING LATERAL RAISES 8

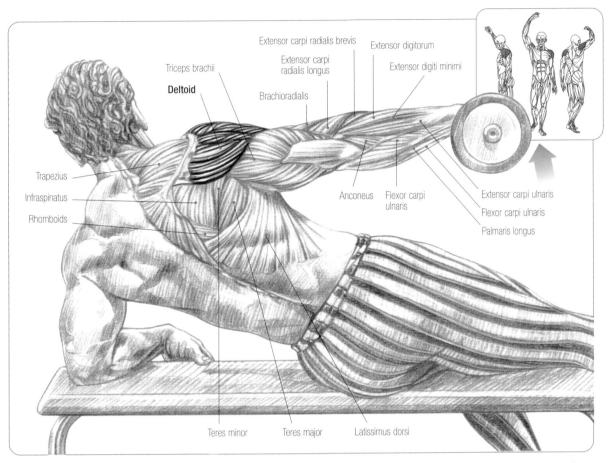

Extensor carpi radialis brevis
Extensor digitorum
Extensor carpi radialis longus
Extensor digiti minimi
Triceps brachii
Deltoid
Brachioradialis
Trapezius
Infraspinatus
Rhomboids
Anconeus
Flexor carpi ulnaris
Extensor carpi ulnaris
Flexor carpi ulnaris
Palmaris longus
Teres minor
Teres major
Latissimus dorsi

Lie on one side on the floor or on a bench holding a dumbbell with an overhand grip:

- Inhale and raise the arm to vertical.
- Exhale at the end of the movement.

Unlike standing raises, which progressively work the muscle to maximum intensity at the end of the movement (when the arm reaches horizontal), this exercise works the deltoid differently by focusing the effort at the beginning of the raise. Sets of 10 to 12 repetitions work best.

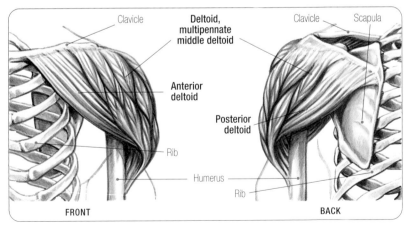

Clavicle
Deltoid, multipennate middle deltoid
Clavicle
Scapula
Anterior deltoid
Posterior deltoid
Rib
Humerus
Rib
FRONT
BACK

Comment: This movement contracts the supraspinatus, the muscle mainly responsible for initiating abduction. Varying the initial position (dumbbell in front of or behind the thigh) allows you to work all the deltoid fibers.

9 LOW-PULLEY LATERAL RAISES

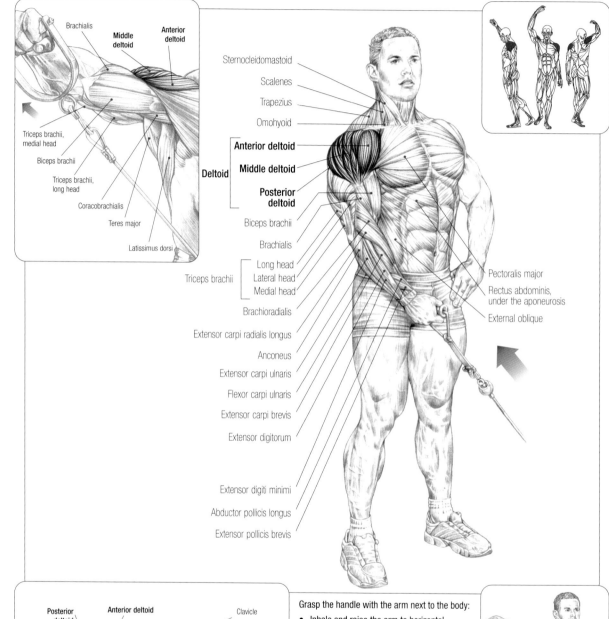

Brachialis

Middle deltoid

Anterior deltoid

Triceps brachii, medial head

Biceps brachii

Triceps brachii, long head

Coracobrachialis

Teres major

Latissimus dorsi

Sternocleidomastoid

Scalenes

Trapezius

Omohyoid

Deltoid — Anterior deltoid

Middle deltoid

Posterior deltoid

Biceps brachii

Brachialis

Triceps brachii — Long head / Lateral head / Medial head

Brachioradialis

Extensor carpi radialis longus

Anconeus

Extensor carpi ulnaris

Flexor carpi ulnaris

Extensor carpi brevis

Extensor digitorum

Extensor digiti minimi

Abductor pollicis longus

Extensor pollicis brevis

Pectoralis major

Rectus abdominis, under the aponeurosis

External oblique

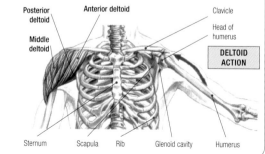

Posterior deltoid

Anterior deltoid

Middle deltoid

Clavicle

Head of humerus

DELTOID ACTION

Sternum   Scapula   Rib   Glenoid cavity   Humerus

Grasp the handle with the arm next to the body:
- Inhale and raise the arm to horizontal.
- Exhale out at the end of the movement.

This exercise mainly develops the middle deltoid. Because the muscle is multipennate, composed of many fibers in the shape of a feather, it is best to vary the working angles in order to work all the fibers.

FINAL POSITION

LOW-PULLEY FRONT RAISES 10

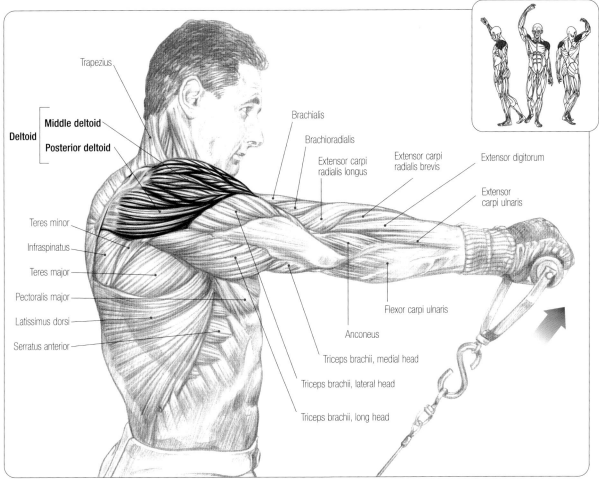

Trapezius

Deltoid
- **Middle deltoid**
- **Posterior deltoid**

Brachialis

Brachioradialis

Extensor carpi radialis longus

Extensor carpi radialis brevis

Extensor digitorum

Extensor carpi ulnaris

Teres minor

Infraspinatus

Teres major

Pectoralis major

Latissimus dorsi

Serratus anterior

Flexor carpi ulnaris

Anconeus

Triceps brachii, medial head

Triceps brachii, lateral head

Triceps brachii, long head

Stand with the feet slightly apart, arms next to the body. Grasp the handle with an overhand grip with one hand:

- Inhale and raise the arm up to eye level.
- Exhale at the end of the movement.

This exercise contracts the deltoid (mainly the anterior deltoid) as well as the clavicular head of the pectoralis major and, to a lesser degree, the short head of the biceps brachii.

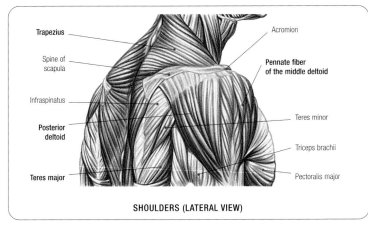

Trapezius

Spine of scapula

Infraspinatus

Posterior deltoid

Teres major

Acromion

Pennate fiber of the middle deltoid

Teres minor

Triceps brachii

Pectoralis major

SHOULDERS (LATERAL VIEW)

11 HIGH-PULLEY LATERAL EXTENSIONS

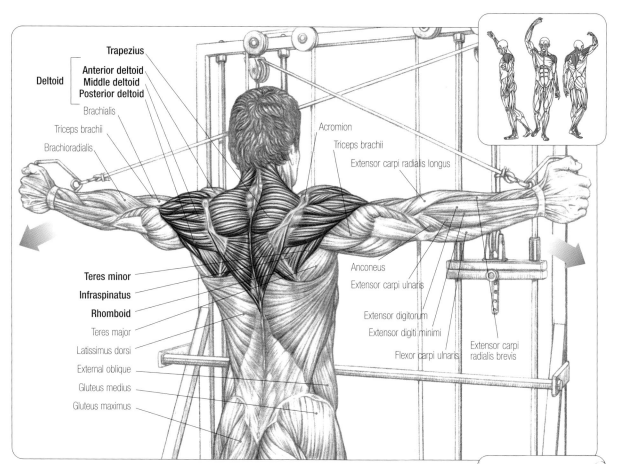

Trapezius

Deltoid
- Anterior deltoid
- Middle deltoid
- Posterior deltoid

Brachialis

Triceps brachii

Brachioradialis

Acromion

Triceps brachii

Extensor carpi radialis longus

Teres minor

Infraspinatus

Rhomboid

Teres major

Latissimus dorsi

External oblique

Gluteus medius

Gluteus maximus

Anconeus

Extensor carpi ulnaris

Extensor digitorum

Extensor digiti minimi

Flexor carpi ulnaris

Extensor carpi radialis brevis

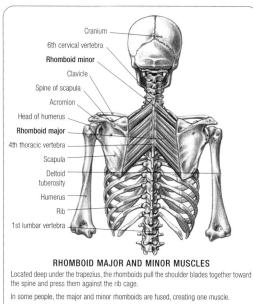

Cranium

6th cervical vertebra

Rhomboid minor

Clavicle

Spine of scapula

Acromion

Head of humerus

Rhomboid major

4th thoracic vertebra

Scapula

Deltoid tuberosity

Humerus

Rib

1st lumbar vertebra

RHOMBOID MAJOR AND MINOR MUSCLES

Located deep under the trapezius, the rhomboids pull the shoulder blades together toward the spine and press them against the rib cage.

In some people, the major and minor rhomboids are fused, creating one muscle.

Stand facing the pulleys with the arms extended to the front, gripping the right handle with the left hand and the left handle with the right hand:

- Inhale and extend arms to the side and back.
- Exhale at the end of the movement.

Return to the initial position with a controlled movement and begin again.

This exercise mainly contracts the posterior deltoid, infraspinatus, teres minor, and, at the end of the movement as the shoulder blades come together, the trapezius and deeper in, the rhomboids.

INITIAL POSITION

Comment: People who carry their shoulders forward because of chest muscle development can perform this exercise in addition to posterior shoulder work at a machine to help rebalance their posture.

To realign shoulders where they belong, work with moderate weights, and at the end of the movement squeeze the shoulders back.

LOW-PULLEY BENT-OVER LATERAL RAISES 12

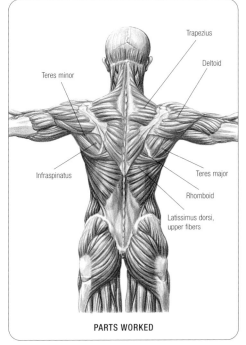

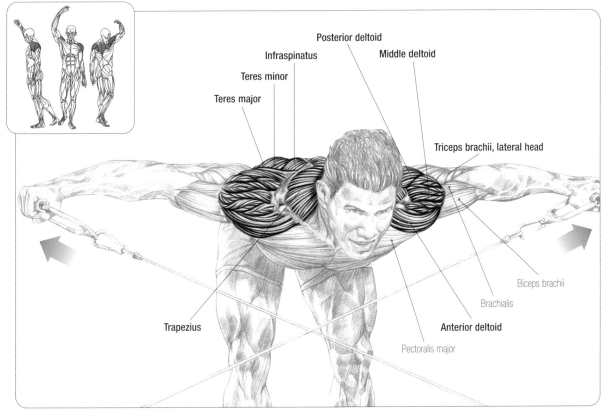

Posterior deltoid

Middle deltoid

Infraspinatus

Teres minor

Teres major

Triceps brachii, lateral head

Biceps brachii

Brachialis

Trapezius

Anterior deltoid

Pectoralis major

Trapezius

Deltoid

Teres minor

Infraspinatus

Teres major

Rhomboid

Latissimus dorsi, upper fibers

PARTS WORKED

Stand with the feet apart, legs slightly bent, and lean forward from the waist, keeping a flat back. Grip a handle in each hand with the cables crossed:

- Inhale and raise the arms to the side to horizontal.
- Exhale at the end of the effort.

This exercise mainly works the posterior deltoid. At the end of the movement, as the shoulder blades squeeze together, the trapezius (middle and lower portions) and the rhomboids contract.

13 ONE-DUMBBELL FRONT RAISES

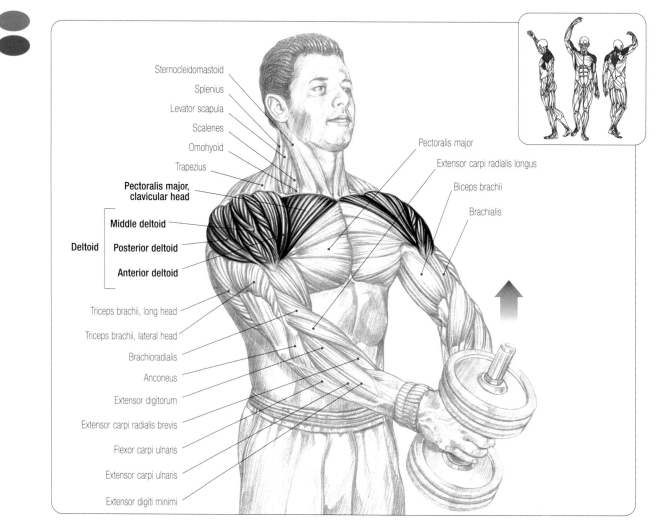

Sternocleidomastoid

Splenius

Levator scapula

Scalenes

Omohyoid

Trapezius

Pectoralis major, clavicular head

Deltoid {
Middle deltoid

Posterior deltoid

Anterior deltoid
}

Triceps brachii, long head

Triceps brachii, lateral head

Brachioradialis

Anconeus

Extensor digitorum

Extensor carpi radialis brevis

Flexor carpi ulnaris

Extensor carpi ulnaris

Extensor digiti minimi

Pectoralis major

Extensor carpi radialis longus

Biceps brachii

Brachialis

Stand with the legs slightly apart, a straight back, and the abdominal muscles contracted. With arms extended, grasp a dumbbell in both hands with fingers crossed over each other as it rests against the thighs:

- Inhale and raise the dumbbell to eye level.
- Lower gently, avoiding abrupt movements.
- Exhale at the end of the movement.

This exercise mainly contracts the anterior deltoid, the clavicular head of the pectoralis major, and the short head of the biceps.

Note that all the fixators of the scapula are used during the isometric contraction, which allows the humerus to move from a stable position.

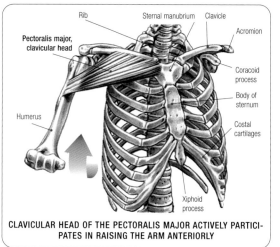

Rib

Sternal manubrium

Clavicle

Acromion

Pectoralis major, clavicular head

Coracoid process

Body of sternum

Costal cartilages

Humerus

Xiphoid process

CLAVICULAR HEAD OF THE PECTORALIS MAJOR ACTIVELY PARTICI-
PATES IN RAISING THE ARM ANTERIORLY

BARBELL FRONT RAISES 14

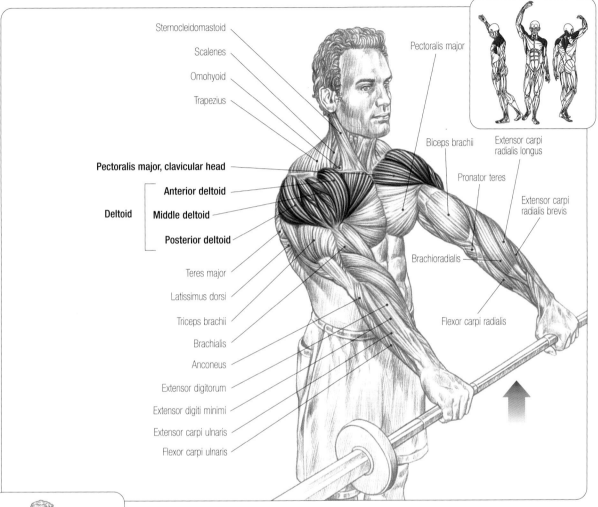

Sternocleidomastoid

Scalenes

Omohyoid

Trapezius

Pectoralis major

Pectoralis major, clavicular head

Deltoid
Anterior deltoid

Middle deltoid

Posterior deltoid

Teres major

Latissimus dorsi

Triceps brachii

Brachialis

Anconeus

Extensor digitorum

Extensor digiti minimi

Extensor carpi ulnaris

Flexor carpi ulnaris

Biceps brachii

Pronator teres

Extensor carpi radialis longus

Extensor carpi radialis brevis

Brachioradialis

Flexor carpi radialis

VARIATION
Front raise at a low pulley.

Stand with the legs slightly apart and the back straight, contracting the abdominal muscles. Hold the barbell with an overhand grip as it rests against the thighs:

- Inhale and raise the barbell with extended arms to eye level.
- Exhale at the end of the movement.

This exercise contracts the anterior deltoid, the clavicular head of the pectoralis major, the infraspinatus, and, to a lesser degree, the trapezius, serratus anterior, and short head of biceps.

If you continue raising the arms, the posterior deltoid contracts, reinforcing the work of the other muscles and allowing you to raise the arms to vertical.

The exercise may also be performed with your back to a low pulley and the cable passing between the legs.

1 Begin   2 End

THE MOVEMENT

Comment: The biceps brachii participates to a lesser degree in all anterior arm raises.

15 UPRIGHT ROWS

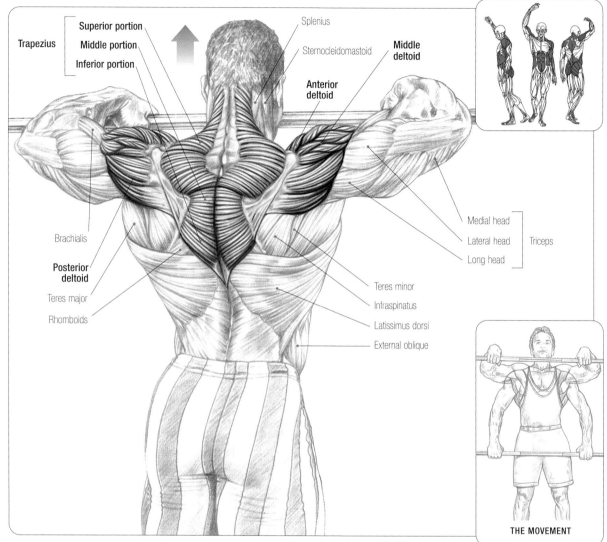

Trapezius
- Superior portion
- Middle portion
- Inferior portion

Splenius

Sternocleidomastoid

Middle deltoid

Anterior deltoid

Brachialis

Posterior deltoid

Teres major

Rhomboids

Medial head
Lateral head — Triceps
Long head

Teres minor

Infraspinatus

Latissimus dorsi

External oblique

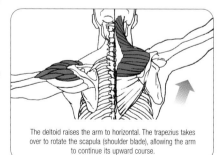

THE MOVEMENT

Stand with the legs slightly apart and back straight. Grasp the barbell with an overhand grip slightly wider than shoulder width as it rests against the thighs:

- Inhale and pull the barbell up along the body to the chin keeping the elbows as high as possible.
- Lower the bar in a controlled manner without abrupt movements.
- Exhale at the end of the effort.

This exercise mainly uses the deltoid, trapezius, and biceps, and to a lesser degree, the muscles of the forearms, the gluteal muscles, the lumbosacralis group, and the abdominal muscles.

This is a fundamental exercise that is comprehensive and helps develop a "Hercules" physique.

The deltoid raises the arm to horizontal. The trapezius takes over to rotate the scapula (shoulder blade), allowing the arm to continue its upward course.

NAUTILUS LATERAL RAISES 16

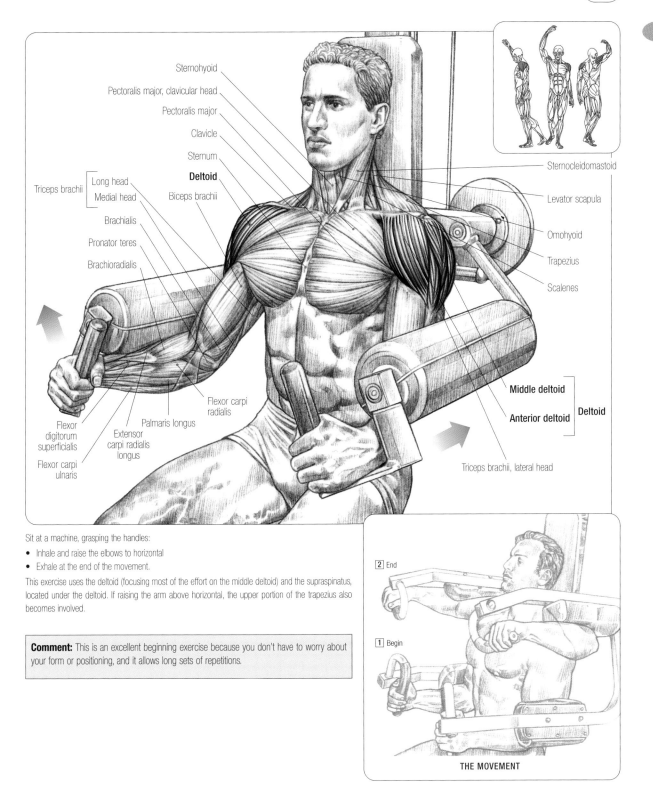

Sternohyoid

Pectoralis major, clavicular head

Pectoralis major

Clavicle

Sternum

Deltoid

Triceps brachii

Long head

Medial head

Biceps brachii

Brachialis

Pronator teres

Brachioradialis

Flexor digitorum superficialis

Extensor carpi radialis longus

Palmaris longus

Flexor carpi ulnaris

Flexor carpi radialis

Sternocleidomastoid

Levator scapula

Omohyoid

Trapezius

Scalenes

Middle deltoid

Anterior deltoid

Deltoid

Triceps brachii, lateral head

Sit at a machine, grasping the handles:

- Inhale and raise the elbows to horizontal
- Exhale at the end of the movement.

This exercise uses the deltoid (focusing most of the effort on the middle deltoid) and the supraspinatus, located under the deltoid. If raising the arm above horizontal, the upper portion of the trapezius also becomes involved.

Comment: This is an excellent beginning exercise because you don't have to worry about your form or positioning, and it allows long sets of repetitions.

2 End

1 Begin

THE MOVEMENT

17 PEC DECK REAR-DELT LATERALS

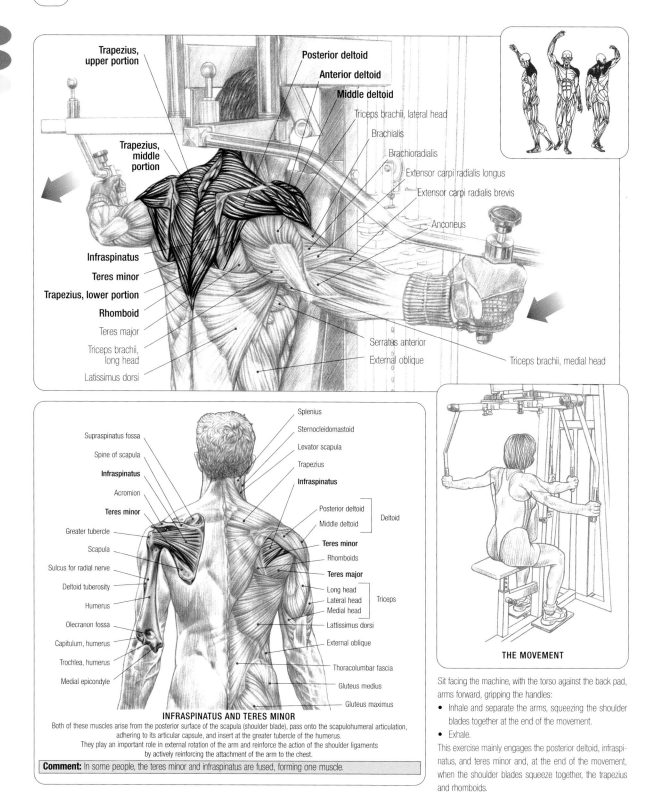

Trapezius, upper portion

Posterior deltoid

Anterior deltoid

Middle deltoid

Triceps brachii, lateral head

Brachialis

Trapezius, middle portion

Brachioradialis

Extensor carpi radialis longus

Extensor carpi radialis brevis

Anconeus

Infraspinatus

Teres minor

Trapezius, lower portion

Rhomboid

Teres major

Serratus anterior

Triceps brachii, long head

External oblique

Triceps brachii, medial head

Latissimus dorsi

Supraspinatus fossa

Splenius

Sternocleidomastoid

Spine of scapula

Levator scapula

Infraspinatus

Trapezius

Acromion

Infraspinatus

Teres minor

Posterior deltoid

Middle deltoid

Deltoid

Greater tubercle

Scapula

Teres minor

Sulcus for radial nerve

Rhomboids

Deltoid tuberosity

Teres major

Humerus

Long head

Olecranon fossa

Lateral head

Medial head

Triceps

Capitulum, humerus

Lattissimus dorsi

Trochlea, humerus

External oblique

Medial epicondyle

Thoracolumbar fascia

Gluteus medius

Gluteus maximus

INFRASPINATUS AND TERES MINOR

Both of these muscles arise from the posterior surface of the scapula (shoulder blade), pass onto the scapulohumeral articulation, adhering to its articular capsule, and insert at the greater tubercle of the humerus. They play an important role in external rotation of the arm and reinforce the action of the shoulder ligaments by actively reinforcing the attachment of the arm to the chest.

Comment: In some people, the teres minor and infraspinatus are fused, forming one muscle.

THE MOVEMENT

Sit facing the machine, with the torso against the back pad, arms forward, gripping the handles:

- Inhale and separate the arms, squeezing the shoulder blades together at the end of the movement.
- Exhale.

This exercise mainly engages the posterior deltoid, infraspinatus, and teres minor and, at the end of the movement, when the shoulder blades squeeze together, the trapezius and rhomboids.

3
CHEST

1 INCLINE PRESSES

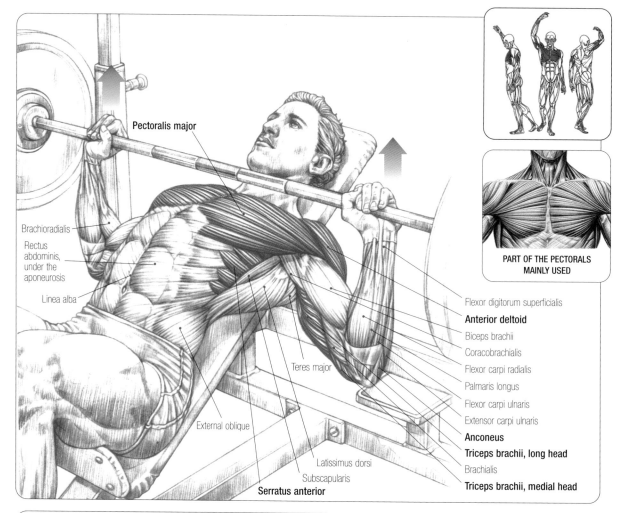

Pectoralis major

Brachioradialis

Rectus abdominis, under the aponeurosis

Linea alba

External oblique

Teres major

Latissimus dorsi

Subscapularis

Serratus anterior

Flexor digitorum superficialis

Anterior deltoid

Biceps brachii

Coracobrachialis

Flexor carpi radialis

Palmaris longus

Flexor carpi ulnaris

Extensor carpi ulnaris

Anconeus

Triceps brachii, long head

Brachialis

Triceps brachii, medial head

PART OF THE PECTORALS MAINLY USED

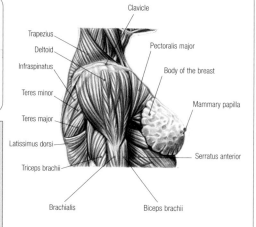

Clavicle

Trapezius

Deltoid

Infraspinatus

Teres minor

Teres major

Latissimus dorsi

Triceps brachii

Brachialis

Pectoralis major

Body of the breast

Mammary papilla

Serratus anterior

Biceps brachii

Comment: Contrary to popular lore, the incline press does not tone the breasts and in no way prevents their sagging. Breasts are composed of adipose tissue containing the mammary glands, all of which is contained in a net of connective tissue that rests on top of the pectoralis major.

Sit on an incline bench angled at 45 to 60 degrees, grasp the barbell with an overhand grip wider than shoulder width:

- Inhale and lower the barbell to the sternal notch.
- Extend the arms.
- Exhale at the end of the movement.

This exercise mainly solicits the clavicular head of the pectoralis major, anterior deltoid, triceps brachii, serratus anterior, and pectoralis minor. This exercise may be done at a frame that guides the bar.

PECTORALIS MAJOR TEAR

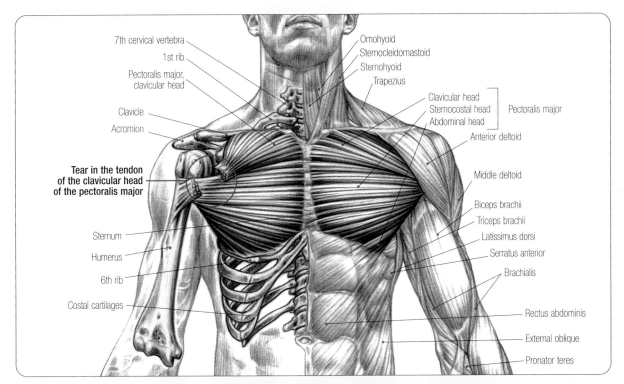

7th cervical vertebra
1st rib
Pectoralis major, clavicular head
Clavicle
Acromion
Tear in the tendon of the clavicular head of the pectoralis major
Sternum
Humerus
6th rib
Costal cartilages

Omohyoid
Sternocleidomastoid
Sternohyoid
Trapezius
Clavicular head
Sternocostal head] Pectoralis major
Abdominal head
Anterior deltoid
Middle deltoid
Biceps brachii
Triceps brachii
Latissimus dorsi
Serratus anterior
Brachialis
Rectus abdominis
External oblique
Pronator teres

The pectoralis major originates at the anterior surface of the rib cage and inserts at the anterior surface of the upper end of the humerus.

It is a powerful muscle whose main function is to bring the arms together in front of the rib cage. (It is the hugging muscle.)

Unlike most sports, where pectoralis major injuries are rare, weightlifting, especially the bench press, can lead to small tears and even partial rupture of its tendon.

This ultimate injury is seen only in relatively powerful athletes using abnormally rapid force before the tendon has had time to strengthen. Sometimes it is associated with a low-calorie diet aimed at increased muscle definition. (These diets tend to weaken the muscles, tendons, and joints.)

The injury, which always occurs during heavy bench-pressing, generally affects only the tendon of the clavicular head of the pectoralis major.

A torn tendon is extremely painful, and the athlete may faint. Swelling and bruising often appear on the anterior surface of the arm, and retraction of the clavicular head leads to a hollow that is medial to the anterior deltoid.

The problem with this injury is that doctors often misdiagnose it. This mistake is unfortunately common but is understandable because during the posttraumatic examination the injured party is able to perform all the movements that indicate full motor function of the pectoralis major. Therefore, the injury appears to be a simple muscle tear rather than the more serious tear of the tendinous insertion.

For example, despite a tear of the clavicular head of the pectoralis major, anterior elevation of the arm, which is part of its function, is compensated for by the anterior deltoid. And abduction is performed by the sternal and abdominal heads of the pectoralis major.

If the tendon of the clavicular head of the pectoralis major is torn, it must be surgically reinserted onto the humerus as soon as possible. If this is not done promptly, retraction and fibrosis of the muscle occurs, and the operation will no longer be possible.

Although you can move your arm through its full range of motion without the superior head of the pectoralis major, you will never recover your initial strength and will be at a serious disadvantage if you want to continue heavy weight training.

Head of the humerus
Lesser tubercle
Greater tubercle
Anatomical neck
Bicipital groove
Section of the muscle corresponding to the clavicular head (susceptible to tearing)
Section of the muscle corresponding to the sternal portion
Section of the muscle corresponding to the chondro-abdominal portion
insertion of the pectoralis major

INSERTION OF THE PECTORALIS MAJOR MUSCLE ON THE HUMERUS DISPLAYING HOW THE TENDON TWISTS ON ITSELF CREATING A U-SHAPE

During bench presses or flys, the most lateral part of the pectoralis major tendon, which corresponds to the clavicular head, is put under the most stress.

Therefore, when lifting heavy weights, this is the tendon that tears or pulls away from its insertion.

2 BENCH PRESSES

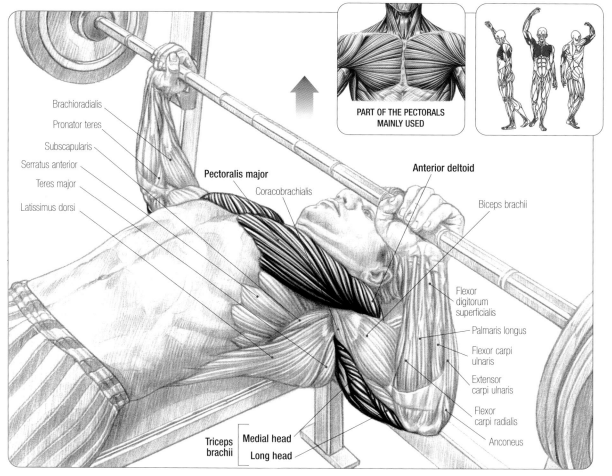

Brachioradialis

Pronator teres

Subscapularis

Serratus anterior

Teres major

Latissimus dorsi

Pectoralis major

Coracobrachialis

Anterior deltoid

Biceps brachii

Flexor digitorum superficialis

Palmaris longus

Flexor carpi ulnaris

Extensor carpi ulnaris

Flexor carpi radialis

Anconeus

Triceps brachii — Medial head / Long head

PART OF THE PECTORALS MAINLY USED

Lie faceup on a horizontal bench, with buttocks on the bench and feet flat on the ground:

- Grasp the barbell with an overhand grip wider than shoulder width.
- Inhale and lower the bar to the chest with a controlled movement.
- Extend the arms and exhale at the end of the effort.

This exercise engages the complete pectoralis major muscle, pectoralis minor, anterior deltoid, serratus anterior, and coracobrachialis.

THE MOVEMENT

Variations

1. This movement may be performed while arching the back power-lifter style. This position brings the more powerful lower part of the pectoral muscle into play, allowing you to lift heavier weights.
2. Executing the extension with the elbows next to the body concentrates the work onto the anterior deltoid.
3. Varying the width of the hands isolates different parts of the muscle:
   - Hands closer together isolates the central part of the pectorals.
   - Hands wider apart isolates the lateral part of the pectorals.
4. Varying the angle of the barbell isolates different parts of the muscle:
   - Lowering the bar to the chondrocostal border of the rib cage isolates the lower part of the pectorals.
   - Lowering the barbell onto the middle part of the pectorals isolates the midline fibers.
   - Lowering the bar onto the sternal notch isolates the clavicular head of the muscle.
5. If you have back problems or want to isolate the pectorals, perform the extension with the legs raised.
6. Perform the extension at a frame that guides the bar.

CLASSIC POSITION

ARCHED-BACK VARIATION

Executing the bench press with an arched back, power-lifter style, limits the range of the movement and allows you to lift significantly heavier weights because it uses mainly the lower part of the pectorals, which are the strongest. In competition, the feet and the head should not move, and the buttocks should remain in contact with the bench. People with back problems should not perform this variation.

RAISED-LEG VARIATION

Performing the movement with raised legs helps prevent excessive arching, which can cause low back pain.

This variation diminishes the effort of the lower pectorals by working the middle and superior fibers more.

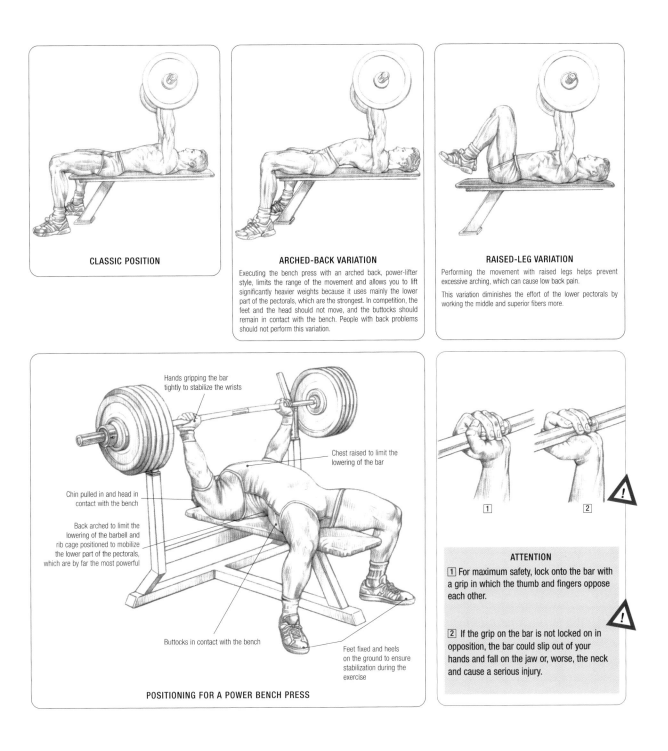

Hands gripping the bar tightly to stabilize the wrists

Chest raised to limit the lowering of the bar

Chin pulled in and head in contact with the bench

Back arched to limit the lowering of the barbell and rib cage positioned to mobilize the lower part of the pectorals, which are by far the most powerful

Buttocks in contact with the bench

Feet fixed and heels on the ground to ensure stabilization during the exercise

POSITIONING FOR A POWER BENCH PRESS

1

2

ATTENTION

1 For maximum safety, lock onto the bar with a grip in which the thumb and fingers oppose each other.

2 If the grip on the bar is not locked on in opposition, the bar could slip out of your hands and fall on the jaw or, worse, the neck and cause a serious injury.

3 CLOSE-GRIP BENCH PRESSES

Flexor digitorum superficialis

Flexor carpi ulnaris

Anconeus

Biceps brachii

Medial head

Triceps brachii   **Lateral head**

Long head

Teres major

Posterior deltoid

Serratus anterior

Latissimus dorsi

Subscapularis

Palmaris longus

Brachioradialis

Flexor carpi radialis

Pronator teres

Brachialis

Pectoralis major

PART OF THE PECTORAL MUSCLES
THAT ARE MAINLY USED

EXECUTION WITH ELBOWS
OPEN TO THE SIDES TO BETTER
ISOLATE THE TRICEPS BRACHII

Lie on a horizontal bench with the buttocks on the bench and the feet on the ground, gripping the barbell with an overhand grip and wrists 4 to 15 inches apart, depending on the flexibility of the wrists: Inhale and lower the bar with a controlled movement to the chest, with the elbows out to the side. Extend and exhale at the end of the effort. This exercise develops the pectoral muscles at the sternal notch and the triceps brachii. (With this in mind, it may be included in a program for the arms.) By extending and keeping the elbows next to the body, a greater part of the work is performed by the anterior deltoid. This movement may be performed at a frame that guides the bar.

Attention: Depending on your physical structure, the narrow grip may cause wrist pain. In this case, use a wider grip.

Bench Presses and Elbow Pain
Elbow pain most often develops after bench pressing. This overuse injury is generally related to excessive training with long sets. In bench pressing, locking the extended arms at the end of the movement subjects the elbow to rubbing and microtrauma, which over time may lead to inflammation.

Comment: Occasionally, this condition can lead to intra-articular calcifications, which are particularly crippling. In this case, surgery is often the only solution for regaining complete arm extension.

At the first sign of elbow pain, avoid for several days exercises that involve arm extension in order to prevent serious injury.

When you resume exercises that include arm extension, avoid completely extending the forearms at the end of the movement until the pain has completely disappeared.

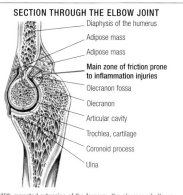

SECTION THROUGH THE ELBOW JOINT

Diaphysis of the humerus

Adipose mass

Adipose mass

**Main zone of friction prone
to inflammation injuries**

Olecranon fossa

Olecranon

Articular cavity

Trochlea, cartilage

Coronoid process

Ulna

With repeated extension of the forearm, the olecranon butts up against the olecranon fossa of the humerus. The articulation then suffers from microtrauma, which over time may generate painful inflammation at the dorsal surface of the elbow.

DECLINE PRESSES | 4

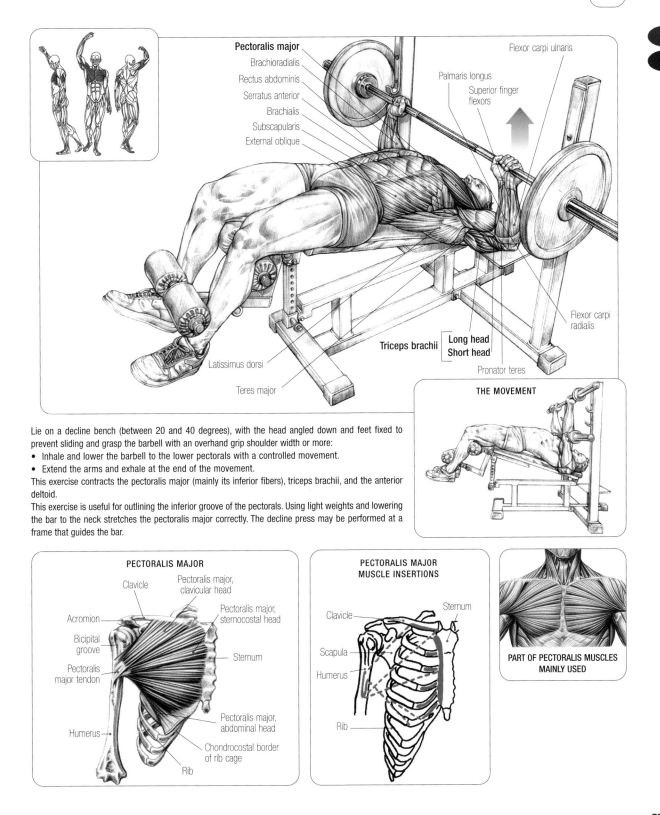

Pectoralis major
Brachioradialis
Rectus abdominis
Serratus anterior
Brachialis
Subscapularis
External oblique

Flexor carpi ulnaris
Palmaris longus
Superior finger flexors

Flexor carpi radialis

Triceps brachii   Long head
                   Short head

Pronator teres

Latissimus dorsi
Teres major

THE MOVEMENT

Lie on a decline bench (between 20 and 40 degrees), with the head angled down and feet fixed to prevent sliding and grasp the barbell with an overhand grip shoulder width or more:
- Inhale and lower the barbell to the lower pectorals with a controlled movement.
- Extend the arms and exhale at the end of the movement.

This exercise contracts the pectoralis major (mainly its inferior fibers), triceps brachii, and the anterior deltoid.

This exercise is useful for outlining the inferior groove of the pectorals. Using light weights and lowering the bar to the neck stretches the pectoralis major correctly. The decline press may be performed at a frame that guides the bar.

PECTORALIS MAJOR

Clavicle
Pectoralis major, clavicular head
Acromion
Pectoralis major, sternocostal head
Bicipital groove
Pectoralis major tendon
Sternum
Humerus
Pectoralis major, abdominal head
Chondrocostal border of rib cage
Rib

PECTORALIS MAJOR MUSCLE INSERTIONS

Sternum
Clavicle
Scapula
Humerus
Rib

PART OF PECTORALIS MUSCLES MAINLY USED

5 PUSH-UPS

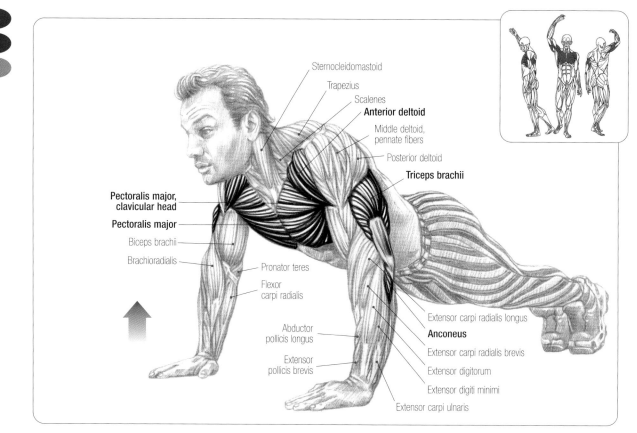

Sternocleidomastoid

Trapezius

Scalenes

Anterior deltoid

Middle deltoid, pennate fibers

Posterior deltoid

Triceps brachii

Pectoralis major, clavicular head

Pectoralis major

Biceps brachii

Brachioradialis

Pronator teres

Flexor carpi radialis

Abductor pollicis longus

Extensor pollicis brevis

Extensor carpi radialis longus

Anconeus

Extensor carpi radialis brevis

Extensor digitorum

Extensor digiti minimi

Extensor carpi ulnaris

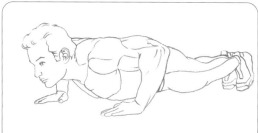

INITIAL POSITION

Support yourself facedown on the ground, with arms extended, hands shoulder-width (or more) apart, and feet touching or slightly apart:

- Inhale and bend the elbows to bring the rib cage close to the ground without arching the low back excessively.
- Push back up to complete arm extension.
- Exhale at the end of the movement.

This movement is excellent for the pectoralis major and the triceps brachii.

PART OF THE PECTORAL MUSCLES MAINLY USED

Varying the tilt of the chest focuses the work on different parts of the pectorals:

- Feet higher isolates the the clavicular head of the pectoralis major.
- Chest higher isolates the inferior part of the pectoralis major.

Varying the width of the hands focuses the work on different parts of the pectorals:

- Hands wider isolates the lateral part of the pectoralis major.
- Hands closer together isolates the sternal head of the pectoralis major.

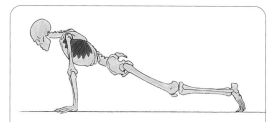

While performing push-ups the serratus anterior contracts to maintain the scapula against the rib cage, locking the arms onto the torso.

PARALLEL BAR DIPS 6

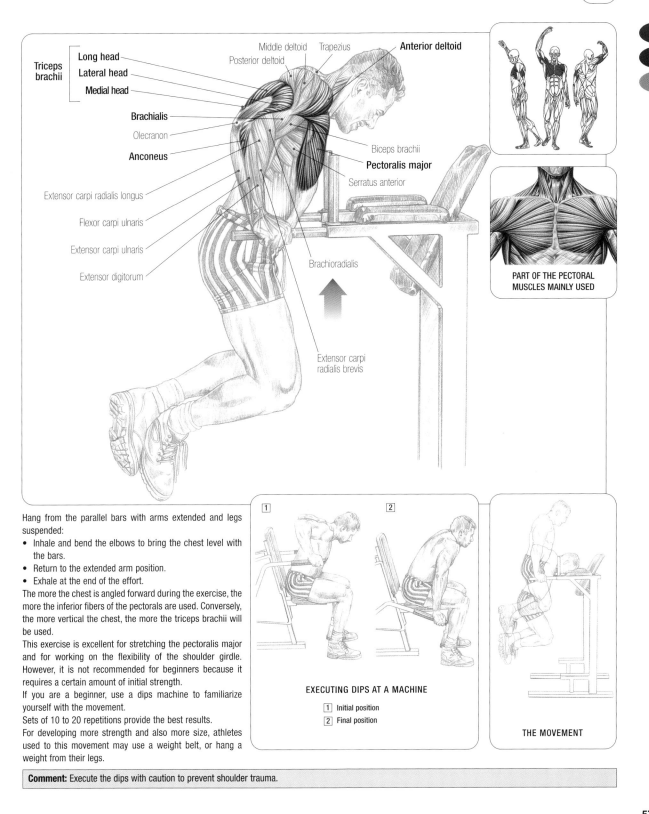

Triceps brachii
- Long head
- Lateral head
- Medial head

Brachialis

Olecranon

Anconeus

Extensor carpi radialis longus

Flexor carpi ulnaris

Extensor carpi ulnaris

Extensor digitorum

Middle deltoid   Trapezius

Posterior deltoid

Anterior deltoid

Biceps brachii

Pectoralis major

Serratus anterior

Brachioradialis

Extensor carpi radialis brevis

PART OF THE PECTORAL MUSCLES MAINLY USED

Hang from the parallel bars with arms extended and legs suspended:

- Inhale and bend the elbows to bring the chest level with the bars.
- Return to the extended arm position.
- Exhale at the end of the effort.

The more the chest is angled forward during the exercise, the more the inferior fibers of the pectorals are used. Conversely, the more vertical the chest, the more the triceps brachii will be used.

This exercise is excellent for stretching the pectoralis major and for working on the flexibility of the shoulder girdle. However, it is not recommended for beginners because it requires a certain amount of initial strength.

If you are a beginner, use a dips machine to familiarize yourself with the movement.

Sets of 10 to 20 repetitions provide the best results.

For developing more strength and also more size, athletes used to this movement may use a weight belt, or hang a weight from their legs.

EXECUTING DIPS AT A MACHINE

1 Initial position
2 Final position

THE MOVEMENT

Comment: Execute the dips with caution to prevent shoulder trauma.

7 DUMBBELL PRESSES

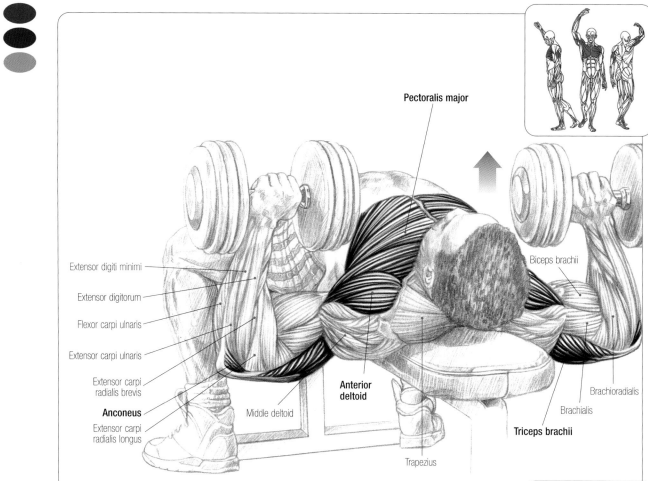

Pectoralis major

Extensor digiti minimi

Extensor digitorum

Flexor carpi ulnaris

Extensor carpi ulnaris

Extensor carpi radialis brevis

Anconeus

Extensor carpi radialis longus

Middle deltoid

Anterior deltoid

Trapezius

Biceps brachii

Brachioradialis

Brachialis

Triceps brachii

Lie faceup on a horizontal bench, with feet flat on the ground for stability and elbows bent, holding dumbbells with an overhand grip at the chest level:

- Inhale and extend the arms vertically while rotating the forearms so that the palms face each other.
- Once the hands face each other, perform an isometric contraction to focus the effort on the sternal head of the pectoralis major.
- Exhale at the end of the movement.

This exercise is similar to the bench press, but with its greater range of motion, it stretches the pectoralis muscles.

Although not contracted as intensely, the triceps brachii and anterior deltoid are also used.

VARIATION
Executing the exercise without rotating the forearms.

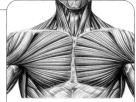

PART OF THE PECTORAL MUSCLES MAINLY USED

DUMBBELL FLYS 8

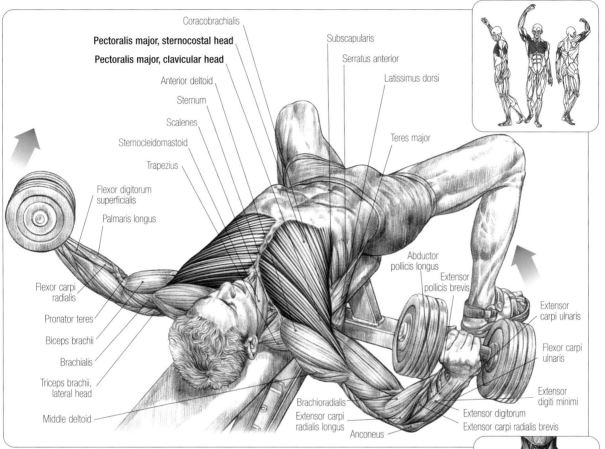

- Coracobrachialis
- **Pectoralis major, sternocostal head**
- **Pectoralis major, clavicular head**
- Anterior deltoid
- Sternum
- Scalenes
- Sternocleidomastoid
- Trapezius
- Flexor digitorum superficialis
- Palmaris longus
- Flexor carpi radialis
- Pronator teres
- Biceps brachii
- Brachialis
- Triceps brachii, lateral head
- Middle deltoid
- Subscapularis
- Serratus anterior
- Latissimus dorsi
- Teres major
- Abductor pollicis longus
- Extensor pollicis brevis
- Extensor carpi ulnaris
- Flexor carpi ulnaris
- Extensor digiti minimi
- Extensor digitorum
- Extensor carpi radialis brevis
- Brachioradialis
- Extensor carpi radialis longus
- Anconeus

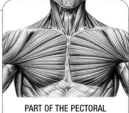

PART OF THE PECTORAL MUSCLES MAINLY USED

Lie on a narrow bench that won't interfere with the shoulder movement and hold a dumbbell in each hand with arms extended or slightly bent to relieve stress on the joint:

- Inhale and open the arms to horizontal.
- Raise the arms to vertical while exhaling.
- Perform a small isometric contraction at the end of the movement to emphasize the work on the sternal head of the pectoralis major.

This exercise is never performed with heavy weights.

This exercise focuses the work on the pectoralis major. It serves as a basic exercise to increase thoracic expansion, which contributes to increased pulmonary capacity. It also develops muscle flexibility.

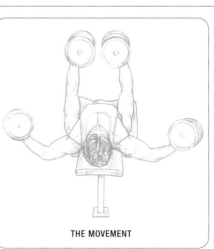

THE MOVEMENT

Comment: To avoid the risk of tearing the pectoral muscles, perform the exercise with extreme caution when using heavier weights.

9 INCLINE DUMBBELL PRESSES

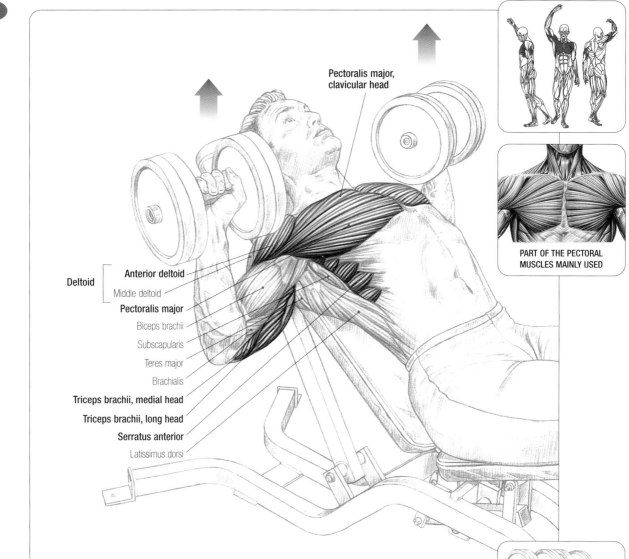

Pectoralis major,
clavicular head

Deltoid
- Anterior deltoid
- Middle deltoid

Pectoralis major
Biceps brachii
Subscapularis
Teres major
Brachialis
Triceps brachii, medial head
Triceps brachii, long head
Serratus anterior
Latissimus dorsi

PART OF THE PECTORAL
MUSCLES MAINLY USED

Sit on a bench with an angle of no more than 60 degrees (to prevent too much work with the deltoid), with elbows bent and grasping the dumbbells with an overhand grip:

- Inhale and extend the arms vertically, bringing the dumbbells together.
- Exhale at the end of the movement.

This exercise, which is midway between an incline press and incline dumbbell fly, works the pectorals (mainly the clavicular head) and increases their flexibility. It also contracts the anterior deltoid, the serratus anterior, and the pectoralis minor (these last two muscles are fixators of the scapula, which stabilize the arm at the torso). It also uses the triceps brachii, but not as intensely as the barbell press does.

Variation: Beginning the press with the hands in an underhand grip and rotating the wrists halfway to an overhand grip so that the dumbbells face each other focuses the effort on the sternal head of the pectoralis major.

FINAL POSITION

INCLINE DUMBBELL FLYS 10

Flexor pollicis longus
Extensor carpi radialis longus
Brachioradialis
Flexor digitorum superficialis
Palmaris longus
Flexor carpi ulnaris
Flexor carpi radialis
Biceps brachii, aponeurotic expansion
Medial epicondyle
Pronator teres

Deltoid
Coracobrachialis
Biceps brachii

Brachialis

Triceps brachii
Medial head
Long head

Teres major
Subscapularis
Latissimus dorsi
Serratus anterior
Pectoralis major

Sit on a bench angled between 45 and 60 degrees, dumbbells in hand and arms extended vertically or slightly bent to ease stress when bringing the arms together:

• Inhale and extend the arms to horizontal.
• Raise the arms to vertical while exhaling.

This movement should not be performed with heavy weights. It focuses the effort mainly on the clavicular head of the pectoralis major. Along with the pullover, it is a fundamental exercise for developing thoracic expansion.

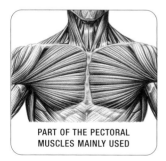

PART OF THE PECTORAL MUSCLES MAINLY USED

FINAL POSITION

11 PEC DECK FLYS

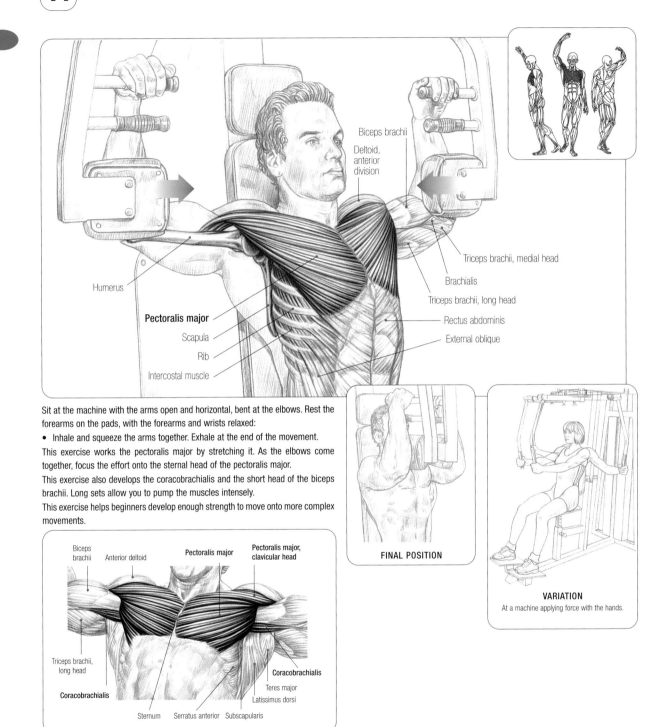

Biceps brachii

Deltoid, anterior division

Triceps brachii, medial head

Brachialis

Triceps brachii, long head

Rectus abdominis

External oblique

Humerus

Pectoralis major

Scapula

Rib

Intercostal muscle

Sit at the machine with the arms open and horizontal, bent at the elbows. Rest the forearms on the pads, with the forearms and wrists relaxed:

• Inhale and squeeze the arms together. Exhale at the end of the movement.

This exercise works the pectoralis major by stretching it. As the elbows come together, focus the effort onto the sternal head of the pectoralis major.

This exercise also develops the coracobrachialis and the short head of the biceps brachii. Long sets allow you to pump the muscles intensely.

This exercise helps beginners develop enough strength to move onto more complex movements.

FINAL POSITION

VARIATION
At a machine applying force with the hands.

Biceps brachii

Anterior deltoid

Pectoralis major

Pectoralis major, clavicular head

Triceps brachii, long head

Coracobrachialis

Teres major

Latissimus dorsi

Coracobrachialis

Sternum

Serratus anterior

Subscapularis

CABLE CROSSOVER FLYS 12

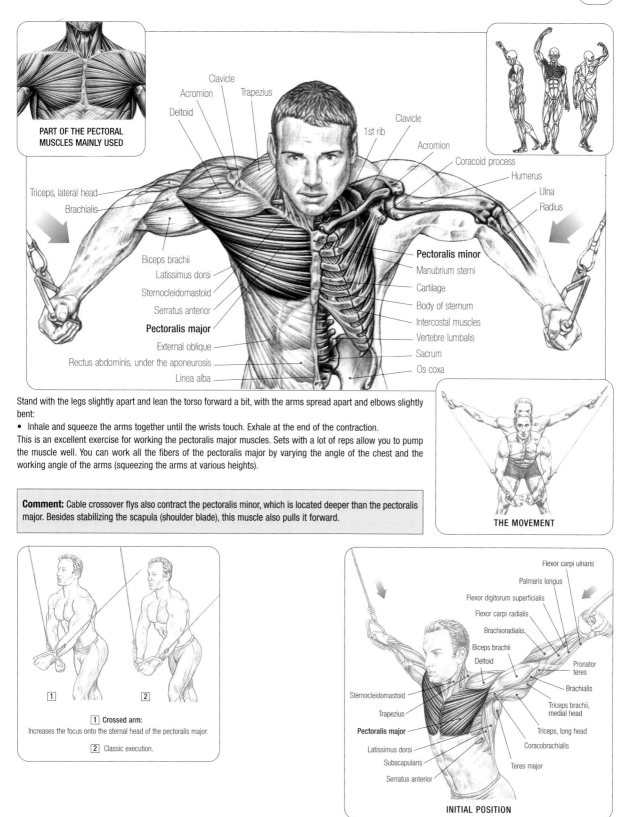

PART OF THE PECTORAL MUSCLES MAINLY USED

Clavicle
Acromion
Deltoid
Trapezius
Clavicle
1st rib
Acromion
Coracoid process
Humerus
Ulna
Radius
Triceps, lateral head
Brachialis
Biceps brachii
Latissimus dorsi
Sternocleidomastoid
Serratus anterior
Pectoralis major
External oblique
Rectus abdominis, under the aponeurosis
Linea alba
Pectoralis minor
Manubrium sterni
Cartilage
Body of sternum
Intercostal muscles
Vertebre lumbalis
Sacrum
Os coxa

Stand with the legs slightly apart and lean the torso forward a bit, with the arms spread apart and elbows slightly bent:

• Inhale and squeeze the arms together until the wrists touch. Exhale at the end of the contraction.

This is an excellent exercise for working the pectoralis major muscles. Sets with a lot of reps allow you to pump the muscle well. You can work all the fibers of the pectoralis major by varying the angle of the chest and the working angle of the arms (squeezing the arms at various heights).

Comment: Cable crossover flys also contract the pectoralis minor, which is located deeper than the pectoralis major. Besides stabilizing the scapula (shoulder blade), this muscle also pulls it forward.

THE MOVEMENT

1 Crossed arm:
Increases the focus onto the sternal head of the pectoralis major.

2 Classic execution.

Flexor carpi ulnaris
Palmaris longus
Flexor digitorum superficialis
Flexor carpi radialis
Brachioradialis
Biceps brachii
Deltoid
Pronator teres
Brachialis
Triceps brachii, medial head
Triceps, long head
Coracobrachialis
Teres major
Sternocleidomastoid
Trapezius
Pectoralis major
Latissimus dorsi
Subscapularis
Serratus anterior

INITIAL POSITION

13 DUMBBELL PULLOVERS

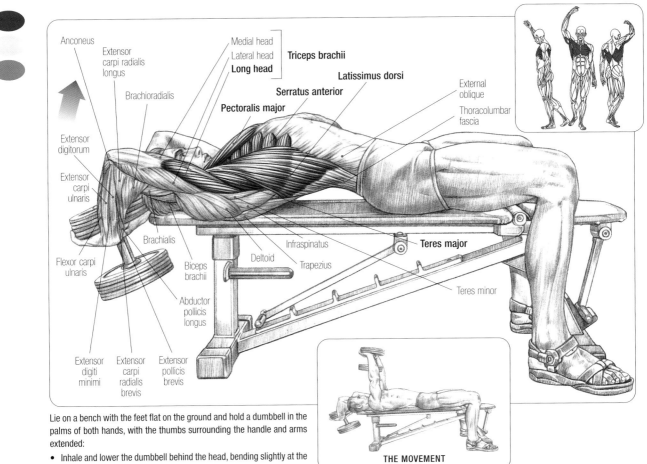

Anconeus
Extensor carpi radialis longus
Brachioradialis
Extensor digitorum
Extensor carpi ulnaris
Flexor carpi ulnaris
Brachialis
Biceps brachii
Abductor pollicis longus
Extensor digiti minimi
Extensor carpi radialis brevis
Extensor pollicis brevis

Medial head
Lateral head
Long head
Triceps brachii
Latissimus dorsi
Serratus anterior
Pectoralis major
External oblique
Thoracolumbar fascia
Infraspinatus
Deltoid
Trapezius
Teres major
Teres minor

THE MOVEMENT

Lie on a bench with the feet flat on the ground and hold a dumbbell in the palms of both hands, with the thumbs surrounding the handle and arms extended:

- Inhale and lower the dumbbell behind the head, bending slightly at the elbows.
- Exhale and return to the initial position.

This exercise develops the bulk of the pectoralis major, long head of triceps brachii, teres major, latissimus dorsi, serratus anterior, rhomboids, and pectoralis minor. The last three muscles stabilize the scapula so that the humerus can move from a stable base.

STABILIZERS OF THE SHOULDER BLADES

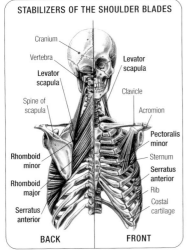

Cranium
Vertebra
Levator scapula
Levator scapula
Clavicle
Spine of scapula
Acromion
Pectoralis minor
Rhomboid minor
Sternum
Serratus anterior
Rhomboid major
Rib
Serratus anterior
Costal cartilage

BACK   FRONT

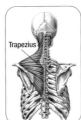

Trapezius

If you use this exercise to open the rib cage, you must work with light weights and avoid bending too much at the elbows. If possible, use a convex bench or place yourself across a horizontal bench and position the pelvis lower than the shoulder girdle. Take in a deep breath at the beginning of the movement and breathe out only at the end of the execution.

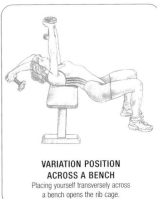

PERFORMING THE MOVEMENT AT A MACHINE

VARIATION POSITION ACROSS A BENCH
Placing yourself transversely across a bench opens the rib cage.

BARBELL PULLOVERS 14

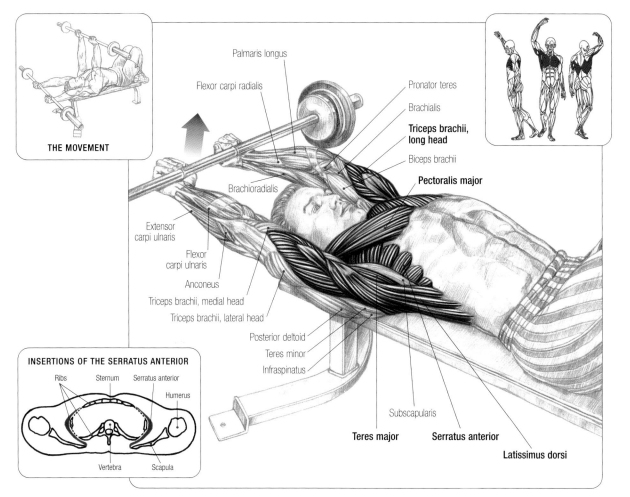

THE MOVEMENT

Palmaris longus

Flexor carpi radialis

Pronator teres

Brachialis

Triceps brachii, long head

Biceps brachii

Pectoralis major

Brachioradialis

Extensor carpi ulnaris

Flexor carpi ulnaris

Anconeus

Triceps brachii, medial head

Triceps brachii, lateral head

Posterior deltoid

Teres minor

Infraspinatus

Subscapularis

Teres major   **Serratus anterior**

Latissimus dorsi

INSERTIONS OF THE SERRATUS ANTERIOR

Ribs   Sternum   Serratus anterior

Humerus

Vertebra   Scapula

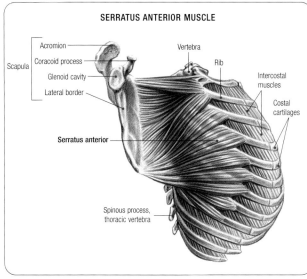

SERRATUS ANTERIOR MUSCLE

Acromion

Coracoid process

Glenoid cavity

Lateral border

Scapula

Vertebra

Rib

Intercostal muscles

Costal cartilages

Serratus anterior

Spinous process, thoracic vertebra

With arms extended, hold the barbell with an overhand grip and hands shoulder-width apart:

- Inhale and expand the chest as much as possible, lowering the barbell behind the head bending slightly at the elbows.
- Exhale while returning to the initial position.

This exercise develops the pectoralis major, long head of the triceps brachii, teres major, latissimus dorsi, serratus anterior, rhomboids, and pectoralis minor.

This is an excellent movement for developing the flexibility and expansion of the rib cage. It should be performed with light weights using proper form and breathing.

4 BACK

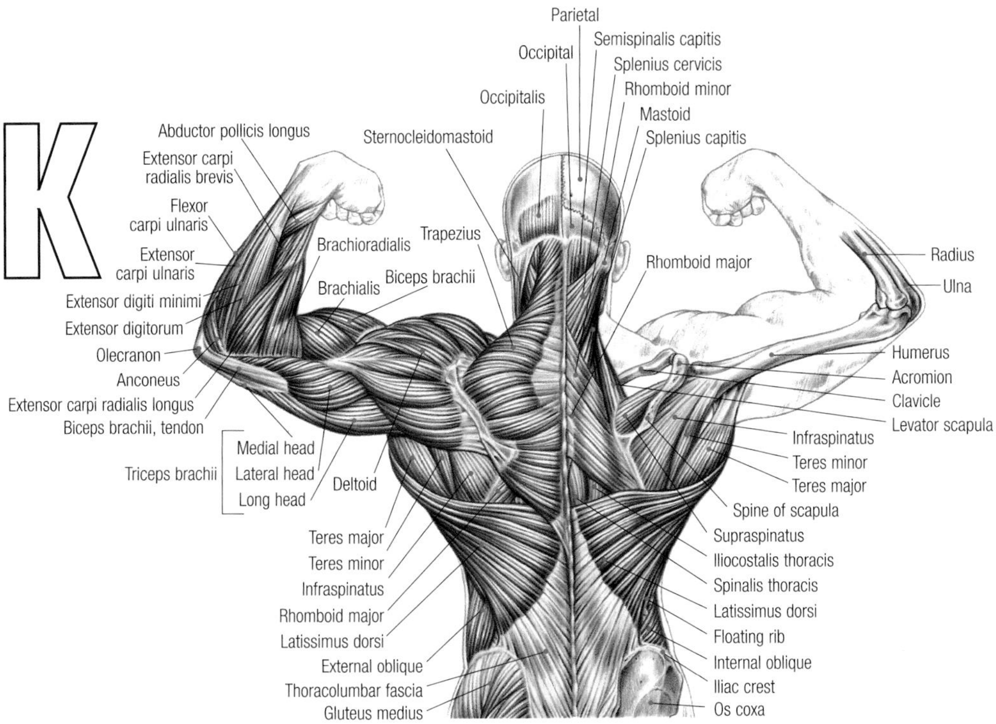

Parietal
Occipital
Semispinalis capitis
Splenius cervicis
Rhomboid minor
Mastoid
Splenius capitis
Occipitalis
Sternocleidomastoid
Abductor pollicis longus
Extensor carpi radialis brevis
Flexor carpi ulnaris
Extensor carpi ulnaris
Brachioradialis
Trapezius
Rhomboid major
Biceps brachii
Brachialis
Extensor digiti minimi
Extensor digitorum
Olecranon
Anconeus
Extensor carpi radialis longus
Biceps brachii, tendon
Radius
Ulna
Humerus
Acromion
Clavicle
Levator scapula
Infraspinatus
Teres minor
Teres major
Spine of scapula
Supraspinatus
Iliocostalis thoracis
Spinalis thoracis
Latissimus dorsi
Floating rib
Internal oblique
Iliac crest
Os coxa
Medial head
Lateral head
Long head
Triceps brachii
Deltoid
Teres major
Teres minor
Infraspinatus
Rhomboid major
Latissimus dorsi
External oblique
Thoracolumbar fascia
Gluteus medius

REVERSE CHIN-UPS 1

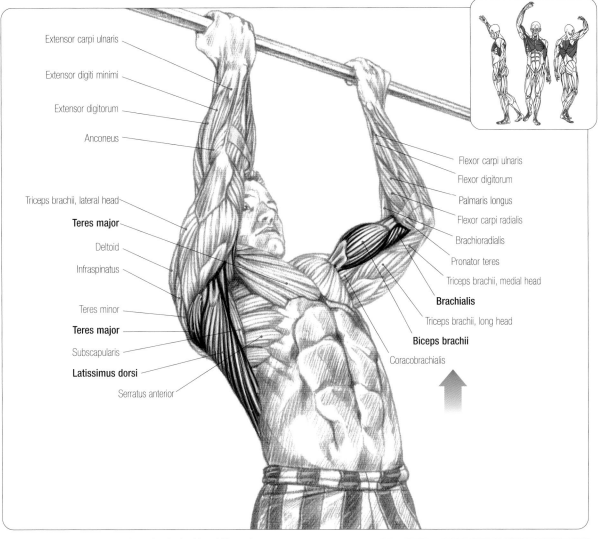

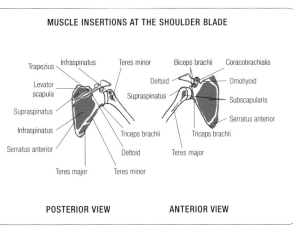

Extensor carpi ulnaris

Extensor digiti minimi

Extensor digitorum

Anconeus

Triceps brachii, lateral head

Teres major

Deltoid

Infraspinatus

Teres minor

Teres major

Subscapularis

Latissimus dorsi

Serratus anterior

Flexor carpi ulnaris

Flexor digitorum

Palmaris longus

Flexor carpi radialis

Brachioradialis

Pronator teres

Triceps brachii, medial head

Brachialis

Triceps brachii, long head

Biceps brachii

Coracobrachialis

Hang from a bar with an underhand grip, hands shoulder-width apart:

• Inhale and push out the chest as you raise the chin to the bar.

• Exhale at the end of the movement.

This movement develops the latissimus dorsi and teres major and is associated with the intense work of the biceps brachii and brachialis.

Therefore, it could be included in an arm workout program.

This exercise also contracts the middle and lower portions of the trapezius, the rhomboids, and the pectorals.

Performing this exercise takes a certain amount of strength; use a high pulley to make it easier.

MUSCLE INSERTIONS AT THE SHOULDER BLADE

Trapezius

Infraspinatus

Levator scapula

Supraspinatus

Infraspinatus

Serratus anterior

Teres major

Teres minor

Deltoid

Teres minor

Biceps brachii

Coracobrachialis

Deltoid

Omohyoid

Supraspinatus

Subscapularis

Serratus anterior

Triceps brachii

Triceps brachii

Teres major

POSTERIOR VIEW

ANTERIOR VIEW

2 CHIN-UPS

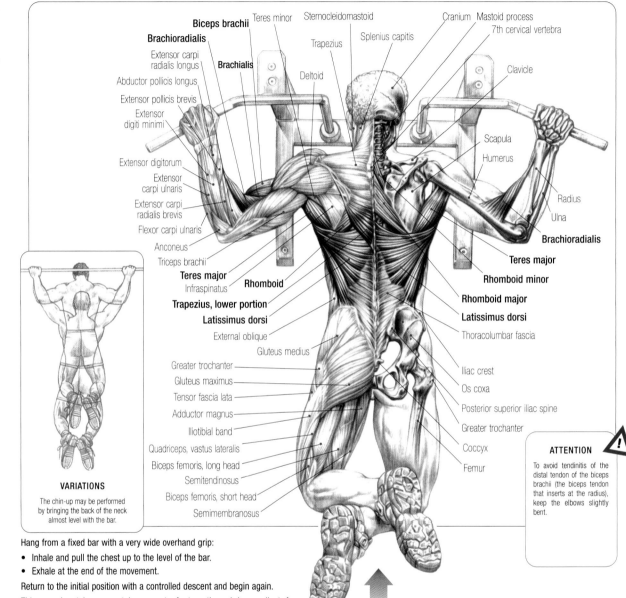

Biceps brachii
Teres minor
Sternocleidomastoid
Cranium Mastoid process
7th cervical vertebra
Brachioradialis
Splenius capitis
Extensor carpi
radialis longus
Trapezius
Clavicle
Brachialis
Abductor pollicis longus
Deltoid
Extensor pollicis brevis
Extensor
digiti minimi
Scapula
Humerus
Extensor digitorum
Extensor
carpi ulnaris
Extensor carpi
radialis brevis
Radius
Flexor carpi ulnaris
Ulna
Anconeus
Brachioradialis
Triceps brachii
Teres major
Teres major
Rhomboid minor
Infraspinatus
Rhomboid
Trapezius, lower portion
Rhomboid major
Latissimus dorsi
Latissimus dorsi
External oblique
Thoracolumbar fascia
Gluteus medius
Greater trochanter
Iliac crest
Gluteus maximus
Os coxa
Tensor fascia lata
Posterior superior iliac spine
Adductor magnus
Greater trochanter
Iliotibial band
Coccyx
Quadriceps, vastus lateralis
Femur
Biceps femoris, long head
Semitendinosus
Biceps femoris, short head
Semimembranosus

VARIATIONS

The chin-up may be performed
by bringing the back of the neck
almost level with the bar.

ATTENTION

To avoid tendinitis of the
distal tendon of the biceps
brachii (the biceps tendon
that inserts at the radius),
keep the elbows slightly
bent.

Hang from a fixed bar with a very wide overhand grip:

- Inhale and pull the chest up to the level of the bar.
- Exhale at the end of the movement.

Return to the initial position with a controlled descent and begin again.

This exercise takes a certain amount of strength and is excellent for developing the latissimus dorsi and teres major and, when the shoulder blades come together at the top of the chin-up, the rhomboids and middle and lower portions of the trapezius. It also works the biceps brachii, brachialis, and brachioradialis.

Variations: By sticking out the chest you can raise your chest to chin level. To increase the intensity, wear a weight belt. Keeping the elbows in next to the body during the movement contracts mainly the external fibers of the latissimus dorsi and develops the width of the back.

Bringing the elbows back and the chest out as you raise the chin to the bar mainly solicits the upper and central fibers of the latissimus dorsi and those of the teres major. This exercise develops the bulk of the back when the shoulder blades come together and the rhomboids and the upper and lower portion of the trapezius are used equally.

Comment: Although not as strongly contracted, the pectoralis major works with the latissimus dorsi and teres major to create the angle between the arm and the trunk.

BRINGING THE BAR TO THE NECK WITH ARMS ALONGSIDE THE BODY

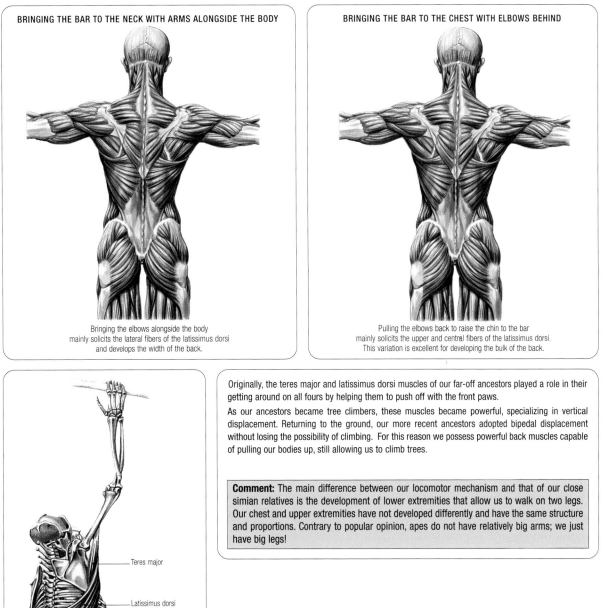

Bringing the elbows alongside the body
mainly solicits the lateral fibers of the latissimus dorsi
and develops the width of the back.

BRINGING THE BAR TO THE CHEST WITH ELBOWS BEHIND

Pulling the elbows back to raise the chin to the bar
mainly solicits the upper and central fibers of the latissimus dorsi.
This variation is excellent for developing the bulk of the back.

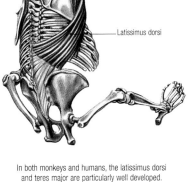

Teres major

Latissimus dorsi

In both monkeys and humans, the latissimus dorsi
and teres major are particularly well developed.

Originally, the teres major and latissimus dorsi muscles of our far-off ancestors played a role in their getting around on all fours by helping them to push off with the front paws.

As our ancestors became tree climbers, these muscles became powerful, specializing in vertical displacement. Returning to the ground, our more recent ancestors adopted bipedal displacement without losing the possibility of climbing. For this reason we possess powerful back muscles capable of pulling our bodies up, still allowing us to climb trees.

Comment: The main difference between our locomotor mechanism and that of our close simian relatives is the development of lower extremities that allow us to walk on two legs. Our chest and upper extremities have not developed differently and have the same structure and proportions. Contrary to popular opinion, apes do not have relatively big arms; we just have big legs!

3 LAT PULL-DOWNS

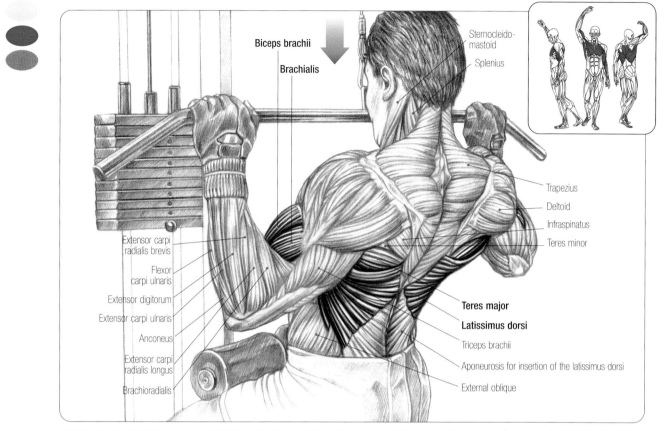

Biceps brachii
Brachialis
Sternocleido-mastoid
Splenius
Trapezius
Deltoid
Infraspinatus
Teres minor
Teres major
Latissimus dorsi
Triceps brachii
Aponeurosis for insertion of the latissimus dorsi
External oblique

Extensor carpi radialis brevis
Flexor carpi ulnaris
Extensor digitorum
Extensor carpi ulnaris
Anconeus
Extensor carpi radialis longus
Brachioradialis

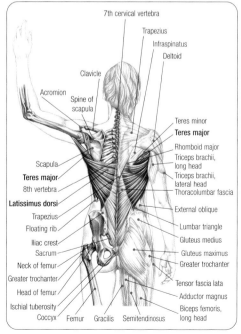

7th cervical vertebra
Trapezius
Infraspinatus
Deltoid
Clavicle
Acromion
Spine of scapula
Scapula
Teres major
8th vertebra
Latissimus dorsi
Trapezius
Floating rib
Iliac crest
Sacrum
Neck of femur
Greater trochanter
Head of femur
Ischial tuberosity
Coccyx Femur Gracilis Semitendinosus

Teres minor
Teres major
Rhomboid major
Triceps brachii, long head
Triceps brachii, lateral head
Thoracolumbar fascia
External oblique
Lumbar triangle
Gluteus medius
Gluteus maximus
Greater trochanter
Tensor fascia lata
Adductor magnus
Biceps femoris, long head

Sit facing the machine with the legs positioned under the pads, gripping the bar in with a wide overhand grip: Inhale and pull the bar down to the sternal notch while puffing out the chest and pulling the elbows back. Exhale at the end of the movement.

This exercise develops the bulk of the back. It mainly works the upper and central fibers of the latissimus dorsi. The middle and lower portions of the trapezius, the rhomboids, the biceps brachii, the brachialis, and, to a lesser extent, the pectorals also contract.

Ulna
Radius
Humerus
Spine of scapula
Acromion
Teres major
Scapula

The teres major gets its name from its circular transverse section.

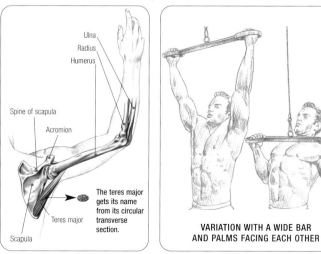

VARIATION WITH A WIDE BAR AND PALMS FACING EACH OTHER

BACK LAT PULL-DOWNS 4

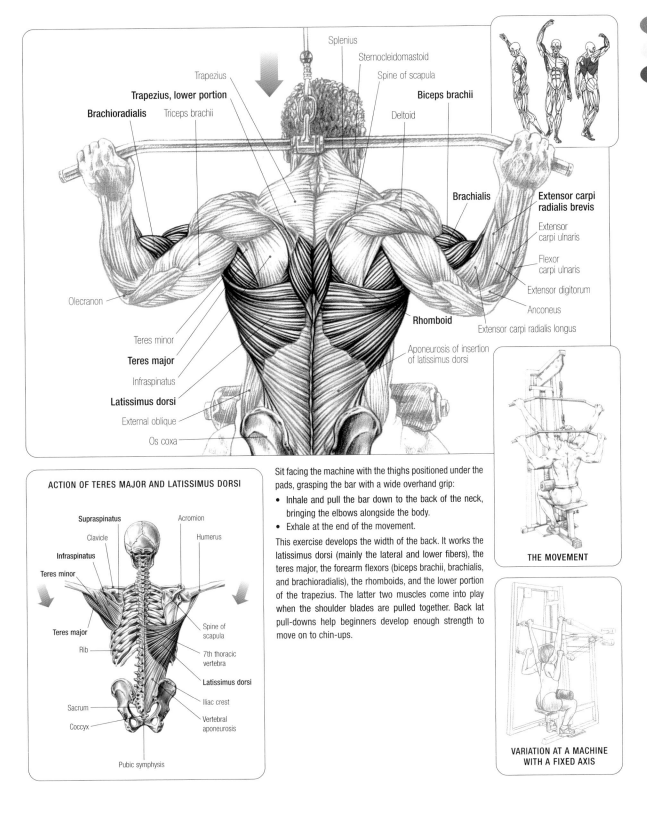

Splenius

Sternocleidomastoid

Trapezius

Spine of scapula

Trapezius, lower portion

Biceps brachii

Brachioradialis

Triceps brachii

Deltoid

Olecranon

Teres minor

Teres major

Infraspinatus

Latissimus dorsi

External oblique

Os coxa

Brachialis

Extensor carpi radialis brevis

Extensor carpi ulnaris

Flexor carpi ulnaris

Extensor digitorum

Anconeus

Extensor carpi radialis longus

Rhomboid

Aponeurosis of insertion of latissimus dorsi

ACTION OF TERES MAJOR AND LATISSIMUS DORSI

Supraspinatus

Acromion

Clavicle

Humerus

Infraspinatus

Teres minor

Teres major

Rib

Spine of scapula

7th thoracic vertebra

Latissimus dorsi

Iliac crest

Sacrum

Coccyx

Vertebral aponeurosis

Pubic symphysis

Sit facing the machine with the thighs positioned under the pads, grasping the bar with a wide overhand grip:

- Inhale and pull the bar down to the back of the neck, bringing the elbows alongside the body.
- Exhale at the end of the movement.

This exercise develops the width of the back. It works the latissimus dorsi (mainly the lateral and lower fibers), the teres major, the forearm flexors (biceps brachii, brachialis, and brachioradialis), the rhomboids, and the lower portion of the trapezius. The latter two muscles come into play when the shoulder blades are pulled together. Back lat pull-downs help beginners develop enough strength to move on to chin-ups.

THE MOVEMENT

VARIATION AT A MACHINE WITH A FIXED AXIS

TRICEPS BRACHII TEARS

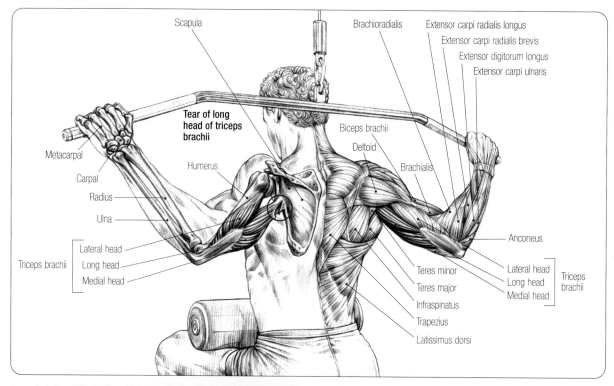

Heavy training of the back and injury to the long head of the triceps brachii

Although it is not the most-used muscle when working the back, the long head of the triceps brachii is the most frequently injured muscle during back lat pull-downs with heavy weights or during chin-ups with added weight.

The latissimus dorsi is a powerful, fan-shaped muscle that attaches the arm to the rib cage, and whose distal tendon is strongly attached to the humerus.

This is the main climbing muscle.

The long head of the triceps brachii, on the other hand, is a smaller muscle whose main function is to extend the forearm and secondarily to bring the arm toward the rib cage. In this way it complements the action of the latissimus dorsi.

Tearing of the long head of the triceps occurs when the muscle is fatigued, most frequently after an improper warm-up.

It only takes a sudden relaxation of the latissimus dorsi during chin-ups with added weight to immediately shift the tension to the long head of the triceps.

This tendon may partially tear, most often close to its insertion on the scapula. (Fortunately complete tears are infrequent.)

Unlike incapacitating shoulder injuries, which may completely halt upper-body training, a tear in the long head of the biceps is less devastating.

You can still perform back exercises such as seated rows or T-bar rows and movements for the triceps such as forearm extensions at a high pulley with the elbows next to the body despite the injury as long as you begin with lighter weights.

However, a brief rest period is recommended before beginning upper-body training.

Comment: Tearing the long head of the triceps may also occur during bench presses. To prevent this triceps tear, warm up with stretching exercises

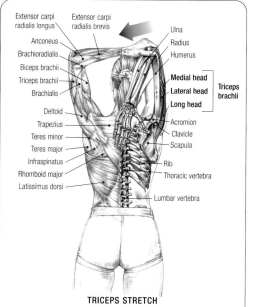

TRICEPS STRETCH

Stand or sit with your back straight and one arm raised vertically beside your head. Bend the arm at the elbow and touch the top of the back with your hand. With the other hand grasp the elbow and slowly try to pull it behind your head. This stretches the teres major, the long head of the triceps brachii, and, to a lesser extent, the latissimus dorsi.

Variation: Pull the hand rather than the elbow. For greater intensity, place the raised arm against a wall.

CLOSE-GRIP LAT PULL-DOWNS 5

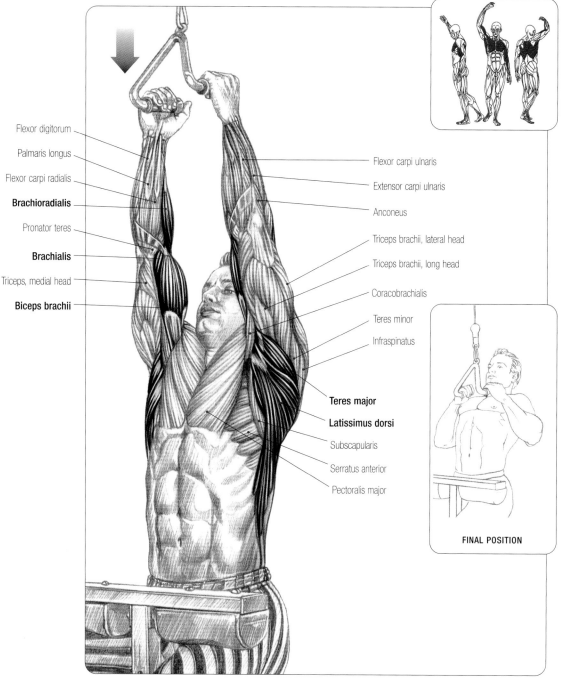

Flexor digitorum

Palmaris longus

Flexor carpi radialis

Brachioradialis

Pronator teres

Brachialis

Triceps, medial head

Biceps brachii

Flexor carpi ulnaris

Extensor carpi ulnaris

Anconeus

Triceps brachii, lateral head

Triceps brachii, long head

Coracobrachialis

Teres minor

Infraspinatus

Teres major

Latissimus dorsi

Subscapularis

Serratus anterior

Pectoralis major

FINAL POSITION

Sit and face the machine with knees positioned under the pads.

• Inhale and bring the handle to the sternum while expanding the chest and leaning slightly back with the torso.

• Exhale at the end of the movement.

This exercise develops the latissimus dorsi and teres major.

When the shoulder blades come together, the trapezius and the posterior deltoid contract.

As with every pulling exercise, the biceps brachii and brachialis contract, and when the palms face each other, the brachioradialis comes into play.

6 | STRAIGHT-ARM LAT PULL-DOWNS

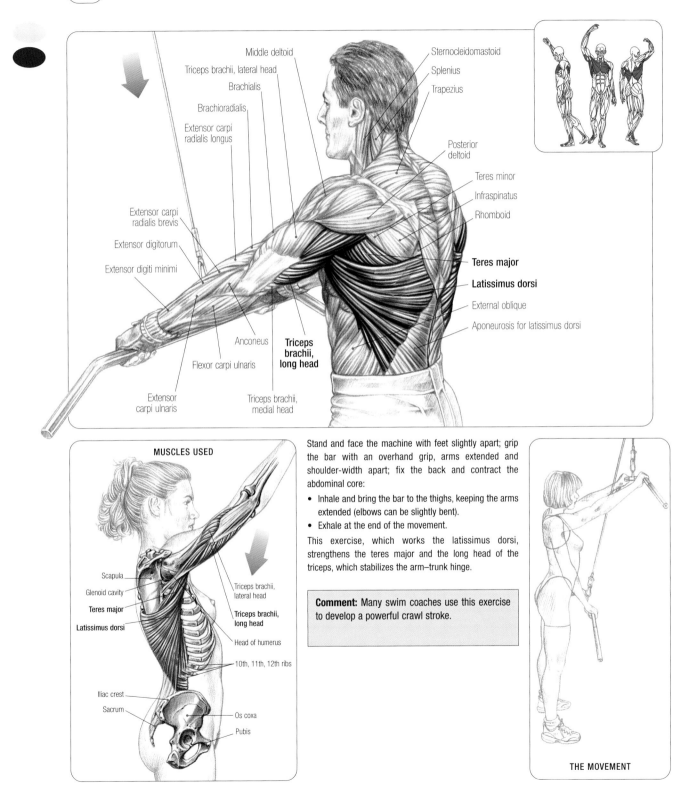

Middle deltoid

Triceps brachii, lateral head

Brachialis

Brachioradialis

Extensor carpi radialis longus

Extensor carpi radialis brevis

Extensor digitorum

Extensor digiti minimi

Anconeus

Flexor carpi ulnaris

Extensor carpi ulnaris

Triceps brachii, long head

Triceps brachii, medial head

Sternocleidomastoid

Splenius

Trapezius

Posterior deltoid

Teres minor

Infraspinatus

Rhomboid

Teres major

Latissimus dorsi

External oblique

Aponeurosis for latissimus dorsi

MUSCLES USED

Scapula

Glenoid cavity

Teres major

Latissimus dorsi

Triceps brachii, lateral head

Triceps brachii, long head

Head of humerus

10th, 11th, 12th ribs

Iliac crest

Sacrum

Os coxa

Pubis

Stand and face the machine with feet slightly apart; grip the bar with an overhand grip, arms extended and shoulder-width apart; fix the back and contract the abdominal core:

- Inhale and bring the bar to the thighs, keeping the arms extended (elbows can be slightly bent).
- Exhale at the end of the movement.

This exercise, which works the latissimus dorsi, strengthens the teres major and the long head of the triceps, which stabilizes the arm–trunk hinge.

Comment: Many swim coaches use this exercise to develop a powerful crawl stroke.

THE MOVEMENT

SEATED ROWS 7

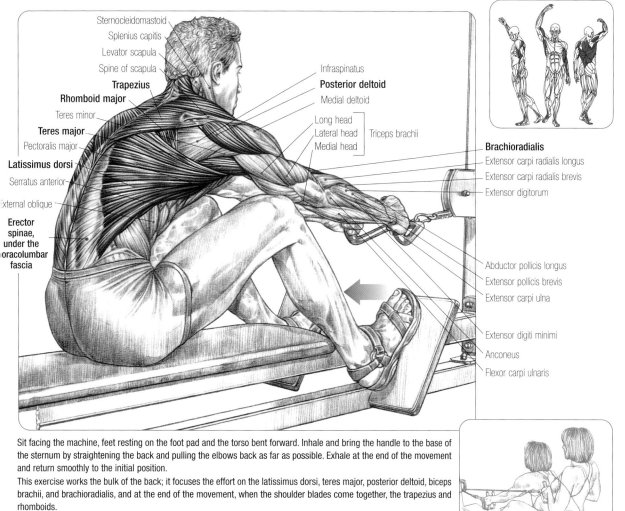

Sternocleidomastoid
Splenius capitis
Levator scapula
Spine of scapula
Trapezius
Rhomboid major
Teres minor
Teres major
Pectoralis major
Latissimus dorsi
Serratus anterior
External oblique
Erector spinae, under the thoracolumbar fascia

Infraspinatus
Posterior deltoid
Medial deltoid
Long head
Lateral head — Triceps brachii
Medial head

Brachioradialis
Extensor carpi radialis longus
Extensor carpi radialis brevis
Extensor digitorum

Abductor pollicis longus
Extensor pollicis brevis
Extensor carpi ulna

Extensor digiti minimi
Anconeus
Flexor carpi ulnaris

Sit facing the machine, feet resting on the foot pad and the torso bent forward. Inhale and bring the handle to the base of the sternum by straightening the back and pulling the elbows back as far as possible. Exhale at the end of the movement and return smoothly to the initial position.

This exercise works the bulk of the back; it focuses the effort on the latissimus dorsi, teres major, posterior deltoid, biceps brachii, and brachioradialis, and at the end of the movement, when the shoulder blades come together, the trapezius and rhomboids.

While raising the chest, the spinal muscles (erector spinae) also contribute.

Allowing the weight to pull you on the return helps develop back flexibility.

Attention: To prevent back injury, never round the back when performing seated rows with heavy weights. ⚠

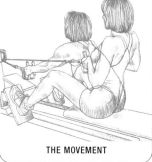

THE MOVEMENT

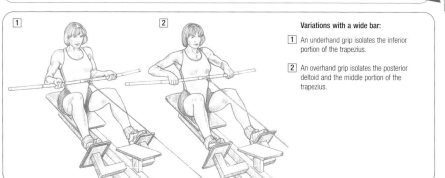

Variations with a wide bar:

1 An underhand grip isolates the inferior portion of the trapezius.

2 An overhand grip isolates the posterior deltoid and the middle portion of the trapezius.

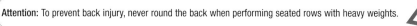

8 ONE-ARM DUMBBELL ROWS

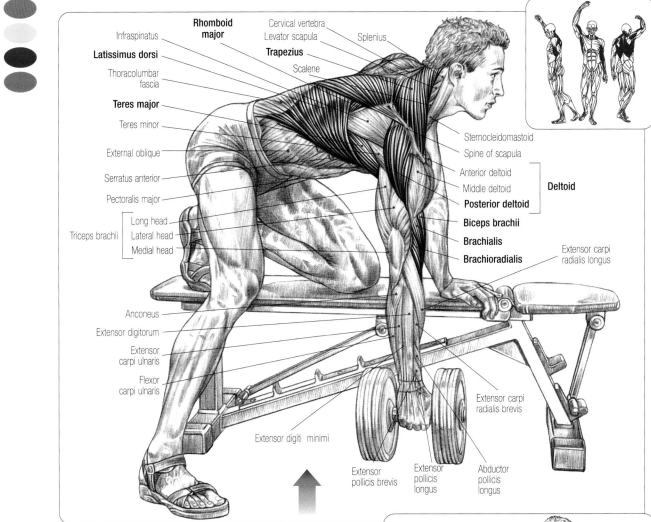

Rhomboid major
Cervical vertebra
Levator scapula
Splenius
Infraspinatus
Trapezius
Latissimus dorsi
Scalene
Thoracolumbar fascia
Teres major
Teres minor
External oblique
Serratus anterior
Pectoralis major
Sternocleidomastoid
Spine of scapula
Anterior deltoid
Middle deltoid
Posterior deltoid
Deltoid
Biceps brachii
Brachialis
Brachioradialis
Extensor carpi radialis longus
Long head
Lateral head
Medial head
Triceps brachii
Anconeus
Extensor digitorum
Extensor carpi ulnaris
Flexor carpi ulnaris
Extensor carpi radialis brevis
Extensor digiti minimi
Extensor pollicis brevis
Extensor pollicis longus
Abductor pollicis longus

Grasp a barbell with the palm facing in; use the opposite hand and knee on the bench to support the back:

• Inhale and lift the upper arm and elbow as high as possible next to the body with the elbow bent.
• Exhale at the end of the movement.

To maximize the contraction, rotate the torso slightly toward the working side at the end of the row.

This exercise mainly works the latissimus dorsi, teres major, and posterior deltoid, and, at the end of the contraction, the trapezius and rhomboids. The forearm flexors (biceps brachii, brachialis, and brachioradialis) are also used.

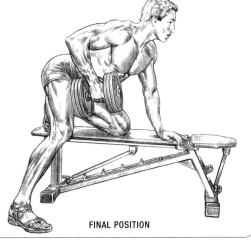

FINAL POSITION

BENT ROWS 9

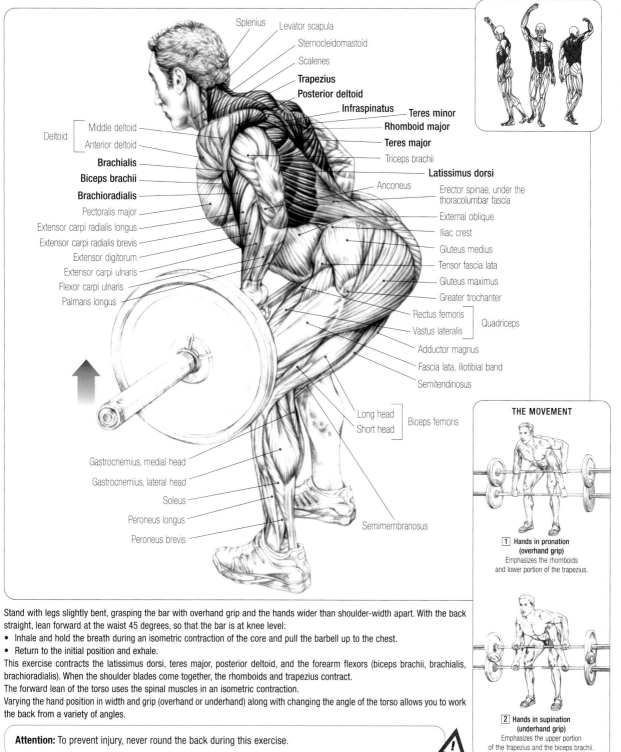

Splenius
Levator scapula
Sternocleidomastoid
Scalenes
Trapezius
Posterior deltoid
Infraspinatus
Teres minor
Rhomboid major
Teres major
Triceps brachii
Latissimus dorsi
Anconeus
Erector spinae, under the thoracolumbar fascia
External oblique
Iliac crest
Gluteus medius
Tensor fascia lata
Gluteus maximus
Greater trochanter
Rectus femoris
Vastus lateralis
Quadriceps
Adductor magnus
Fascia lata, iliotibial band
Semitendinosus

Deltoid
Middle deltoid
Anterior deltoid
Brachialis
Biceps brachii
Brachioradialis
Pectoralis major
Extensor carpi radialis longus
Extensor carpi radialis brevis
Extensor digitorum
Extensor carpi ulnaris
Flexor carpi ulnaris
Palmaris longus

Long head
Short head
Biceps femoris

Gastrocnemius, medial head
Gastrocnemius, lateral head
Soleus
Peroneus longus
Peroneus brevis

Semimembranosus

THE MOVEMENT

1 Hands in pronation (overhand grip)
Emphasizes the rhomboids and lower portion of the trapezius.

2 Hands in supination (underhand grip)
Emphasizes the upper portion of the trapezius and the biceps brachii.

Stand with legs slightly bent, grasping the bar with overhand grip and the hands wider than shoulder-width apart. With the back straight, lean forward at the waist 45 degrees, so that the bar is at knee level:
• Inhale and hold the breath during an isometric contraction of the core and pull the barbell up to the chest.
• Return to the initial position and exhale.
This exercise contracts the latissimus dorsi, teres major, posterior deltoid, and the forearm flexors (biceps brachii, brachialis, brachioradialis). When the shoulder blades come together, the rhomboids and trapezius contract.
The forward lean of the torso uses the spinal muscles in an isometric contraction.
Varying the hand position in width and grip (overhand or underhand) along with changing the angle of the torso allows you to work the back from a variety of angles.

Attention: To prevent injury, never round the back during this exercise.

10 FREESTANDING T-BAR ROWS

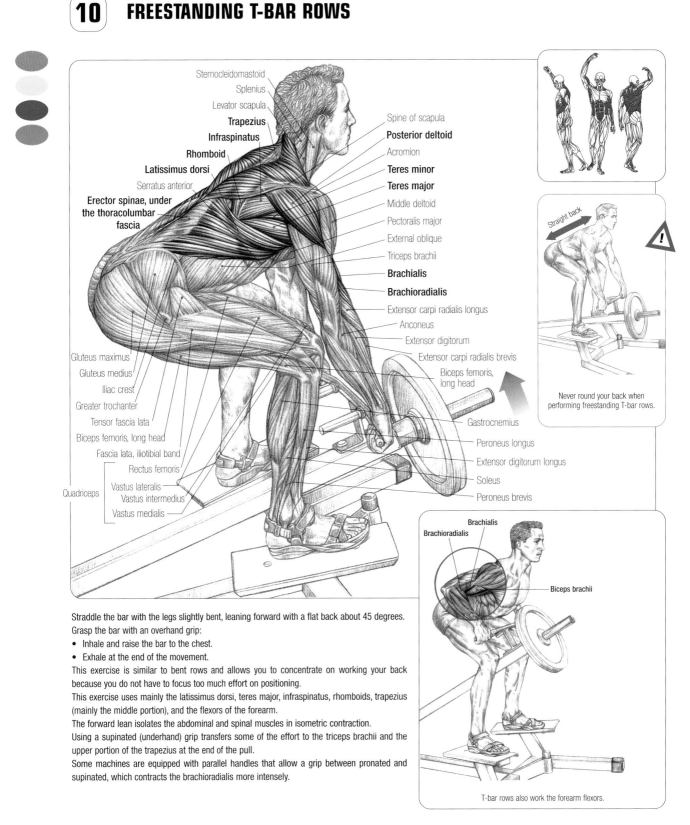

Sternocleidomastoid
Splenius
Levator scapula
Trapezius
Infraspinatus
Rhomboid
Latissimus dorsi
Serratus anterior
Erector spinae, under the thoracolumbar fascia

Spine of scapula
Posterior deltoid
Acromion
Teres minor
Teres major
Middle deltoid
Pectoralis major
External oblique
Triceps brachii
Brachialis
Brachioradialis
Extensor carpi radialis longus
Anconeus
Extensor digitorum
Extensor carpi radialis brevis
Biceps femoris, long head
Gastrocnemius
Peroneus longus
Extensor digitorum longus
Soleus
Peroneus brevis

Gluteus maximus
Gluteus medius
Iliac crest
Greater trochanter
Tensor fascia lata
Biceps femoris, long head
Fascia lata, iliotibial band
Rectus femoris
Vastus lateralis
Vastus intermedius
Vastus medialis
Quadriceps

Straight back

Never round your back when performing freestanding T-bar rows.

Brachialis
Brachioradialis
Biceps brachii

T-bar rows also work the forearm flexors.

Straddle the bar with the legs slightly bent, leaning forward with a flat back about 45 degrees. Grasp the bar with an overhand grip:

- Inhale and raise the bar to the chest.
- Exhale at the end of the movement.

This exercise is similar to bent rows and allows you to concentrate on working your back because you do not have to focus too much effort on positioning.

This exercise uses mainly the latissimus dorsi, teres major, infraspinatus, rhomboids, trapezius (mainly the middle portion), and the flexors of the forearm.

The forward lean isolates the abdominal and spinal muscles in isometric contraction.

Using a supinated (underhand) grip transfers some of the effort to the triceps brachii and the upper portion of the trapezius at the end of the pull.

Some machines are equipped with parallel handles that allow a grip between pronated and supinated, which contracts the brachioradialis more intensely.

T-BAR ROWS WITH ABDOMINAL SUPPORT 11

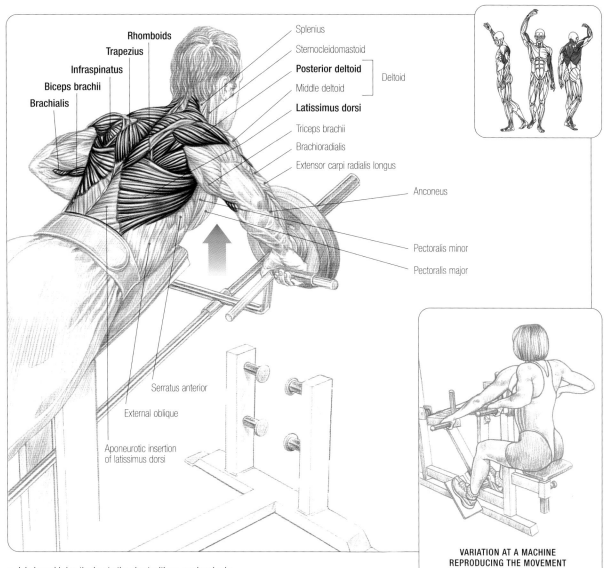

Rhomboids
Trapezius
Infraspinatus
Biceps brachii
Brachialis

Splenius
Sternocleidomastoid
Posterior deltoid } Deltoid
Middle deltoid
Latissimus dorsi
Triceps brachii
Brachioradialis
Extensor carpi radialis longus
Anconeus
Pectoralis minor
Pectoralis major

Serratus anterior
External oblique
Aponeurotic insertion
of latissimus dorsi

**VARIATION AT A MACHINE
REPRODUCING THE MOVEMENT
AS PERFORMED AT A T-BAR**

- Inhale and bring the bar to the chest with an overhand grip.
- Exhale at the end of the movement.

This exercise is similar to bent rows and allows you to concentrate on working your back because you do not have to focus too much effort on positioning.

It mainly uses the latissimus dorsi, teres major, posterior deltoid, arm flexors, trapezius, and rhomboids. Some machines are equipped with an abdominal support, which eliminates the work of the abdominal and spinal muscles. However, when using heavy weights, the rib cage is compressed against the abdominal-support pad, which interferes with breathing and makes the exercise painful to perform.

Comment: A pronated (overhand) hold shifts some of the effort to the biceps brachii and the upper portion of the trapezius at the end of the pull.

12 STIFF-LEGGED DEADLIFTS

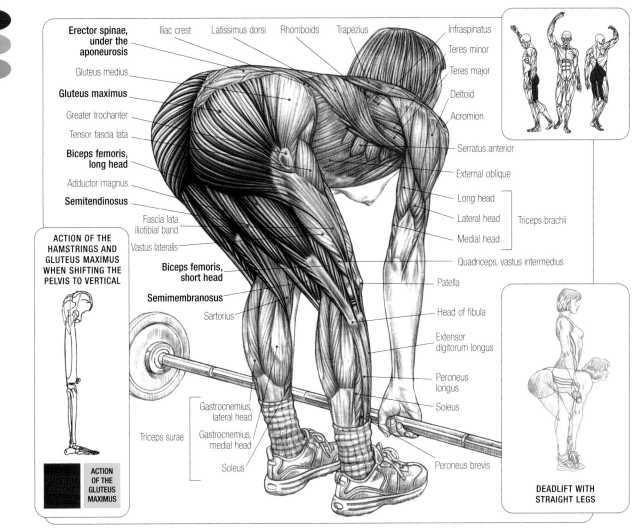

Erector spinae, under the aponeurosis
Iliac crest
Latissimus dorsi
Rhomboids
Trapezius
Infraspinatus
Teres minor
Teres major
Gluteus medius
Gluteus maximus
Deltoid
Greater trochanter
Acromion
Tensor fascia lata
Serratus anterior
Biceps femoris, long head
External oblique
Adductor magnus
Long head
Semitendinosus
Lateral head
Triceps brachii
Fascia lata iliotibial band
Medial head
Vastus lateralis
Quadriceps, vastus intermedius
Biceps femoris, short head
Patella
Semimembranosus
Head of fibula
Sartorius
Extensor digitorum longus
Peroneus longus
Soleus
Gastrocnemius, lateral head
Triceps surae
Gastrocnemius, medial head
Soleus
Peroneus brevis

ACTION OF THE HAMSTRINGS AND GLUTEUS MAXIMUS WHEN SHIFTING THE PELVIS TO VERTICAL

ACTION OF THE GLUTEUS MAXIMUS

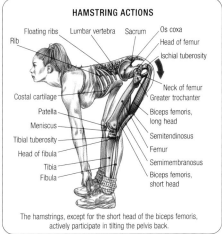

DEADLIFT WITH STRAIGHT LEGS

Stand with the feet slightly apart in front of the bar as it rests on the ground:

- Inhale and bend forward at the waist with the chest forward, back arched, and legs as straight as possible.
- Grasp the bar with an overhand grip. Keeping the arms relaxed, stand up straight by rotating the hips. Keep the abdominal muscles tight and a slight arch in the back for support.
- Exhale out at the end of the movement.
- Bend forward and return to the initial position, but without returning the bar to the floor.

To avoid injury, keep the back straight.

This exercise contracts the deep spinal muscles on either side of the spinal column that straighten the spine.

Straightening the torso by tilting the pelvis from front to back contracts the gluteus maximus and hamstrings (except the short head of the biceps femoris).

Deadlifting from the ground with extended knees stretches the back of the thighs.

To increase the intensity, stand on a box so that the feet are higher than the bar on the ground.

HAMSTRING ACTIONS

Floating ribs
Lumbar vertebra
Sacrum
Os coxa
Rib
Head of femur
Ischial tuberosity
Costal cartilage
Neck of femur
Greater trochanter
Patella
Biceps femoris, long head
Meniscus
Semitendinosus
Tibial tuberosity
Femur
Head of fibula
Semimembranosus
Tibia
Biceps femoris, short head
Fibula

The hamstrings, except for the short head of the biceps femoris, actively participate in tilting the pelvis back.

Comment: To stretch the hamstrings, perform the stiff-legged deadlift with very light weights. The greater the weight, the more the gluteal muscles take over from the hamstrings to straighten the pelvis to vertical.

SUMO DEADLIFTS 13

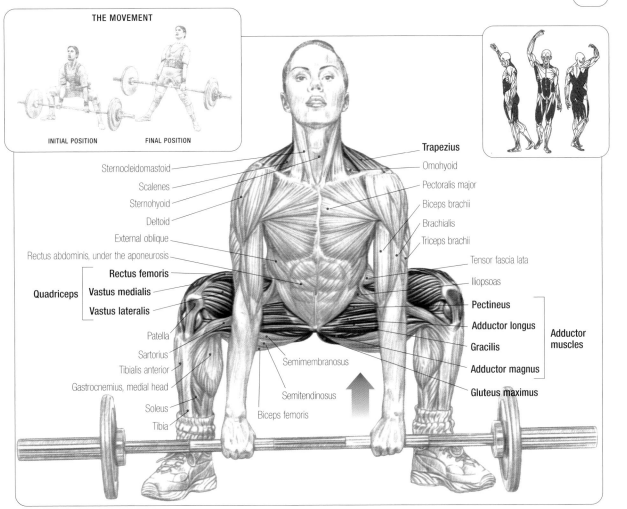

THE MOVEMENT

INITIAL POSITION   FINAL POSITION

Sternocleidomastoid

Scalenes

Sternohyoid

Deltoid

External oblique

Rectus abdominis, under the aponeurosis

Rectus femoris

Quadriceps **Vastus medialis**

Vastus lateralis

Patella

Sartorius

Tibialis anterior

Gastrocnemius, medial head

Soleus

Tibia

Trapezius

Omohyoid

Pectoralis major

Biceps brachii

Brachialis

Triceps brachii

Tensor fascia lata

Iliopsoas

Pectineus

Adductor longus   Adductor muscles

Gracilis

Adductor magnus

Gluteus maximus

Semimembranosus

Semitendinosus

Biceps femoris

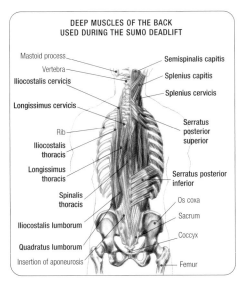

**DEEP MUSCLES OF THE BACK
USED DURING THE SUMO DEADLIFT**

Mastoid process

Vertebra

Iliocostalis cervicis

Longissimus cervicis

Rib

Iliocostalis thoracis

Longissimus thoracis

Spinalis thoracis

Iliocostalis lumborum

Quadratus lumborum

Insertion of aponeurosis

Semispinalis capitis

Splenius capitis

Splenius cervicis

Serratus posterior superior

Serratus posterior inferior

Os coxa

Sacrum

Coccyx

Femur

Stand facing the bar, with legs wider than shoulder-width apart and toes pointing out in line with the knees:

- Inhale and bend the legs until the thighs are horizontal to the ground; grasp the bar with an overhand grip about shoulder-width apart. If you are lifting very heavy weights, use a reverse grip (grasping the bar with one overhand and one underhand grip) to keep the bar from rolling.
- Hold your breath and contract the core, slightly round the back, and extend the legs, bringing the torso vertical and pulling the shoulders back.
- Exhale at the end of the movement.
- Return the bar to the ground holding your breath and never round your back.

The difference between this and the classic deadlift is that this exercise works the quadriceps and adductor muscles intensely. Because the pelvis is not as tilted, it works the back less.

Comment: When beginning the movement, slide the bar along the shins. High reps (10 maximum) with light weights strengthen the lumbar region and work the thighs and the gluteal muscles.

When using heavy weights, perform this exercise with great caution to prevent injuries to the hip joints, adductor group of the thighs, and the lumbosacral junction. The sumo deadlift is one of the three power-lifting movements.

14 DEADLIFTS

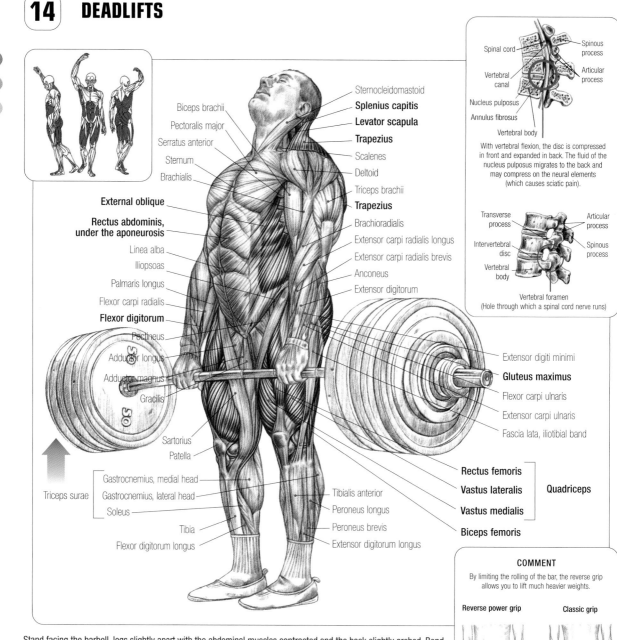

Sternocleidomastoid
Splenius capitis
Levator scapula
Trapezius
Scalenes
Deltoid
Triceps brachii
Trapezius
Brachioradialis
Extensor carpi radialis longus
Extensor carpi radialis brevis
Anconeus
Extensor digitorum

Biceps brachii
Pectoralis major
Serratus anterior
Sternum
Brachialis
External oblique
Rectus abdominis, under the aponeurosis
Linea alba
Iliopsoas
Palmaris longus
Flexor carpi radialis
Flexor digitorum
Pectineus
Adductor longus
Adductor magnus
Gracilis
Sartorius
Patella

Extensor digiti minimi
Gluteus maximus
Flexor carpi ulnaris
Extensor carpi ulnaris
Fascia lata, iliotibial band

Rectus femoris
Vastus lateralis — Quadriceps
Vastus medialis
Biceps femoris

Triceps surae
Gastrocnemius, medial head
Gastrocnemius, lateral head
Soleus
Tibia
Flexor digitorum longus

Tibialis anterior
Peroneus longus
Peroneus brevis
Extensor digitorum longus

Spinal cord
Spinous process
Vertebral canal
Articular process
Nucleus pulposus
Annulus fibrosus
Vertebral body

With vertebral flexion, the disc is compressed in front and expanded in back. The fluid of the nucleus pulposus migrates to the back and may compress on the neural elements (which causes sciatic pain).

Transverse process
Articular process
Intervertebral disc
Spinous process
Vertebral body
Vertebral foramen
(Hole through which a spinal cord nerve runs)

COMMENT

By limiting the rolling of the bar, the reverse grip allows you to lift much heavier weights.

Reverse power grip   Classic grip

Stand facing the barbell, legs slightly apart with the abdominal muscles contracted and the back slightly arched. Bend the knees until the thighs are horizontal with the floor. This position will vary depending on the flexibility at the ankles and your physical structure. (The thighs will be horizontal for someone with short femurs and arms. The thighs will be above than horizontal for someone with long femurs and arms.) Grasp the barbell with extended arms in an overhand grip a little wider than shoulder-width apart (reversing the grip of one hand—one overhand and one underhand—keeps the bar from rolling, which allows you to use much heavier weights):

- Inhale, hold the breath, and contract the abdominal muscles and low back and raise the bar by straightening the legs and allowing the bar to slide up the shins. When the bar reaches the knees, straighten the torso while straightening the legs.
- Exhale at the end of the effort.

Throughout the exercise, keep your back straight.

This exercise works nearly every muscle in the body and is effective for developing the lumbosacral and trapezius muscles. It also works the gluteal muscles and quadriceps intensely.

The deadlift, along with the bench press and the squat, make up the exercises in power-lifting competitions.

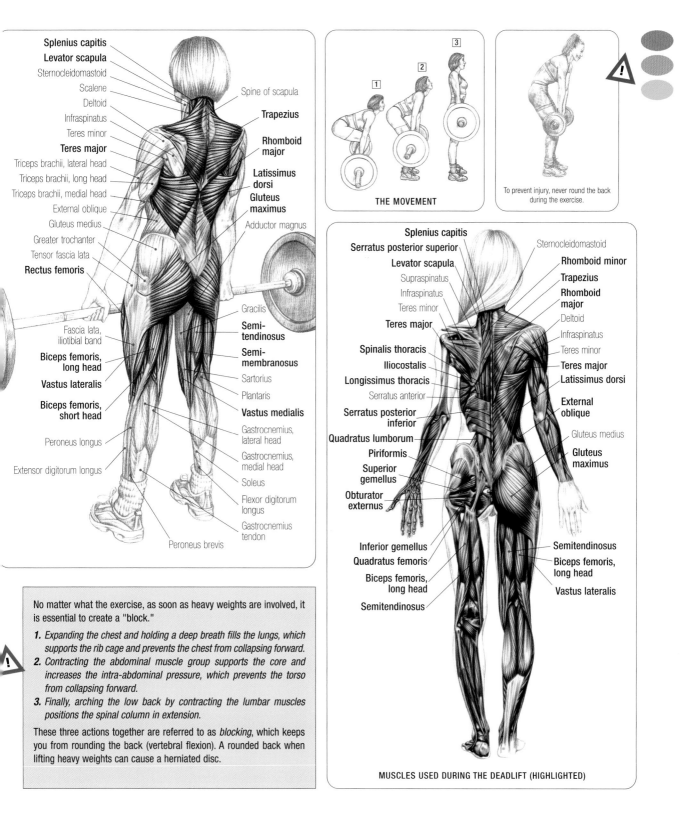

Splenius capitis
Levator scapula
Sternocleidomastoid
Scalene
Deltoid
Infraspinatus
Teres minor
Teres major
Triceps brachii, lateral head
Triceps brachii, long head
Triceps brachii, medial head
External oblique
Gluteus medius
Greater trochanter
Tensor fascia lata
Rectus femoris

Spine of scapula
Trapezius
Rhomboid major
Latissimus dorsi
Gluteus maximus
Adductor magnus

Fascia lata, iliotibial band
Biceps femoris, long head
Vastus lateralis
Biceps femoris, short head
Peroneus longus
Extensor digitorum longus

Gracilis
Semi-tendinosus
Semi-membranosus
Sartorius
Plantaris
Vastus medialis
Gastrocnemius, lateral head
Gastrocnemius, medial head
Soleus
Flexor digitorum longus
Gastrocnemius tendon
Peroneus brevis

THE MOVEMENT

To prevent injury, never round the back during the exercise.

Splenius capitis
Serratus posterior superior
Levator scapula
Supraspinatus
Infraspinatus
Teres minor
Teres major
Spinalis thoracis
Iliocostalis
Longissimus thoracis
Serratus anterior
Serratus posterior inferior
Quadratus lumborum
Piriformis
Superior gemellus
Obturator externus

Sternocleidomastoid
Rhomboid minor
Trapezius
Rhomboid major
Deltoid
Infraspinatus
Teres minor
Teres major
Latissimus dorsi
External oblique
Gluteus medius
Gluteus maximus

Inferior gemellus
Quadratus femoris
Biceps femoris, long head
Semitendinosus

Semitendinosus
Biceps femoris, long head
Vastus lateralis

MUSCLES USED DURING THE DEADLIFT (HIGHLIGHTED)

No matter what the exercise, as soon as heavy weights are involved, it is essential to create a "block."

1. *Expanding the chest and holding a deep breath fills the lungs, which supports the rib cage and prevents the chest from collapsing forward.*

2. *Contracting the abdominal muscle group supports the core and increases the intra-abdominal pressure, which prevents the torso from collapsing forward.*

3. *Finally, arching the low back by contracting the lumbar muscles positions the spinal column in extension.*

These three actions together are referred to as *blocking*, which keeps you from rounding the back (vertebral flexion). A rounded back when lifting heavy weights can cause a herniated disc.

✚ BICEPS BRACHII TENDON TEAR

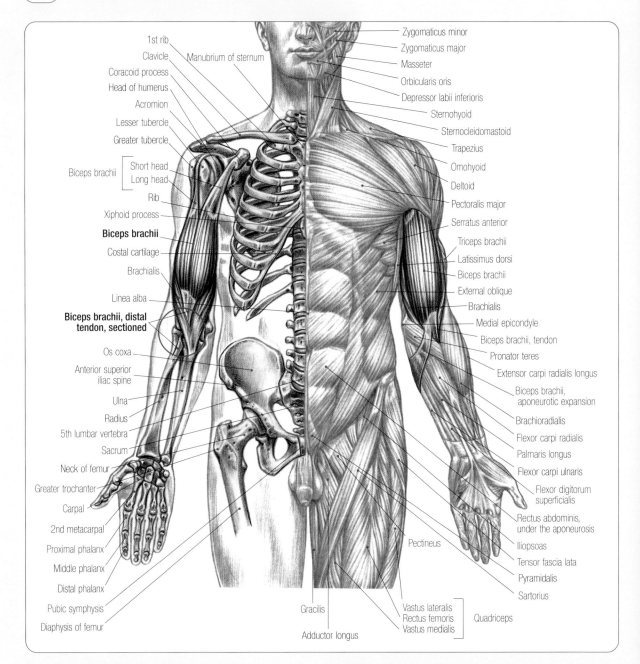

1st rib
Clavicle
Manubrium of sternum
Coracoid process
Head of humerus
Acromion
Lesser tubercle
Greater tubercle
Biceps brachii — Short head, Long head
Rib
Xiphoid process
Biceps brachii
Costal cartilage
Brachialis
Linea alba
Biceps brachii, distal tendon, sectioned
Os coxa
Anterior superior iliac spine
Ulna
Radius
5th lumbar vertebra
Sacrum
Neck of femur
Greater trochanter
Carpal
2nd metacarpal
Proximal phalanx
Middle phalanx
Distal phalanx
Pubic symphysis
Diaphysis of femur

Zygomaticus minor
Zygomaticus major
Masseter
Orbicularis oris
Depressor labii inferioris
Sternohyoid
Sternocleidomastoid
Trapezius
Omohyoid
Deltoid
Pectoralis major
Serratus anterior
Triceps brachii
Latissimus dorsi
Biceps brachii
External oblique
Brachialis
Medial epicondyle
Biceps brachii, tendon
Pronator teres
Extensor carpi radialis longus
Biceps brachii, aponeurotic expansion
Brachioradialis
Flexor carpi radialis
Palmaris longus
Flexor carpi ulnaris
Flexor digitorum superficialis
Rectus abdominis, under the aponeurosis
Iliopsoas
Tensor fascia lata
Pyramidalis
Sartorius

Pectineus
Gracilis
Adductor longus
Vastus lateralis
Rectus femoris
Vastus medialis
Quadriceps

Tearing the long head of the biceps brachii is by far the most common serious sport-related biceps injury.

Generally, it occurs in a muscle, already weakened by tendinitis, after a sudden backward movement of the arm, e.g., during a throw. This movement is relatively common in baseball, tennis, and any sport involving a throwing action, but it also occurs in the snatch in weightlifting. During this motion, tension is suddenly placed on the long head of the biceps brachii, most often where its tendon passes through the bicipital groove of the humerus.

Weightlifting, specifically the deadlift, with heavy weights can cause another characteristic biceps brachii injury.

A common practice when using heavy weights in the deadlift that prevents the bar from rolling in the hands is to use a reverse grip (one overhand grip and one underhand grip).

This technique, although usually safe, can in rare instances cause the tearing or the pulling away of the inferior tendon of the biceps brachii where the muscle inserts onto the humerus.

During the positive phase of the deadlift, the effort is mainly exerted by the muscles of the legs and gluteal muscles, the back, and the abdominal muscles. The arms hang down, completely extended and relaxed.

Unfortunately, the slight shortening caused by contracting either head of the biceps brings the hand into supination (the biceps being the strongest supinator), which with extra heavy weights may cause complete rupture of the tendon at the radius.

This injury occurs at the distal attachment because as the arms hang next to the body, the proximal tension is divided between the short and long heads of the biceps brachii whereas, distally, only one tendinous insertion supports the tension.

Compared to other tendon tears such as the pectoralis major or the adductors of the thigh in which the pain is unbearable and stops the athlete from continuing, the pain of a biceps tendon tear is relatively mild despite the seriousness of the actual injury.

In competitive power lifting, athletes have continued their lift despite the biceps tendon tear incurred during that lift.

After the accident the diagnosis is obvious: swelling caused by hemorrhaging appears in the forearm. But what is most striking is the appearance of the biceps brachii, which becomes ball shaped at the upper arm close to pectoralis major and the deltoid, revealing the brachialis muscle lower down.

Despite the tear, the brachialis, brachioradialis, extensor carpi radialis longus and brevis, and pronator teres muscles can still flex the arm, just not as strongly. Supination of the forearm becomes much more of a problem because the end range of this movement relies only on the supinator muscle.

If this injury is not immediately treated with surgery to reattach the biceps tendon onto the radius, irreversible retraction of the muscle will occur with fibrous change. And although moving the arm will still be possible, there will be permanent loss of strength in flexion and supination. It is possible to prevent this injury by regularly working the biceps, not to develop the muscle, but to strengthen its tendon. For this reason add forearm flexion isolations using a bar in a series of "cheats" by leaning the chest back to give the bar a boost. If practiced regularly, this technique reinforces the distal tendon of the biceps by the tension it places on it. Nevertheless it must be performed carefully without rounding the back to avoid injury.

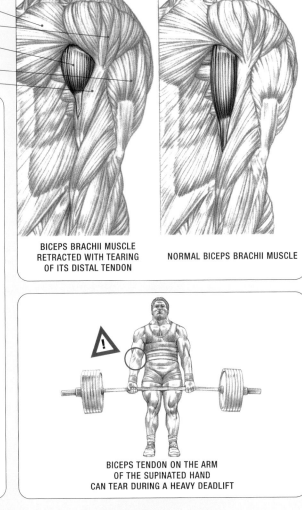

Pectoralis major
Deltoid
Biceps brachii, sectioned and retracted
Triceps brachii
Brachialis

BICEPS BRACHII MUSCLE RETRACTED WITH TEARING OF ITS DISTAL TENDON

NORMAL BICEPS BRACHII MUSCLE

TYPICAL APPEARANCE OF AN UNTREATED DISTAL BICEPS TENDON TEAR
If, after tearing the distal tendon of the biceps brachii, surgery to reattach it to the radius is not performed quickly, permanent retraction and atrophy of the muscle will occur.

BICEPS TENDON ON THE ARM OF THE SUPINATED HAND CAN TEAR DURING A HEAVY DEADLIFT

LOW BACK PAIN

Back pain is the most common problem of the lumbar spine region.

Generally, it is not serious and is most often caused by the shortening of the small, deep vertebral muscles that attach to the transverse processes.

If, during a poorly executed rotation or extension of the spine, one of these muscles is overstretched or is torn, it will automatically shorten along with its neighboring muscles and the superficial erector spinae. The back muscles cramp in pain; however, this cramping limits movement that otherwise might tear or increase the tearing of the small deep muscle.

This general shortening of a portion of the back muscles often disappears when the small deep muscle heals. But sometimes the back pain becomes entrenched, and even after the muscles heal, the local shortening can last several weeks and in some people for years.

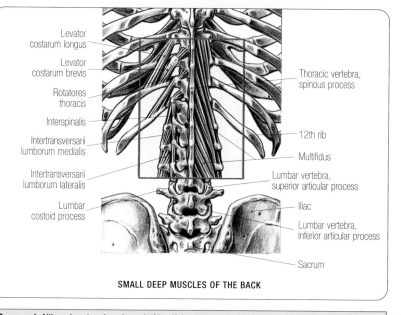

Levator costarum longus
Levator costarum brevis
Rotatores thoracis
Interspinalis
Intertransversarii lumborum medialis
Intertransversarii lumborum lateralis
Lumbar costoid process

Thoracic vertebra, spinous process
12th rib
Multifidus
Lumbar vertebra, superior articular process
Iliac
Lumbar vertebra, inferior articular process
Sacrum

SMALL DEEP MUSCLES OF THE BACK

Comment: Although not serious in and of itself, lumbago, which is a painful contracture of the back muscles, can be part of more serious vertebral injuries such as herniated discs, tears in the paravertebral muscles and ligaments, and fractures.

SHOULD YOU ARCH YOUR BACK?

SHOULD YOU ARCH YOUR BACK?

For people without vertebral problems, arching the back during an exercise is not risky. In fact, with movements such as the squat (page 96) or the deadlift (page 82), where the back tends to round, arching the back can prevent injury. However, for some people arching the back during an exercise can be very dangerous.

- For people suffering from congenital spondylolysis (incomplete fusing of the vertebral arch), putting the lumbar spine in extension can cause the vertebra to slide (spondylolisthesis), which may cause serious nerve compression and lead to sciatica.
- For people who are not fully grown or people experiencing osteoporosis, extending the lumbar spine may lead to spondylolysis because of fractures in the vertebral arch. This fracture in the posterior anchoring system of the vertebra may allow the vertebra to slide forward and seriously compress the neural elements (which leads to sciatica).

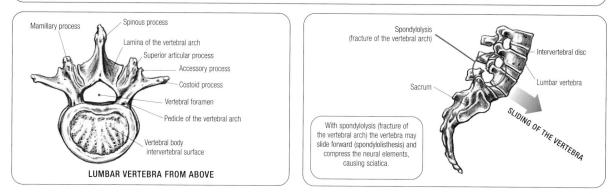

Mamillary process
Spinous process
Lamina of the vertebral arch
Superior articular process
Accessory process
Costoid process
Vertebral foramen
Pedicle of the vertebral arch
Vertebral body intervertebral surface

LUMBAR VERTEBRA FROM ABOVE

Spondylolysis (fracture of the vertebral arch)
Intervertebral disc
Sacrum
Lumbar vertebra
SLIDING OF THE VERTEBRA

With spondylolysis (fracture of the vertebral arch) the vertebra may slide forward (spondylolisthesis) and compress the neural elements, causing sciatica.

BACK EXTENSIONS 15

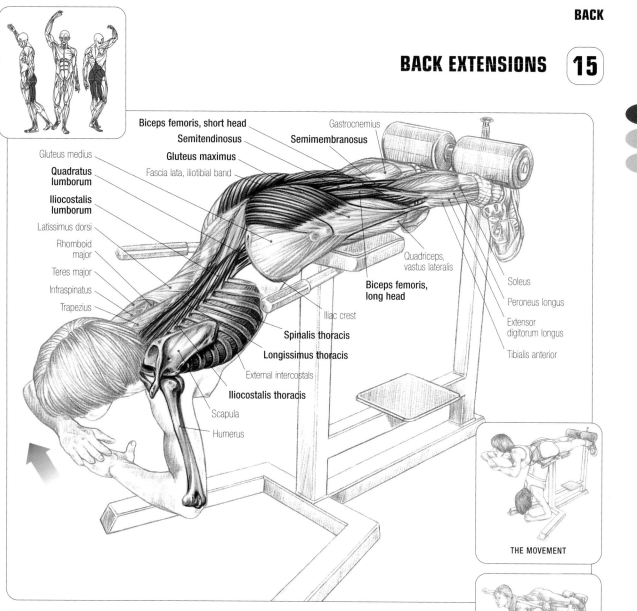

Biceps femoris, short head
Semitendinosus
Gluteus maximus
Gluteus medius
Fascia lata, iliotibial band
Quadratus lumborum
Iliocostalis lumborum
Latissimus dorsi
Rhomboid major
Teres major
Infraspinatus
Trapezius
Iliac crest
Spinalis thoracis
Longissimus thoracis
External intercostals
Iliocostalis thoracis
Scapula
Humerus

Gastrocnemius
Semimembranosus
Quadriceps, vastus lateralis
Biceps femoris, long head
Soleus
Peroneus longus
Extensor digitorum longus
Tibialis anterior

THE MOVEMENT

VARIATION WITH A BAR ACROSS THE SHOULDERS

VARIATION EXTENDING AT AN INCLINE BENCH

Lie facedown on a Roman chair and place the ankles under the roller pads. Because the axis of flexion passes through the coxofemoral joints, the pubic bone should not rest on the support pad:

• With the torso bent forward, extend the back to horizontal. Raise the head and continue into hyperextension by arching the lumbar spine. This must be performed carefully to protect your low back.

This exercise mainly develops the group of paraspinal erectors of the spine (iliocostales, longissimus thoracis, spinalis thoracis, splenius, and semispinalis capitis) and quadratus lumborum and, to a lesser degree, the gluteus maximus and the hamstrings except for the short head of the biceps femoris. Complete flexion of the torso develops the flexibility of the lumbosacral mass. Supporting the pelvis on the bench, so that the axis is displaced to the back of the body, focuses the movement completely at the lumbosacral level but less intensely given the range of motion and the greater power of the lever arm.

To increase the intensity, sustain the horizontal position of the torso at the end of the extension for a few seconds. Using an incline bench makes this exercise easier for beginners to execute.

Variations

• Performing the torso extension with a bar on the shoulders stabilizes the upper back, which focuses the effort on the lower part of the erector spinae muscles.

• The back extension machine allows you to focus on the lumbosacral mass of the spinal muscles (see page 88, Torso Extensions at a Machine).

• To increase the intensity, perform the exercise while holding a weight to the chest or behind the neck.

16 TORSO EXTENSIONS AT A MACHINE

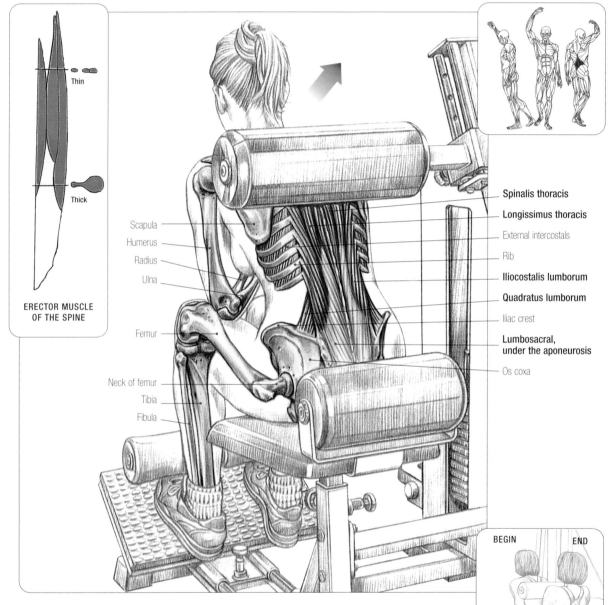

ERECTOR MUSCLE OF THE SPINE

Thin

Thick

Scapula
Humerus
Radius
Ulna

Femur

Neck of femur
Tibia
Fibula

Spinalis thoracis
Longissimus thoracis
External intercostals
Rib
Iliocostalis lumborum
Quadratus lumborum
Iliac crest
Lumbosacral, under the aponeurosis
Os coxa

BEGIN   END

THE MOVEMENT

Sit at the machine, leaning the torso forward and the pad of the machine at shoulder-blade (scapula) level:

• Inhale and press back, straightening the torso as much as possible.
• Return slowly to the initial position while exhaling and begin again.

This exercise works the erector muscles of the spine, focusing the effort on the low back, specifically the lumbosacral mass of the spinal muscles.

This exercise is excellent for beginners. Done in sets of 10 to 12 repetitions, it develops the strength to progress to more technically demanding exercises for the back.

To perform this exercise with heavier weights, reduce the number of repetitions in the set.

Because the machine regulates the range of motion and the weight, the number of repetitions may vary during the same session.

Example: Two series of 15 repetitions with moderate weights and complete range of performance followed by two series of 7 repetitions with more weights and reduced range.

UPRIGHT ROWS (17)

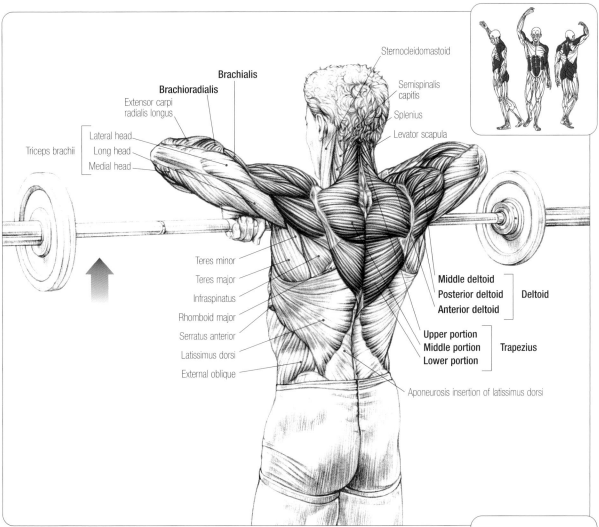

Sternocleidomastoid

Brachialis

Brachioradialis

Extensor carpi
radialis longus

Semispinalis
capitis

Splenius

Levator scapula

Triceps brachii
Lateral head
Long head
Medial head

Teres minor

Teres major

Infraspinatus

Rhomboid major

Serratus anterior

Latissimus dorsi

External oblique

Middle deltoid
Posterior deltoid   Deltoid
Anterior deltoid

Upper portion
Middle portion   Trapezius
Lower portion

Aponeurosis insertion of latissimus dorsi

Stand with the legs slightly apart, keeping the back straight and grasping the barbell with an overhand grip. The grip should be hand width or slightly wider:

- Inhale and pull the barbell up along the front of the body to the chin, raising the elbows as high as possible.
- Exhale and lower the barbell with a controlled movement.

This exercise mainly uses the superior portion of the trapezius as well as the deltoid, levator scapula, biceps brachii, brachialis, muscles of the forearm, abdominal muscles, gluteal muscles, and lumbosacral group.

A wider grip uses the deltoid more than the trapezius.

THE MOVEMENT

18 BARBELL SHRUGS

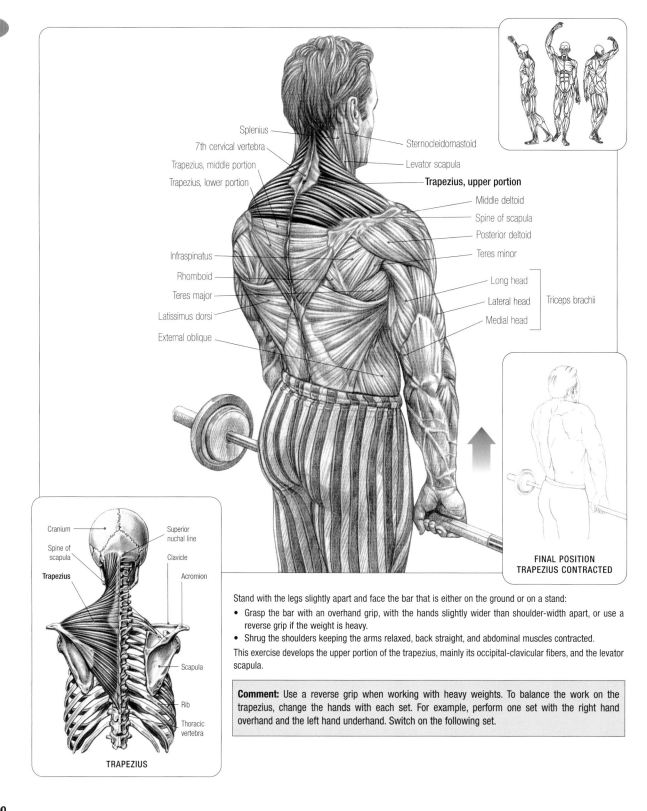

Splenius

7th cervical vertebra

Trapezius, middle portion

Trapezius, lower portion

Sternocleidomastoid

Levator scapula

Trapezius, upper portion

Middle deltoid

Spine of scapula

Posterior deltoid

Teres minor

Infraspinatus

Rhomboid

Teres major

Latissimus dorsi

External oblique

Long head

Lateral head   Triceps brachii

Medial head

**FINAL POSITION
TRAPEZIUS CONTRACTED**

Cranium

Spine of scapula

Trapezius

Superior nuchal line

Clavicle

Acromion

Scapula

Rib

Thoracic vertebra

TRAPEZIUS

Stand with the legs slightly apart and face the bar that is either on the ground or on a stand:

- Grasp the bar with an overhand grip, with the hands slightly wider than shoulder-width apart, or use a reverse grip if the weight is heavy.
- Shrug the shoulders keeping the arms relaxed, back straight, and abdominal muscles contracted.

This exercise develops the upper portion of the trapezius, mainly its occipital-clavicular fibers, and the levator scapula.

Comment: Use a reverse grip when working with heavy weights. To balance the work on the trapezius, change the hands with each set. For example, perform one set with the right hand overhand and the left hand underhand. Switch on the following set.

DUMBBELL SHRUGS (19)

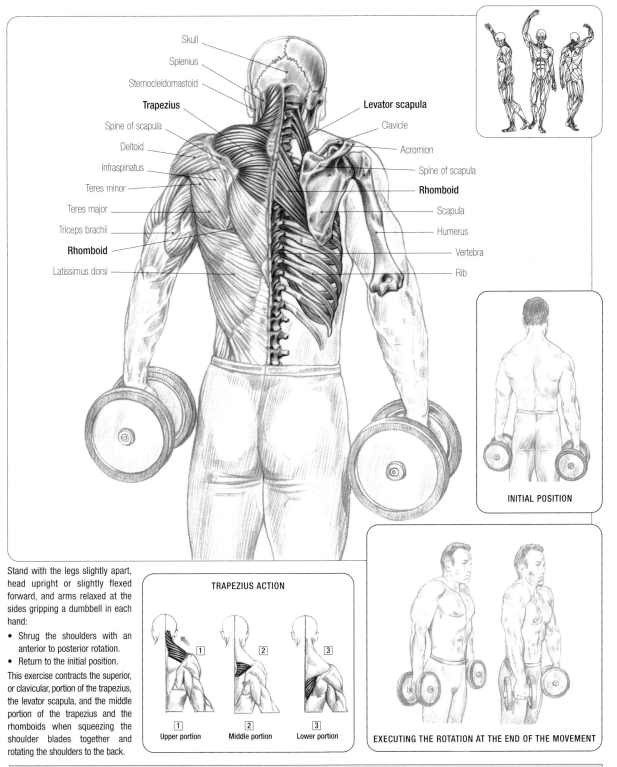

Skull
Splenius
Sternocleidomastoid
Trapezius
Spine of scapula
Deltoid
Infraspinatus
Teres minor
Teres major
Triceps brachii
Rhomboid
Latissimus dorsi

Levator scapula
Clavicle
Acromion
Spine of scapula
Rhomboid
Scapula
Humerus
Vertebra
Rib

INITIAL POSITION

TRAPEZIUS ACTION

1 Upper portion
2 Middle portion
3 Lower portion

EXECUTING THE ROTATION AT THE END OF THE MOVEMENT

Stand with the legs slightly apart, head upright or slightly flexed forward, and arms relaxed at the sides gripping a dumbbell in each hand:

- Shrug the shoulders with an anterior to posterior rotation.
- Return to the initial position.

This exercise contracts the superior, or clavicular, portion of the trapezius, the levator scapula, and the middle portion of the trapezius and the rhomboids when squeezing the shoulder blades together and rotating the shoulders to the back.

Comment: It is impossible to rotate the shoulders when using heavy weights.

20 MACHINE SHRUGS

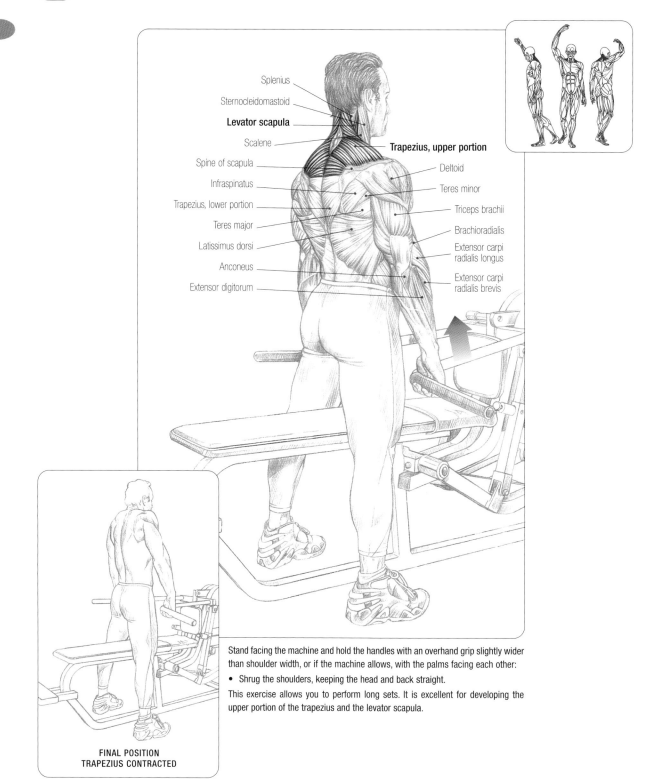

Splenius
Sternocleidomastoid
Levator scapula
Scalene
Spine of scapula
Infraspinatus
Trapezius, lower portion
Teres major
Latissimus dorsi
Anconeus
Extensor digitorum

Trapezius, upper portion
Deltoid
Teres minor
Triceps brachii
Brachioradialis
Extensor carpi radialis longus
Extensor carpi radialis brevis

FINAL POSITION
TRAPEZIUS CONTRACTED

Stand facing the machine and hold the handles with an overhand grip slightly wider than shoulder width, or if the machine allows, with the palms facing each other:

• Shrug the shoulders, keeping the head and back straight.

This exercise allows you to perform long sets. It is excellent for developing the upper portion of the trapezius and the levator scapula.

5 LEGS

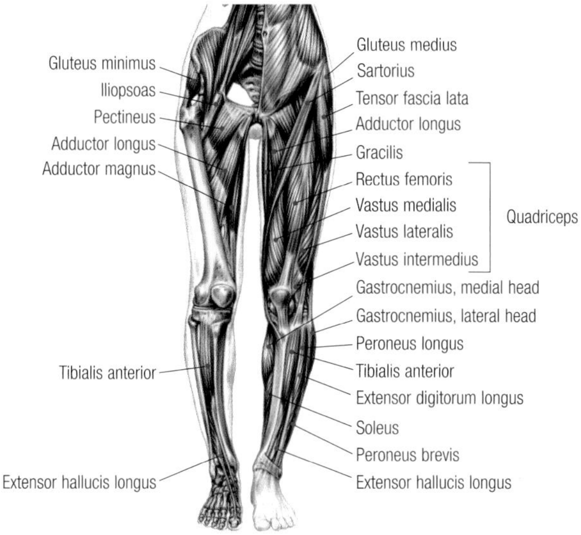

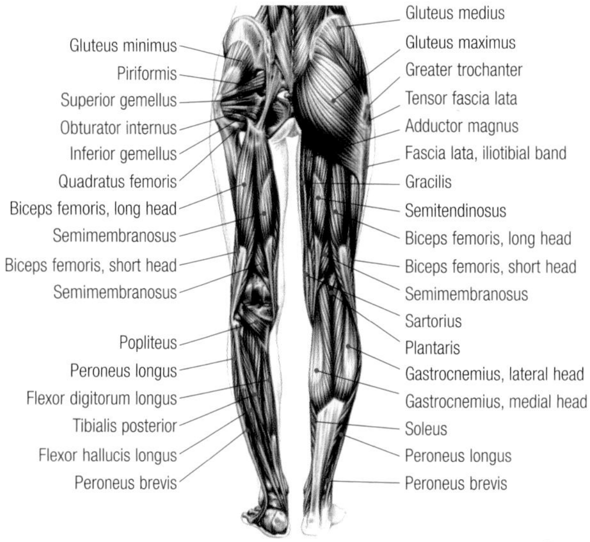

Gluteus minimus
Iliopsoas
Pectineus
Adductor longus
Adductor magnus

Gluteus medius
Sartorius
Tensor fascia lata
Adductor longus
Gracilis
Rectus femoris
Vastus medialis
Vastus lateralis
Vastus intermedius

Quadriceps

Gastrocnemius, medial head
Gastrocnemius, lateral head
Peroneus longus
Tibialis anterior

Tibialis anterior

Extensor hallucis longus

Extensor digitorum longus
Soleus
Peroneus brevis
Extensor hallucis longus

Gluteus minimus
Piriformis
Superior gemellus
Obturator internus
Inferior gemellus
Quadratus femoris
Biceps femoris, long head
Semimembranosus
Biceps femoris, short head
Semimembranosus

Popliteus
Peroneus longus
Flexor digitorum longus
Tibialis posterior
Flexor hallucis longus
Peroneus brevis

Gluteus medius
Gluteus maximus
Greater trochanter
Tensor fascia lata
Adductor magnus
Fascia lata, iliotibial band
Gracilis
Semitendinosus
Biceps femoris, long head
Biceps femoris, short head
Semimembranosus
Sartorius
Plantaris
Gastrocnemius, lateral head
Gastrocnemius, medial head
Soleus
Peroneus longus
Peroneus brevis

1 DUMBBELL SQUATS

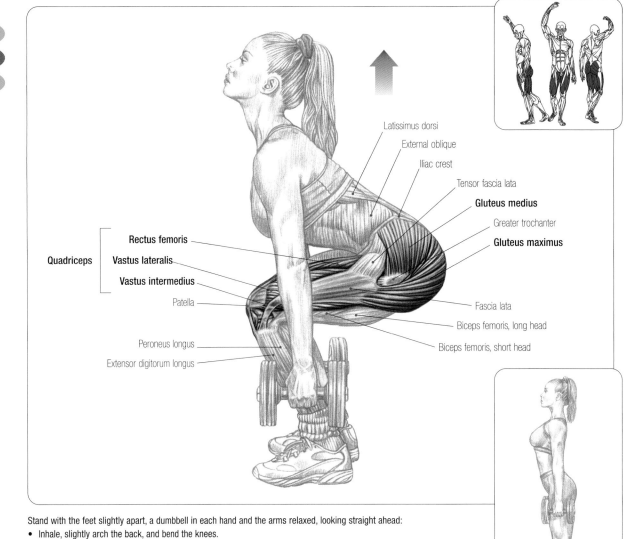

Latissimus dorsi
External oblique
Iliac crest
Tensor fascia lata
Gluteus medius
Greater trochanter
Gluteus maximus
Quadriceps
Rectus femoris
Vastus lateralis
Vastus intermedius
Patella
Fascia lata
Biceps femoris, long head
Biceps femoris, short head
Peroneus longus
Extensor digitorum longus

INITIAL POSITION

Stand with the feet slightly apart, a dumbbell in each hand and the arms relaxed, looking straight ahead:
- Inhale, slightly arch the back, and bend the knees.
- When the thighs reach horizontal, extend the legs to return to the initial position.
- Exhale at the end of the effort.

This exercise mainly works the quadriceps and the gluteal muscles.

Comment: There is no point in working with heavy weights. Working with moderate weights in sets of 10 to 15 repetitions provides the best results.

FRONT SQUATS 2

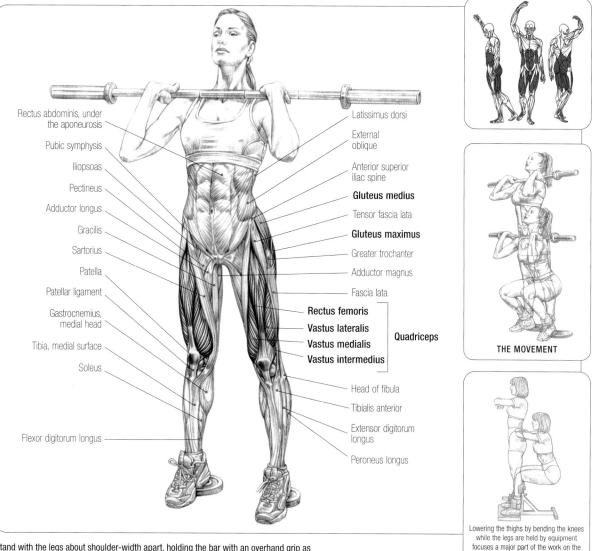

Rectus abdominis, under the aponeurosis

Pubic symphysis

Iliopsoas

Pectineus

Adductor longus

Gracilis

Sartorius

Patella

Patellar ligament

Gastrocnemius, medial head

Tibia, medial surface

Soleus

Flexor digitorum longus

Latissimus dorsi

External oblique

Anterior superior iliac spine

Gluteus medius

Tensor fascia lata

Gluteus maximus

Greater trochanter

Adductor magnus

Fascia lata

Rectus femoris

Vastus lateralis

Vastus medialis   Quadriceps

Vastus intermedius

Head of fibula

Tibialis anterior

Extensor digitorum longus

Peroneus longus

THE MOVEMENT

Lowering the thighs by bending the knees while the legs are held by equipment focuses a major part of the work on the quadriceps muscles.

Stand with the legs about shoulder-width apart, holding the bar with an overhand grip as it rests on the upper pectoral muscles and the anterior deltoid:

- Inhale deeply to maintain intrathoracic pressure, which prevents the torso from collapsing forward, slightly arch the low back, contract the abdominal core, and bend the knees to lower the thighs horizontal to the floor.
- Return to the initial position and breathe out at the end of the movement.

Stick out the chest and to raise the elbows as high as possible to prevent the barbell from sliding forward.

Even though the barbell is in front, keep the back upright and don't lean the torso forward. To make the exercise easier, place blocks under the heels.

This type of squat focuses a greater part of the effort onto the quadriceps and is performed with lighter weights than the classic squat. This exercise contracts the gluteal muscles, hamstring, abdominal core, and the erector spinae. This is a movement frequently used in weight training because it corresponds perfectly with the work the thighs do at the end of a snatch.

CORRECT POSITION   INCORRECT POSITION

3 SQUATS

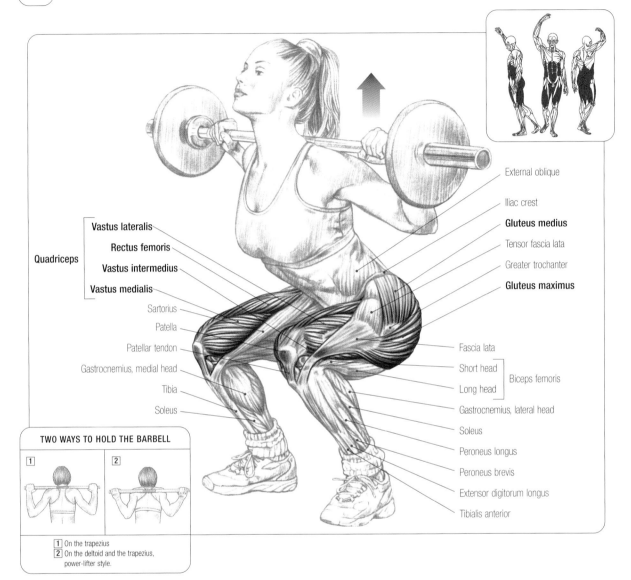

TWO WAYS TO HOLD THE BARBELL

1 | 2

1 On the trapezius
2 On the deltoid and the trapezius,
power-lifter style.

Labels (left side):
- Quadriceps
  - Vastus lateralis
  - Rectus femoris
  - Vastus intermedius
  - Vastus medialis
- Sartorius
- Patella
- Patellar tendon
- Gastrocnemius, medial head
- Tibia
- Soleus

Labels (right side):
- External oblique
- Iliac crest
- **Gluteus medius**
- Tensor fascia lata
- Greater trochanter
- **Gluteus maximus**
- Fascia lata
- Short head / Long head — Biceps femoris
- Gastrocnemius, lateral head
- Soleus
- Peroneus longus
- Peroneus brevis
- Extensor digitorum longus
- Tibialis anterior

The squat is the number one bodybuilding movement: It uses nearly the entire muscular system, and it also works the cardiovascular system. It helps develop thoracic expansion, and therefore, respiratory capacity:

- With the barbell resting on a stand, slide under the bar and place it on the trapezius a bit higher than the posterior deltoid. Grasp the bar firmly with the hands at a comfortable width and the elbows back.
- Inhale deeply (to maintain the intrathoracic pressure, which will prevent the torso from collapsing forward), slightly arch the back by rotating the pelvis forward, contract the abdominal core, look straight ahead, and remove the barbell from the stand.
- Step back one or two steps and stop with both feet parallel to each other (or toes pointing slightly outward) and about shoulder-width apart. Bend forward from the hips (the axis of flexion should pass through the coxofemoral joints) and avoid rounding the back in order to prevent injury.

- When the thighs are horizontal to the floor, straighten the legs and lift the torso to return to the initial position.
- Exhale at the end of the movement.

The squat mainly works the quadriceps, gluteal muscles, adductor group, erector spinae, abdominal muscles, and the hamstrings.

Comment: The squat is one of the best exercises for developing the shape of the buttocks.

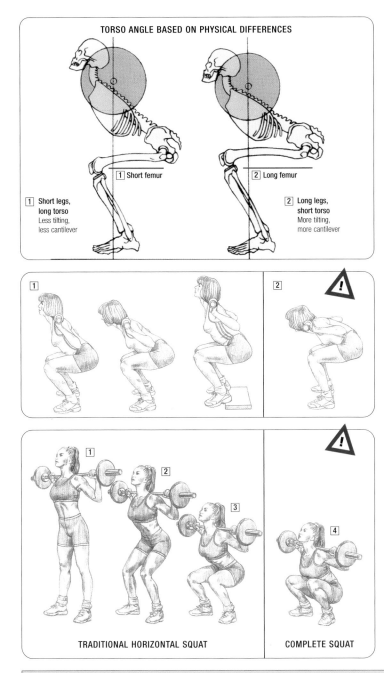

TORSO ANGLE BASED ON PHYSICAL DIFFERENCES

1 Short femur

2 Long femur

1 Short legs, long torso
Less tilting, less cantilever

2 Long legs, short torso
More tilting, more cantilever

1

2 !

1

2

3

4

TRADITIONAL HORIZONTAL SQUAT

COMPLETE SQUAT

Variations:

- People with rigid ankles or long femurs can place a block under their heels to keep from tilting the torso too much. This variation isolates the quadriceps.
- Lowering the bar onto the posterior deltoid increases the leverage of the back, which helps you lift heavier weights. This technique is essential for power lifters.
- The squat can be performed at a frame, which keeps you from tilting the torso and lets you focus on the quadriceps.

FOOT PLACEMENT IN THE SQUAT

When executing the classic squat, that is, with the feet approximately shoulder-width apart, you must place the feet properly. They should be parallel or slightly pointed to the outside. However, you must take into consideration your unique physical structure and make adjustments as necessary to ensure that the feet are in line with the knees.
For example: If you naturally walk with the feet pointed out, perform the squat with the feet pointed out.

1 CORRECT POSITIONS

When executing squats, hold the back straight.

Given the variations in each person's physical structure (different leg lengths and ankle flexibility) and the variations in technique (width of stance, use of heel blocks, barbell higher or lower), the tilt of the torso will vary; however, the lean should start at the hips.

2 INCORRECT POSITION

Never round the back when executing squats.
This mistake is responsible for most lumbar spine injuries, especially herniated discs.

To feel the working of the gluteal muscles, lower the thighs to horizontal.

1-2-3 NEGATIVE PHASE
4 COMPLETE SQUAT

To feel the working of the gluteal muscles even more, lower the thighs past horizontal. However, this technique can only be performed by people with flexible ankles or short femurs. Furthermore, you must perform the complete squat carefully and avoid the tendency to round the low back, which can lead to serious injury.

No matter what the exercise, as soon as heavy weights are involved, it is essential to create a "**block**."

1. Expanding the chest and holding a deep breath fills the lungs, which supports the rib cage and prevents the chest from collapsing forward.
2. Contracting the abdominal muscle group supports the core and increases the intra-abdominal pressure, which prevents the torso from collapsing forward.
3. Finally, arching the low back by contracting the lumbar muscles positions the spinal column in extension.

These three actions together are referred to as *blocking*, which keeps you from rounding the back (vertebral flexion). A rounded back when lifting heavy weights can cause a herniated disc.

4 POWER SQUATS

Rectus abdominis, under the aponeurosis

Internal oblique, under the aponeurosis

Iliopsoas

Pubic symphysis

Pectineus

Quadriceps, rectus femoris

Sartorius

Adductor longus

Quadriceps, vastus medialis

Meniscus

Gracilis

Gastrocnemius, medial head

Tibia, medial surface

Soleus

Adductor magnus

Semimembranosus

Semitendinosus

External oblique

Gluteus medius

Anterior superior iliac spine

Tensor fascia lata

Greater trochanter

Gluteus maximus

Pyramidalis, under the aponeurosis

Fascia lata, iliotibial band

Quadriceps, vastus lateralis

Quadriceps, vastus intermedius

Head of fibula

Patella

Patellar ligament

Peroneus longus

Tibialis anterior

Extensor digitorum longus

Peroneus brevis

This movement is performed the same as the classic squat, except that the legs are farther apart and the toes point out, which works the inner thigh intensely.

The working muscles are as follows:

- quadriceps
- adductor muscle group (adductor magnus, adductor longus, adductor brevis, adductor pectineus, and gracilis)
- gluteal muscles
- hamstrings
- abdominal muscles
- lumbosacral muscle group

THREE FEET POSITIONS FOR SQUATS

Muscles used extensively ▮▮▮   Muscles used ▮▮▮

DISC HERNIATION

Disc herniation is a relatively frequent injury in weightlifting, most often caused by incorrect back position during the squat, deadlift, or bent row.

When executing these exercises, the main thing to avoid is rounding the back (vertebral flexion), which expands the back of the disc and pinches the front of it.

If the intervertebral disc is cracked or aging, the gelatinous liquid of the nucleus pulposus migrates backward and can compress on the spinal cord or the roots of the spinal nerves. Symptoms depend on the type of lesion, the amount of nucleus pulposus pushed out, and the surface that is compressed. The nucleus pulposus can bulge or, worse, explode through the annulus fibrosus, which surrounds it, and sometimes tear the posterior ligament that connects the vertebrae to each other. Compression of the neural elements caused by the tearing of the annulus fibrosus is particularly painful and incapacitating.

In weight training, herniations usually occur at the lumbar level and most frequently between the third and fourth or between the fourth and fifth lumbar vertebrae. The pain is dull and deep, sometimes accompanied by swelling and tingling. The pain is located in the middle of the back or more often to one side, radiating to the gluteal muscles, pelvis, and pubis and down the leg following the path of the sciatic nerve (hence the name sciatica to define this type of pain). Generally, disc herniations are spontaneously reabsorbed, and the pain eventually disappears. But in some cases, the bulge in the disc does not disappear and continues to press painfully against the nerves, or a detached piece of intervertebral cartilage compresses the neural elements.

In both these cases, a surgeon can remove the part that is pressing against the nerves.

To prevent disc herniation, use proper form when performing risky exercises such as the squat, deadlift, good morning, and bent row.

No matter what the exercise, as soon as heavy weights are involved, it is essential to create a "block."

1. *Expanding the chest and holding a deep breath fills the lungs, which supports the rib cage and prevents the chest from collapsing forward.*

2. *Contracting the abdominal muscle group supports the core and increases the intra-abdominal pressure, which prevents the torso from collapsing forward.*

3. *Finally, arching the low back by contracting the lumbar muscles positions the spinal column in extension.*

These three actions together are referred to as blocking, which keeps you from rounding the back (vertebral flexion). A rounded back when lifting heavy weights can cause a herniated disc.

SCIATIC NERVE AND POSTERIOR CUTANEOUS NERVE OF THIGH

Greater sciatic notch

Sciatic nerve, L4-L5-S1-S2-S3

Posterior cutaneous nerve of the thigh, S1-S2-S3

Common peroneal segment of sciatic nerve

Biceps femoris, long head, cut

Adductor magnus

Tibial segment of sciatic nerve

Biceps femoris, short head, cut

Biceps femoris, long head, cut

Common peroneal nerve

Articular branch

Tibial nerve

Lateral sural cutaneous nerve

Peroneal communicating branch

Perianal branches

Adductor magnus

Semitendinosus

Semimembranosus

Medial sural cutaneous nerve

Gastrocnemius

Sural nerve

Soleus

Tibial nerve

Plantar nerves

Lateral calcaneal branch

Lateral dorsal cutaneous nerve

Medial calcaneal branches

To prevent injury at the lumbar level, never round the back when executing a deadlift or squat.

DISC HERNIATION

Spinal cord

Nerve root

Annulus fibrosus

Nucleus pulposus

Intervertebral disc

Costoid process

Spinous process

Articular process

Vertebral flexion using weights can cause a herniated disc, usually in the lumbar vertebrae. These herniations occur most frequently with the squat and deadlift, and most often are the result of incorrect back position because of bad technique.

Comment: After a heavy workout, stretch the back by hanging from a chinning bar and focusing on relaxing the body. This allows the muscles to relax and rebalance the pressures inside the intervertebral discs.

EFFECT OF AGE ON DISC HERNIATION LUMBAR VERTEBRAL SEGMENT (CUT)

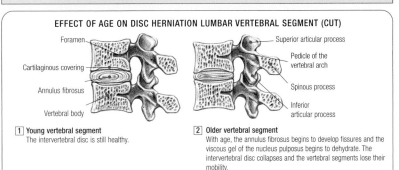

Foramen

Cartilaginous covering

Annulus fibrosus

Vertebral body

Superior articular process

Pedicle of the vertebral arch

Spinous process

Inferior articular process

1 **Young vertebral segment**
The intervertebral disc is still healthy.

2 **Older vertebral segment**
With age, the annulus fibrosus begins to develop fissures and the viscous gel of the nucleus pulposus begins to dehydrate. The intervertebral disc collapses and the vertebral segments lose their mobility.

From the age of 30, the intervertebral discs degenerate, and the annulus fibrosus can crack as the nucleus pulposus begins to dehydrate. The discs of older athletes are more rigid and less elastic, and the mobility of the spine is limited. On the other hand, as the viscous gel of the nucleus pulposus gradually dehydrates, it becomes less likely that it will be displaced and compress against the nerve.

In comparison, disc herniation in a young person involves the movement of a greater amount of the gelatinous fluid of the nucleus pulposus, causing more compression, pain, and incapacity of the neural elements. Disc herniation therefore occurs more frequently with young athletes.

5 | ANGLED LEG PRESSES

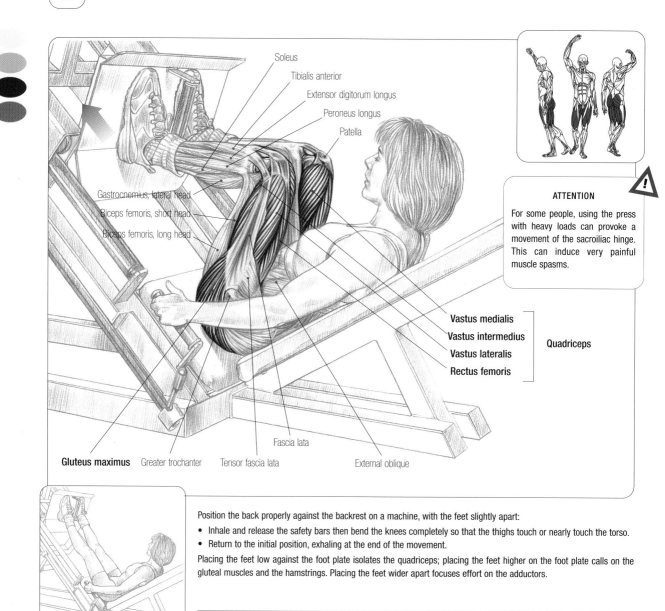

Soleus
Tibialis anterior
Extensor digitorum longus
Peroneus longus
Patella

Gastrocnemius, lateral head
Biceps femoris, short head
Biceps femoris, long head

Vastus medialis
Vastus intermedius
Vastus lateralis
Rectus femoris
Quadriceps

Fascia lata

Gluteus maximus   Greater trochanter   Tensor fascia lata   External oblique

ATTENTION

For some people, using the press with heavy loads can provoke a movement of the sacroiliac hinge. This can induce very painful muscle spasms.

INITIAL POSITION

Position the back properly against the backrest on a machine, with the feet slightly apart:

• Inhale and release the safety bars then bend the knees completely so that the thighs touch or nearly touch the torso.
• Return to the initial position, exhaling at the end of the movement.

Placing the feet low against the foot plate isolates the quadriceps; placing the feet higher on the foot plate calls on the gluteal muscles and the hamstrings. Placing the feet wider apart focuses effort on the adductors.

Comment: People with back pain who are unable to perform squats can do this exercise. However, they must never lift the back off the back pad.

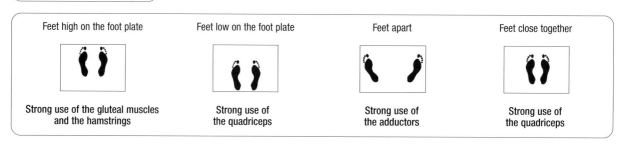

Feet high on the foot plate
Strong use of the gluteal muscles and the hamstrings

Feet low on the foot plate
Strong use of the quadriceps

Feet apart
Strong use of the adductors

Feet close together
Strong use of the quadriceps

HACK SQUATS 6

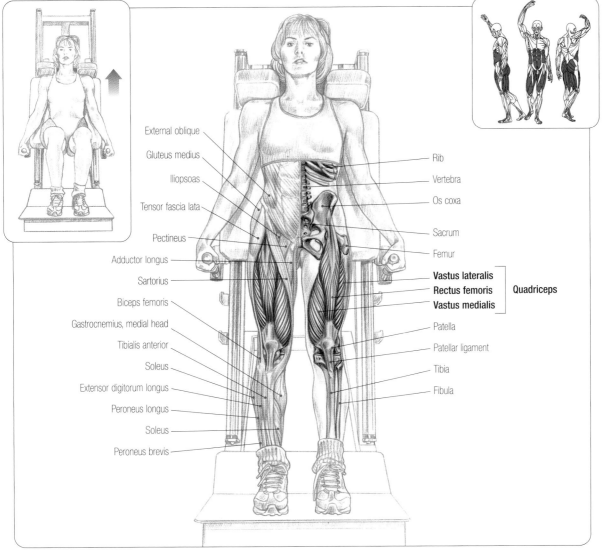

External oblique
Gluteus medius
Iliopsoas
Tensor fascia lata
Pectineus
Adductor longus
Sartorius
Biceps femoris
Gastrocnemius, medial head
Tibialis anterior
Soleus
Extensor digitorum longus
Peroneus longus
Soleus
Peroneus brevis

Rib
Vertebra
Os coxa
Sacrum
Femur
Vastus lateralis
Rectus femoris   Quadriceps
Vastus medialis
Patella
Patellar ligament
Tibia
Fibula

Stand with the legs straight and feet slightly apart, back against the back pad, and shoulders positioned under the shoulder pads. (Hack refers to a "yoke." The pads are reminiscent of the collar placed around the neck of draft animals.):

- Inhale and release the safety catch. Bend the knees, then return to the initial position.
- Exhale at the end of the exercise.

This movement focuses the effort on the quadriceps. The more the feet are forward, the more the gluteal muscles will be used. To protect the back, contract the abdominal core, which eliminates lateral movement of the pelvis or cervical spine.

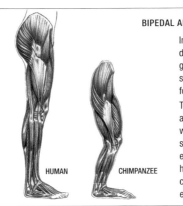

HUMAN   CHIMPANZEE

BIPEDAL ADAPTATION

In the chimpanzee, our closest relative, the well-developed torso is paired with an underdeveloped gluteus maximus, which makes raising the trunk and standing erect difficult and causes an awkward two-footed gait.

The human is the only primate who has completely adapted to walking upright on two legs. Besides the well-developed gluteus maximus, the entire human structure has adapted to walking on two legs. For example, the torso is relatively small, which makes holding it erect easier, and, unlike the gorilla or chimpanzee, humans can lock the knee joint when it is extended, which makes standing much less tiring.

7 LEG EXTENSIONS

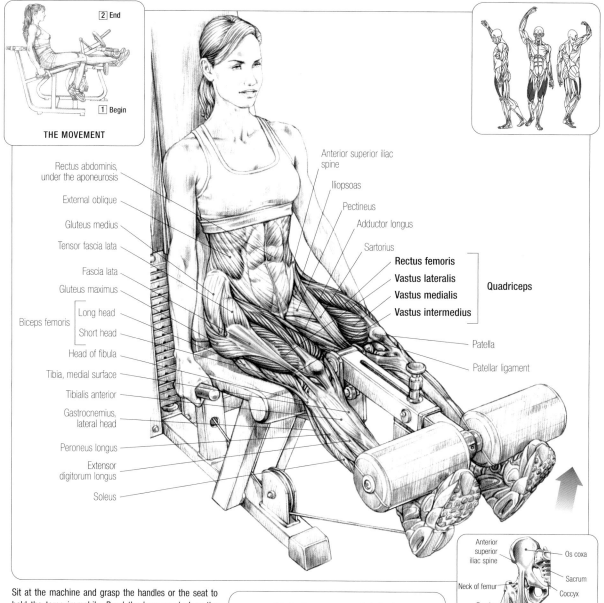

2 End

1 Begin

THE MOVEMENT

Rectus abdominis, under the aponeurosis

External oblique

Gluteus medius

Tensor fascia lata

Fascia lata

Gluteus maximus

Biceps femoris — Long head / Short head

Head of fibula

Tibia, medial surface

Tibialis anterior

Gastrocnemius, lateral head

Peroneus longus

Extensor digitorum longus

Soleus

Anterior superior iliac spine

Iliopsoas

Pectineus

Adductor longus

Sartorius

Rectus femoris

Vastus lateralis

Vastus medialis

Vastus intermedius

Quadriceps

Patella

Patellar ligament

Sit at the machine and grasp the handles or the seat to hold the torso immobile. Bend the knees and place the ankles under the ankle pads.

- Inhale and raise the legs to horizontal.
- Exhale at the end of the exercise.

This is the best exercise for isolating the quadriceps. The greater the angle of the backrest, the farther toward the back the pelvis rotates. This exercise stretches the rectus femoris, which is the midline biarticular portion of the quadriceps, which makes the work on it more intense while extending the legs.

This movement is recommended for beginners so that they can develop enough strength to move on to more technically demanding exercises.

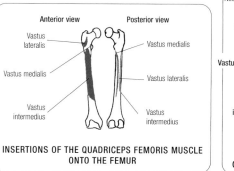

Anterior view   Posterior view

Vastus lateralis

Vastus medialis

Vastus intermedius

Vastus medialis

Vastus lateralis

Vastus intermedius

INSERTIONS OF THE QUADRICEPS FEMORIS MUSCLE ONTO THE FEMUR

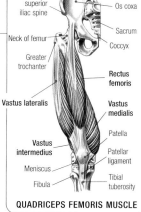

Anterior superior iliac spine

Neck of femur

Greater trochanter

Vastus lateralis

Vastus intermedius

Meniscus

Fibula

Os coxa

Sacrum

Coccyx

Rectus femoris

Vastus medialis

Patella

Patellar ligament

Tibial tuberosity

QUADRICEPS FEMORIS MUSCLE

LYING LEG CURLS 8

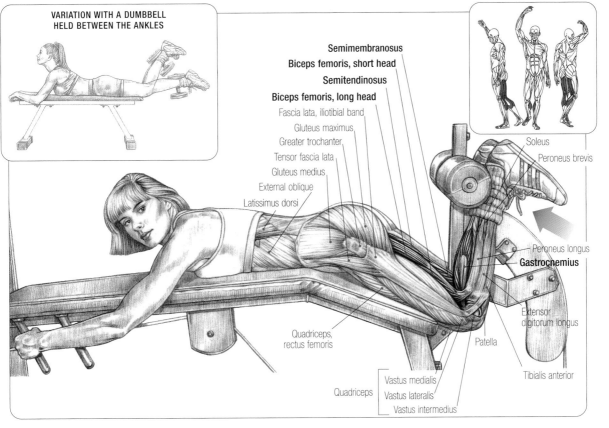

VARIATION WITH A DUMBBELL
HELD BETWEEN THE ANKLES

Semimembranosus
Biceps femoris, short head
Semitendinosus
Biceps femoris, long head
Fascia lata, iliotibial band
Gluteus maximus
Greater trochanter
Tensor fascia lata
Gluteus medius
External oblique
Latissimus dorsi

Soleus
Peroneus brevis

Peroneus longus
Gastrocnemius

Extensor
digitorum longus

Quadriceps,
rectus femoris

Patella

Tibialis anterior

Quadriceps

Vastus medialis
Vastus lateralis
Vastus intermedius

Lie facedown on the machine, holding the handles, legs extended, and ankles positioned under the ankle pads:

- Inhale and bend both legs at the same time, trying to touch the gluteal muscles with the heels.
- Exhale at the end of the effort.
- Return to the initial position with a controlled movement.

This exercise works the hamstring group and gastrocnemius and deeper, the popliteus muscle. In theory, during flexion, it is possible to target the semitendinosus and semimembranosus by internally rotating the feet, or to target the long and short heads of the biceps femoris by externally rotating the feet. But in practice, this proves to be difficult, and only emphasis on the hamstrings and the gastrocnemius can be easily achieved:

- Point the toes (plantar flexion) to feel the effort in the hamstrings.
- Flex the feet (dorisflexion) to feel the effort in the gastrocnemius.

Variation: This exercise may be performed by alternating the legs.

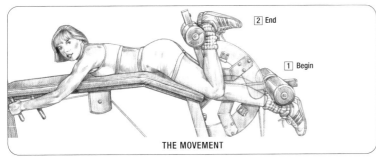

2 End

1 Begin

THE MOVEMENT

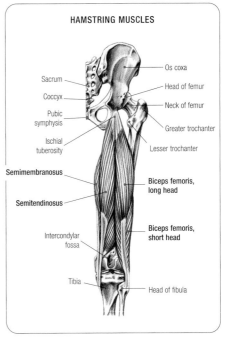

HAMSTRING MUSCLES

Sacrum
Coccyx
Pubic symphysis
Ischial tuberosity

Os coxa
Head of femur
Neck of femur
Greater trochanter
Lesser trochanter

Semimembranosus
Semitendinosus

Biceps femoris, long head

Biceps femoris, short head

Intercondylar fossa

Tibia

Head of fibula

9 STANDING LEG CURLS

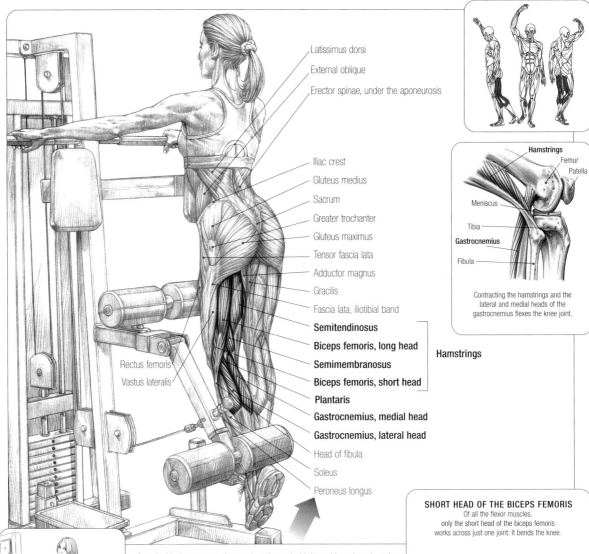

Latissimus dorsi

External oblique

Erector spinae, under the aponeurosis

Iliac crest

Gluteus medius

Sacrum

Greater trochanter

Gluteus maximus

Tensor fascia lata

Adductor magnus

Gracilis

Fascia lata, iliotibial band

Semitendinosus

Biceps femoris, long head

Semimembranosus

Biceps femoris, short head

Plantaris

Gastrocnemius, medial head

Gastrocnemius, lateral head

Head of fibula

Soleus

Peroneus longus

Rectus femoris

Vastus lateralis

Hamstrings

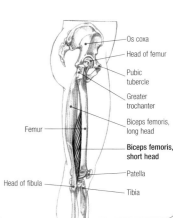

Hamstrings
Femur
Patella
Meniscus
Tibia
Gastrocnemius
Fibula

Contracting the hamstrings and the lateral and medial heads of the gastrocnemius flexes the knee joint.

SHORT HEAD OF THE BICEPS FEMORIS
Of all the flexor muscles, only the short head of the biceps femoris works across just one joint: It bends the knee.

Os coxa
Head of femur
Pubic tubercle
Greater trochanter
Biceps femoris, long head
Femur
Biceps femoris, short head
Head of fibula
Patella
Tibia

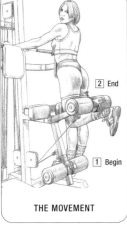

2 End

1 Begin

THE MOVEMENT

Stand with the torso resting against the pad, thigh positioned against the knee pad, the knee straight, and the back of the ankle resting against the ankle roll:

- Inhale and bend at the knee.
- Exhale at the end of the movement.

This exercise uses the hamstring group (semitendinosus and semimembranosus and the long and short heads of the biceps femoris) and, to a lesser extent, the gastrocnemius. To engage the gastrocnemius more, simply bend at the ankle when bending at the knee. To decrease its participation, which is often the goal, simply point the toes.

SEATED LEG CURLS 10

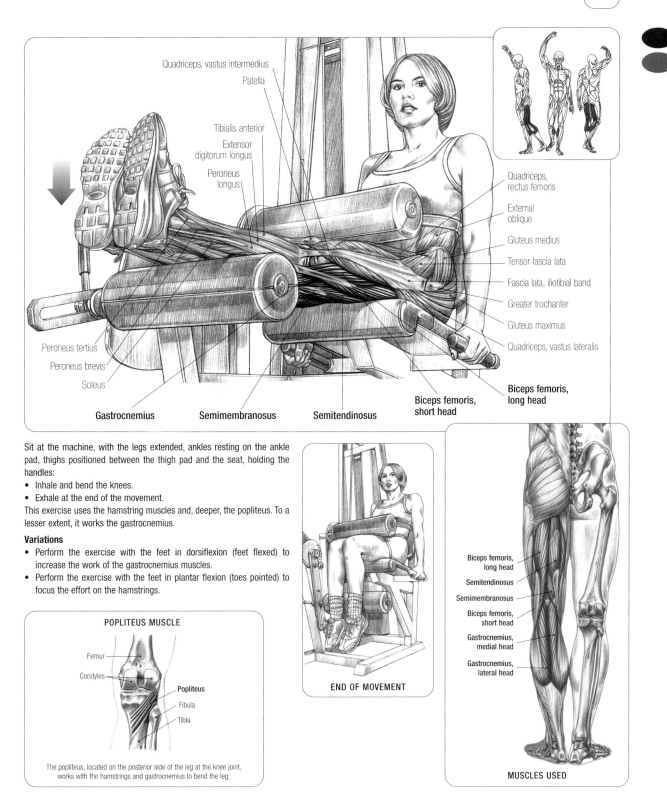

Quadriceps, vastus intermedius

Patella

Tibialis anterior

Extensor digitorum longus

Peroneus longus

Quadriceps, rectus femoris

External oblique

Gluteus medius

Tensor fascia lata

Fascia lata, iliotibial band

Greater trochanter

Gluteus maximus

Quadriceps, vastus lateralis

Peroneus tertius

Peroneus brevis

Soleus

Gastrocnemius

Semimembranosus

Semitendinosus

Biceps femoris, short head

Biceps femoris, long head

Sit at the machine, with the legs extended, ankles resting on the ankle pad, thighs positioned between the thigh pad and the seat, holding the handles:

- Inhale and bend the knees.
- Exhale at the end of the movement.

This exercise uses the hamstring muscles and, deeper, the popliteus. To a lesser extent, it works the gastrocnemius.

Variations

- Perform the exercise with the feet in dorsiflexion (feet flexed) to increase the work of the gastrocnemius muscles.
- Perform the exercise with the feet in plantar flexion (toes pointed) to focus the effort on the hamstrings.

POPLITEUS MUSCLE

Femur

Condyles

Popliteus

Fibula

Tibia

The popliteus, located on the posterior side of the leg at the knee joint, works with the hamstrings and gastrocnemius to bend the leg.

END OF MOVEMENT

Biceps femoris, long head

Semitendinosus

Semimembranosus

Biceps femoris, short head

Gastrocnemius, medial head

Gastrocnemius, lateral head

MUSCLES USED

✚ HAMSTRING MUSCLE TEARS

ACTION OF THE HAMSTRING MUSCLES DURING THE SQUAT

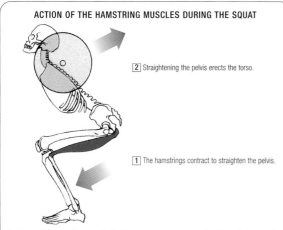

2 Straightening the pelvis erects the torso.

1 The hamstrings contract to straighten the pelvis.

While performing the squat, the hamstring muscles contract to straighten the pelvis, which at the same time prevents the torso from tilting too far forward (as long as pelvis is aligned with the torso by contracting the abdominal and lumbar muscles).

Muscle tearing of the hamstrings

In bodybuilding, hamstring tears occur frequently. This injury occurs most often during the squat when the torso is too far forward. The hamstring muscle group, with the exception of the short head of biceps femoris, is in an extremely stretched position and contracts forcefully to straighten the pelvis. This can lead to tearing, most often at the high or middle portion of the muscle group.

Hamstring tears can also occur when working at a leg curl machine using heavy weights. This most often occurs at the beginning of the movement when the legs are extended and the muscles are stretched.

Although in general, the tears in hamstring muscle fibers are not extensive and not serious (it is rare to see a significant tear in the muscle or its tendinous insertion), they are always painful and prone to complications.

In fact, fibrous scarring frequently occurs after a tear in this muscle group, which creates friction that is especially painful and incapacitating during sport activity. Furthermore, this inelastic scar tissue is liable to tear during intense effort.

Preventing hamstring tearing

To prevent muscle tears, perform either a specific stretching workout or incorporate hamstring stretches during a lifting workout between sets of squats and deadlifts and exercises for the back of the thigh.

Certain weightlifting exercises, such as good mornings or stiff-legged deadlifts, can be considered the best hamstring protectors because of their combined action of muscle strengthening and stretching.

After hamstring tearing

To prevent the formation of fibrous scar tissue in the hamstrings, it is essential to reeducate the muscles as soon as possible. A week after a tear, you must perform gentle stretches for the back of the thighs. The goal is to stretch the injured muscles and especially to soften the scar so that it doesn't tear when you resume training.

HAMSTRING MUSCLES

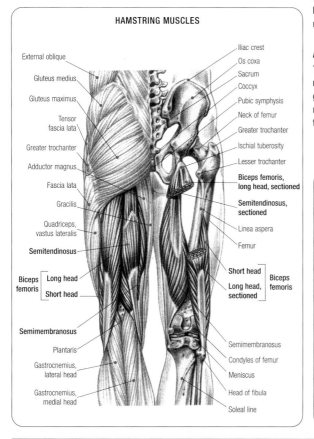

External oblique
Gluteus medius
Gluteus maximus
Tensor fascia lata
Greater trochanter
Adductor magnus
Fascia lata
Gracilis
Quadriceps, vastus lateralis
Semitendinosus
Biceps femoris — Long head / Short head
Semimembranosus
Plantaris
Gastrocnemius, lateral head
Gastrocnemius, medial head

Iliac crest
Os coxa
Sacrum
Coccyx
Pubic symphysis
Neck of femur
Greater trochanter
Ischial tuberosity
Lesser trochanter
Biceps femoris, long head, sectioned
Semitendinosus, sectioned
Linea aspera
Femur
Short head / Long head, sectioned — Biceps femoris
Semimembranosus
Condyles of femur
Meniscus
Head of fibula
Soleal line

RETRACTION OF THE HAMSTRINGS

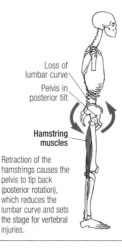

Loss of lumbar curve
Pelvis in posterior tilt
Hamstring muscles
Retraction of the hamstrings causes the pelvis to tip back (posterior rotation), which reduces the lumbar curve and sets the stage for vertebral injuries.

In today's modern world, sitting for long periods during the day can lead to retraction of the hamstring muscles in certain people.

This retraction of the muscles on the back of the thigh tips the pelvis back and reduces the normal curvature of the spine.

This causes the person to adopt poor posture with the pelvis tucked under and the back rounded, which over time can lead to vertebral injuries. To limit this relatively frequently occurring retraction of the hamstrings, stretching movements such as an easy good morning with straight legs and the stiff-legged deadlift are recommended. Hamstring stretches after a hamstring workout are also recommended.

Comment: A massage therapist can also treat fibrous scars by using massage or mechanical techniques aimed at softening the lesion.

GOOD MORNINGS 11

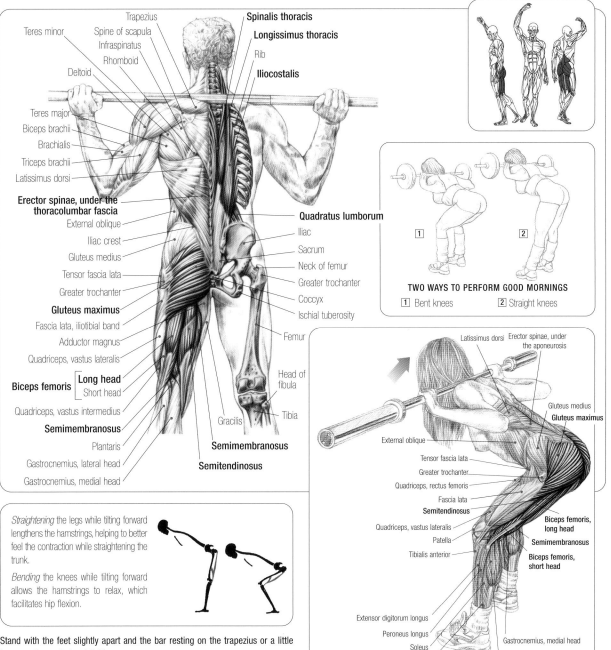

Straightening the legs while tilting forward lengthens the hamstrings, helping to better feel the contraction while straightening the trunk.

Bending the knees while tilting forward allows the hamstrings to relax, which facilitates hip flexion.

TWO WAYS TO PERFORM GOOD MORNINGS
1 Bent knees   2 Straight knees

Stand with the feet slightly apart and the bar resting on the trapezius or a little lower on the posterior deltoid:

- Inhale and bend the torso forward, keeping the back straight. The axis of rotation should pass through the coxofemoral joints.
- Return to the initial position and exhale.

To make the exercise easier, bend slightly at the knees.

This movement, which works the gluteus maximus and the spinal group, is especially noteworthy for the action on the hamstrings (except the short head of the biceps femoris, which only flexes the knee). Besides knee flexion, the main function of the hamstrings is to tip the pelvis back (posterior rotation) and straighten the torso when the pelvis is locked to the torso through isometric contraction of the abdominal core and the lumbosacral muscle group.

To better feel the work of the hamstrings, don't work with heavy weights. In the negative phase, the good morning is excellent for stretching the back of the thighs. Worked regularly, it helps prevent injury when executing a heavy squat.

12 CABLE ADDUCTIONS

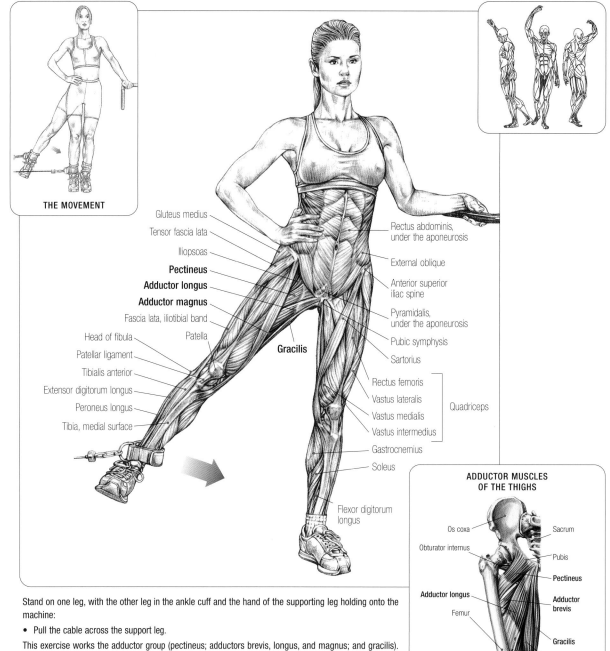

THE MOVEMENT

Gluteus medius
Tensor fascia lata
Iliopsoas
Pectineus
Adductor longus
Adductor magnus
Fascia lata, iliotibial band
Head of fibula
Patellar ligament
Tibialis anterior
Extensor digitorum longus
Peroneus longus
Tibia, medial surface
Patella
Gracilis

Rectus abdominis, under the aponeurosis
External oblique
Anterior superior iliac spine
Pyramidalis, under the aponeurosis
Pubic symphysis
Sartorius
Rectus femoris
Vastus lateralis
Vastus medialis
Vastus intermedius
Gastrocnemius
Soleus
Flexor digitorum longus

Quadriceps

ADDUCTOR MUSCLES OF THE THIGHS

Os coxa
Obturator internus
Adductor longus
Femur
Patella
Fibula

Sacrum
Pubis
Pectineus
Adductor brevis
Gracilis
Adductor magnus
Common insertion
Tibia

Stand on one leg, with the other leg in the ankle cuff and the hand of the supporting leg holding onto the machine:

- Pull the cable across the support leg.

This exercise works the adductor group (pectineus; adductors brevis, longus, and magnus; and gracilis). To develop definition of the inside of the thighs, perform sets of high repetitions.

MACHINE ADDUCTIONS 13

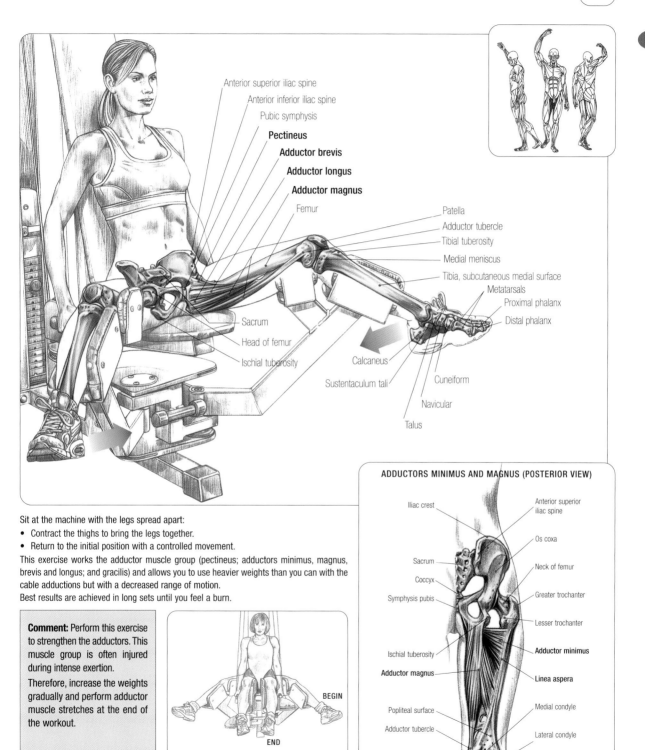

Anterior superior iliac spine
Anterior inferior iliac spine
Pubic symphysis
Pectineus
Adductor brevis
Adductor longus
Adductor magnus
Femur
Sacrum
Head of femur
Ischial tuberosity
Patella
Adductor tubercle
Tibial tuberosity
Medial meniscus
Tibia, subcutaneous medial surface
Metatarsals
Proximal phalanx
Distal phalanx
Calcaneus
Sustentaculum tali
Cuneiform
Navicular
Talus

Sit at the machine with the legs spread apart:
- Contract the thighs to bring the legs together.
- Return to the initial position with a controlled movement.

This exercise works the adductor muscle group (pectineus; adductors minimus, magnus, brevis and longus; and gracilis) and allows you to use heavier weights than you can with the cable adductions but with a decreased range of motion.

Best results are achieved in long sets until you feel a burn.

Comment: Perform this exercise to strengthen the adductors. This muscle group is often injured during intense exertion.

Therefore, increase the weights gradually and perform adductor muscle stretches at the end of the workout.

BEGIN
END
THE MOVEMENT

ADDUCTORS MINIMUS AND MAGNUS (POSTERIOR VIEW)

Iliac crest
Anterior superior iliac spine
Os coxa
Sacrum
Neck of femur
Coccyx
Greater trochanter
Symphysis pubis
Lesser trochanter
Ischial tuberosity
Adductor minimus
Adductor magnus
Linea aspera
Popliteal surface
Medial condyle
Adductor tubercle
Lateral condyle

14 STANDING CALF RAISES

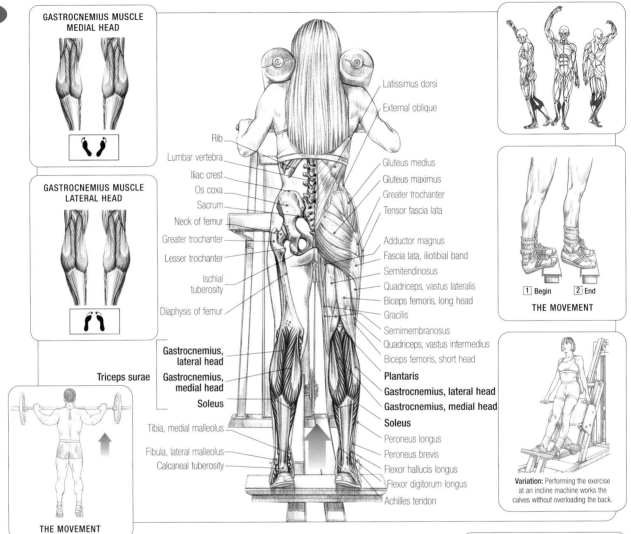

GASTROCNEMIUS MUSCLE
MEDIAL HEAD

GASTROCNEMIUS MUSCLE
LATERAL HEAD

Triceps surae

Latissimus dorsi

External oblique

Rib

Lumbar vertebra

Iliac crest

Os coxa

Sacrum

Neck of femur

Greater trochanter

Lesser trochanter

Ischial tuberosity

Diaphysis of femur

Gluteus medius

Gluteus maximus

Greater trochanter

Tensor fascia lata

Adductor magnus

Fascia lata, iliotibial band

Semitendinosus

Quadriceps, vastus lateralis

Biceps femoris, long head

Gracilis

Semimembranosus

Quadriceps, vastus intermedius

Biceps femoris, short head

Gastrocnemius, lateral head

Gastrocnemius, medial head

Soleus

Tibia, medial malleolus

Fibula, lateral malleolus

Calcaneal tuberosity

Plantaris

Gastrocnemius, lateral head

Gastrocnemius, medial head

Soleus

Peroneus longus

Peroneus brevis

Flexor hallucis longus

Flexor digitorum longus

Achilles tendon

THE MOVEMENT

THE MOVEMENT

1 Begin   2 End

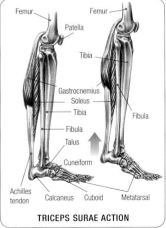

Variation: Performing the exercise at an incline machine works the calves without overloading the back.

Stand at the machine with a straight back, shoulders under the pads, and the balls of the feet on the foot plate, with the calves relaxed and the heels hanging down:

• Rise up by extending (plantar flex) the feet, keeping the knees straight.

This exercise uses the triceps surae (made up of the soleus and the lateral and medial heads of the gastrocnemius). Move the feet through the complete range of flexion with each repetition in order to stretch the muscles properly. In theory, it is possible to isolate the medial gastrocnemius by pointing the toes out and to isolate the lateral gastrocnemius by pointing the toes in. But in practice, this is difficult to achieve. Only separating the work of the soleus and gastrocnemius is easy to achieve. This is done by flexing the knees to relax the gastrocnemius and to put more effort on the soleus.

Variations: Perform the exercise at a frame with a wedge under the feet or with a free bar without the wedge for more balance; however, this reduces the amplitude of movement.

Femur

Femur

Patella

Tibia

Gastrocnemius

Soleus

Tibia

Fibula

Fibula

Talus

Cuneiform

Achilles tendon

Calcaneus   Cuboid   Metatarsal

TRICEPS SURAE ACTION

Comment: The triceps surae is an extremely powerful, tough muscle group that alone raises the entire weight of the body thousands of times in a day when we walk. Don't hesitate to work it with heavy weights.

ONE-LEG TOE RAISES 15

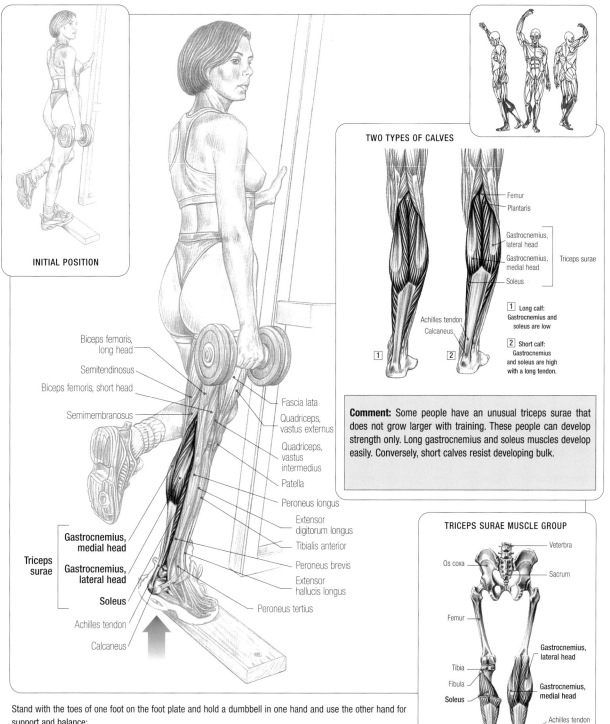

INITIAL POSITION

TWO TYPES OF CALVES

Femur
Plantaris
Gastrocnemius, lateral head
Gastrocnemius, medial head
Soleus
Triceps surae

Achilles tendon
Calcaneus

1 Long calf: Gastrocnemius and soleus are low

2 Short calf: Gastrocnemius and soleus are high with a long tendon.

Comment: Some people have an unusual triceps surae that does not grow larger with training. These people can develop strength only. Long gastrocnemius and soleus muscles develop easily. Conversely, short calves resist developing bulk.

Biceps femoris, long head
Semitendinosus
Biceps femoris, short head
Semimembranosus
Triceps surae
Gastrocnemius, medial head
Gastrocnemius, lateral head
Soleus
Achilles tendon
Calcaneus

Fascia lata
Quadriceps, vastus externus
Quadriceps, vastus intermedius
Patella
Peroneus longus
Extensor digitorum longus
Tibialis anterior
Peroneus brevis
Extensor hallucis longus
Peroneus tertius

TRICEPS SURAE MUSCLE GROUP

Veterbra
Os coxa
Sacrum
Femur
Gastrocnemius, lateral head
Tibia
Fibula
Soleus
Gastrocnemius, medial head
Achilles tendon
Calcaneus

Stand with the toes of one foot on the foot plate and hold a dumbbell in one hand and use the other hand for support and balance:

• Rise up on the toes (plantar flexion), keeping the knee joint straight or slightly flexed.
• Return to the initial position.

This exercise contracts the triceps surae. Completely flex the foot with each repetition in order to stretch the triceps surae properly. Optimal results are obtained through long sets until you feel a burn.

16 DONKEY CALF RAISES

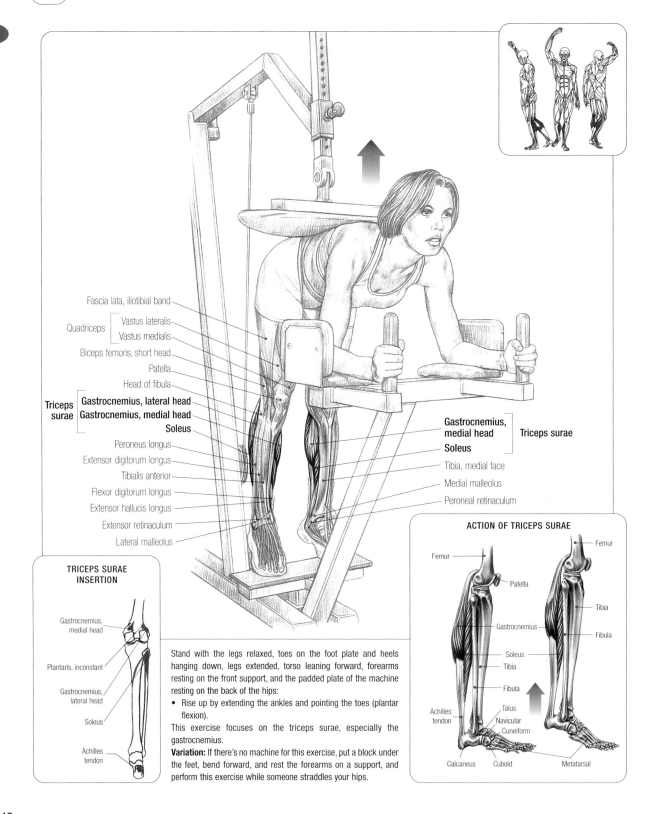

Fascia lata, iliotibial band

Quadriceps {
Vastus lateralis
Vastus medialis
}

Biceps femoris, short head

Patella

Head of fibula

Triceps surae {
Gastrocnemius, lateral head
Gastrocnemius, medial head
Soleus
}

Peroneus longus

Extensor digitorum longus

Tibialis anterior

Flexor digitorum longus

Extensor hallucis longus

Extensor retinaculum

Lateral malleolus

Gastrocnemius, medial head
Soleus
Triceps surae

Tibia, medial face

Medial malleolus

Peroneal retinaculum

TRICEPS SURAE INSERTION

Gastrocnemius, medial head

Plantaris, inconstant

Gastrocnemius, lateral head

Soleus

Achilles tendon

ACTION OF TRICEPS SURAE

Femur

Femur

Patella

Tibia

Gastrocnemius

Fibula

Soleus

Tibia

Fibula

Talus

Achilles tendon

Navicular

Cuneiform

Calcaneus

Cuboid

Metatarsal

Stand with the legs relaxed, toes on the foot plate and heels hanging down, legs extended, torso leaning forward, forearms resting on the front support, and the padded plate of the machine resting on the back of the hips:

• Rise up by extending the ankles and pointing the toes (plantar flexion).

This exercise focuses on the triceps surae, especially the gastrocnemius.

Variation: If there's no machine for this exercise, put a block under the feet, bend forward, and rest the forearms on a support, and perform this exercise while someone straddles your hips.

SEATED CALF RAISES 17

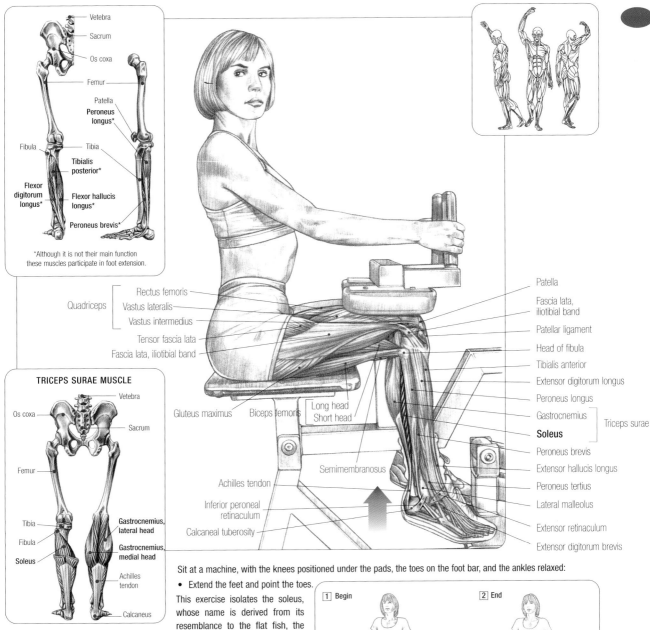

Vetebra
Sacrum
Os coxa
Femur
Patella
Peroneus longus*
Fibula
Tibia
Tibialis posterior*
Flexor digitorum longus*
Flexor hallucis longus*
Peroneus brevis*

*Although it is not their main function these muscles participate in foot extension.

Quadriceps
- Rectus femoris
- Vastus lateralis
- Vastus intermedius
Tensor fascia lata
Fascia lata, iliotibial band

Patella
Fascia lata, iliotibial band
Patellar ligament
Head of fibula
Tibialis anterior
Extensor digitorum longus
Peroneus longus
Gastrocnemius
Soleus
Triceps surae
Peroneus brevis
Extensor hallucis longus
Peroneus tertius
Lateral malleolus
Extensor retinaculum
Extensor digitorum brevis

Gluteus maximus
Biceps femoris
Long head
Short head
Semimembranosus
Achilles tendon
Inferior peroneal retinaculum
Calcaneal tuberosity

TRICEPS SURAE MUSCLE

Vetebra
Os coxa
Sacrum
Femur
Tibia
Fibula
Soleus
Gastrocnemius, lateral head
Gastrocnemius, medial head
Achilles tendon
Calcaneus

Sit at a machine, with the knees positioned under the pads, the toes on the foot bar, and the ankles relaxed:

- Extend the feet and point the toes.

This exercise isolates the soleus, whose name is derived from its resemblance to the flat fish, the sole. (This muscle inserts at the top at the tibia and fibula under the knee joint and attaches at the bottom to the calcaneus by the Achilles tendon. Its purpose is to extend the feet at the ankles.)

Bending at the knees relaxes the gastrocnemius, which attaches at the top above the knee joint and at the bottom onto the Achilles tendon, and reduces its contribution to ankle extension.

Variation: You can also perform this exercise by sitting on a bench with a wedge under the feet and a barbell resting on the thighs. Wrap the bar for comfort.

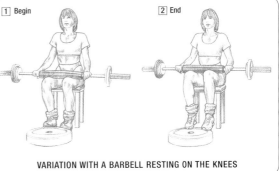

1 Begin

2 End

VARIATION WITH A BARBELL RESTING ON THE KNEES

18 SEATED BARBELL CALF RAISES

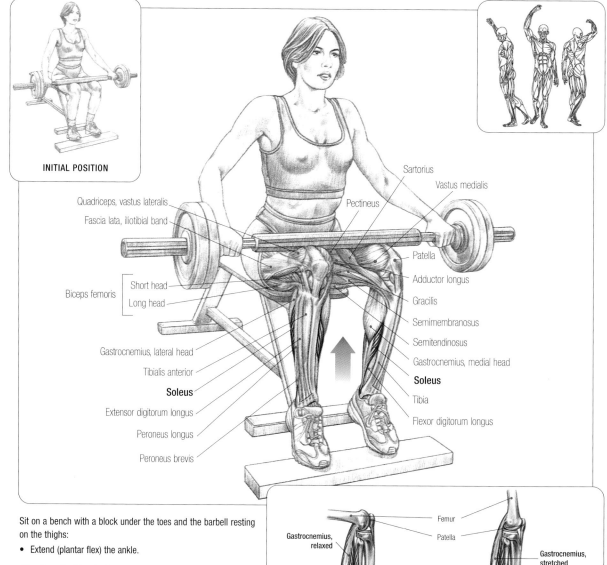

INITIAL POSITION

Quadriceps, vastus lateralis

Fascia lata, iliotibial band

Biceps femoris { Short head / Long head }

Gastrocnemius, lateral head

Tibialis anterior

Soleus

Extensor digitorum longus

Peroneus longus

Peroneus brevis

Sartorius

Vastus medialis

Pectineus

Patella

Adductor longus

Gracilis

Semimembranosus

Semitendinosus

Gastrocnemius, medial head

Soleus

Tibia

Flexor digitorum longus

Sit on a bench with a block under the toes and the barbell resting on the thighs:

• Extend (plantar flex) the ankle.

Attention: Cushion the bar on the thighs with a rubber pad or a folded towel to reduce pain.

This exercise mainly uses the soleus. This muscle, which is part of the triceps surae group, inserts at the top below the knee joint on the tibia and fibula. At the bottom, it attaches to the calcaneus via the Achilles tendon. Its function is to extend the feet at the ankles. Unlike the calf raises, which allow you to work with heavy weights, this exercise does not allow heavy weights because of the awkwardness of the bar position. For best results, work in sets of 15 to 20 repetitions.

Variation: You can also perform this exercise without additional weights while sitting on a chair or bench. In this case, work in very long sets until you feel a burn.

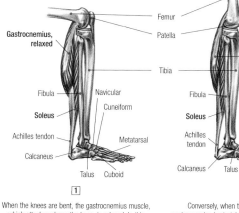

Gastrocnemius, relaxed

Femur

Patella

Fibula

Navicular

Cuneiform

Tibia

Soleus

Achilles tendon

Metatarsal

Calcaneus

Talus   Cuboid

Gastrocnemius, stretched

Fibula

Navicular

Cuneiform

Soleus

Achilles tendon

Metatarsal

Calcaneus   Talus   Cuboid

[1]

When the knees are bent, the gastrocnemius muscle, which attaches above the knee, is relaxed. In this position, it weakly assists ankle extension because most of the work is done by the soleus.

[2]

Conversely, when the knee is straight, the gastrocnemius is stretched. In this position, it actively participates in ankle extension and completes the action of the soleus.

6 BUTTOCKS

Gluteal muscles, a human characteristic

Although some of the larger primates occasionally walk, humans are the only primates and one of the few mammals that has completely adapted to two-legged locomotion. One of the structural features directly related to this way of getting around is the significant development of the gluteus maximus muscle, which has become the biggest and most powerful muscle in the human body.

The development of the gluteal muscles is truly a human characteristic. In comparison, the gluteal muscles in quadrupeds are proportionately underdeveloped, and the hindquarters of the horse, which some consider as typical for animals, is in fact made up of the hamstrings (the back of the thigh in humans).

In humans, the gluteus maximus, which extends the hip, does not play an important role in walking. Instead, the hamstrings play the major role in straightening the pelvis (hip extension) with each stride. Just put your hand on the buttocks while walking, and you can feel that they do not contract much.

However, as soon as the effort becomes significant, such as when walking uphill, walking quickly, or running, the gluteal action is called into play to extend the hip and erect the torso.

These biomechanical points help explain why in exercises for the gluteal muscles and the hamstrings, such as good mornings (see page 107) and leg raises, either the gluteal muscles or the hamstrings are isolated depending on the amount of weight involved.

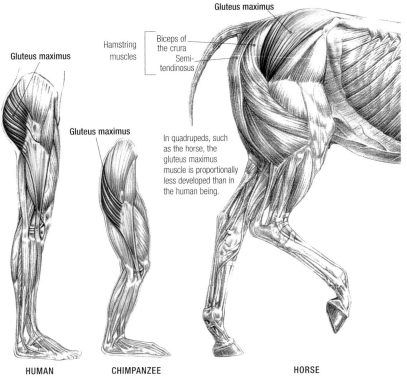

Gluteus maximus

Gluteus maximus

Gluteus maximus

Hamstring muscles

Biceps of the crura

Semi-tendinosus

In quadrupeds, such as the horse, the gluteus maximus muscle is proportionally less developed than in the human being.

HUMAN   CHIMPANZEE   HORSE

1 LUNGES

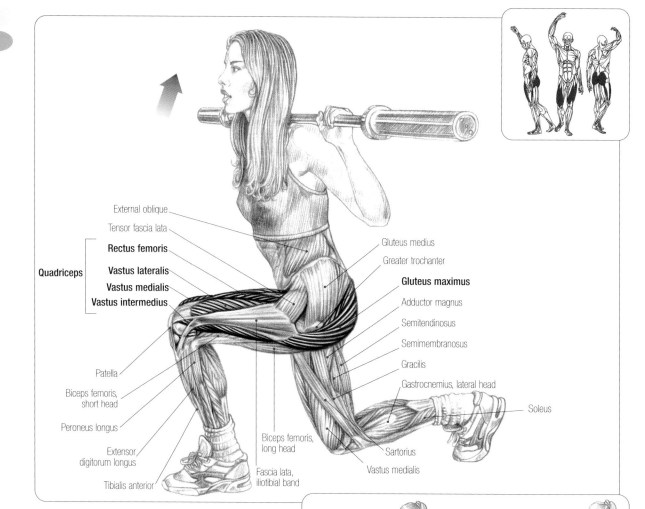

External oblique
Tensor fascia lata
Rectus femoris
Quadriceps
Vastus lateralis
Vastus medialis
Vastus intermedius
Patella
Biceps femoris, short head
Peroneus longus
Extensor digitorum longus
Tibialis anterior

Gluteus medius
Greater trochanter
Gluteus maximus
Adductor magnus
Semitendinosus
Semimembranosus
Gracilis
Gastrocnemius, lateral head
Soleus
Biceps femoris, long head
Sartorius
Vastus medialis
Fascia lata, iliotibial band

Stand with the legs slightly apart and the bar behind the neck resting on the trapezius muscles:

- Inhale and take a big step forward, keeping the trunk as straight as possible.
- Lunge until the front thigh is horizontal to the floor or slightly less.
- Exhale and return to the initial position.

This exercise, which works the gluteus maximus intensely, can be performed two different ways: either by taking a small step (which isolates the quadriceps) or taking a big step (which isolates the hamstrings and gluteus maximus and stretches the rectus femoris and iliopsoas of the back leg).

⚠️ **Comment:** Because the front leg must support almost all the weight in the lunge position and the exercise demands a good sense of balance, begin with very light weights.

1️⃣ EXECUTION WITH A SMALL STEP: PREDOMINANTLY WORKS THE QUADRICEPS

2️⃣ EXECUTION WITH A BIG STEP: PREDOMINANTLY WORKS THE GLUTEUS MAXIMUS

DUMBBELL LUNGES 2

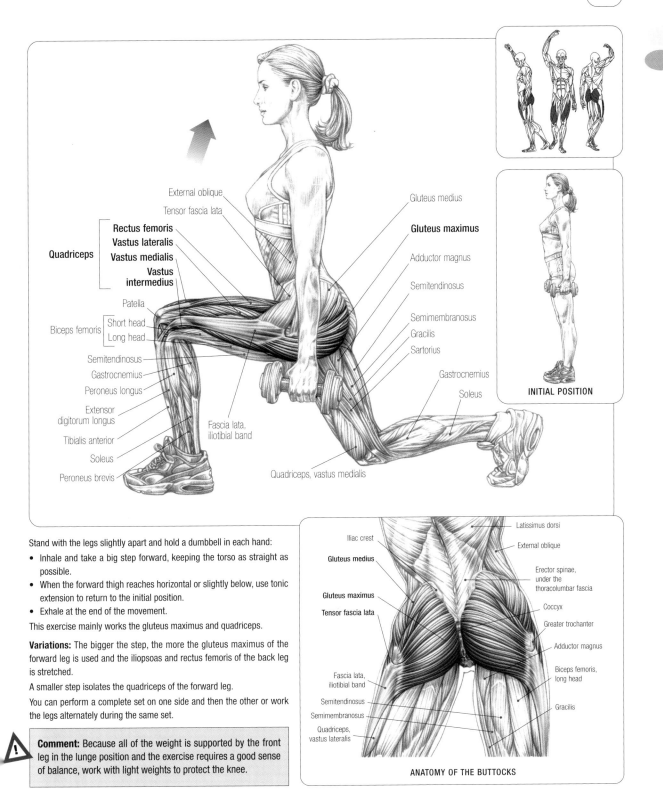

External oblique

Tensor fascia lata

Rectus femoris
Vastus lateralis
Vastus medialis
Vastus intermedius

Quadriceps

Patella

Biceps femoris — Short head / Long head

Semitendinosus

Gastrocnemius

Peroneus longus

Extensor digitorum longus

Tibialis anterior

Soleus

Peroneus brevis

Fascia lata, iliotibial band

Quadriceps, vastus medialis

Gluteus medius

Gluteus maximus

Adductor magnus

Semitendinosus

Semimembranosus
Gracilis
Sartorius

Gastrocnemius

Soleus

INITIAL POSITION

Latissimus dorsi

Iliac crest

External oblique

Gluteus medius

Erector spinae, under the thoracolumbar fascia

Gluteus maximus

Tensor fascia lata

Coccyx

Greater trochanter

Adductor magnus

Fascia lata, iliotibial band

Biceps femoris, long head

Semitendinosus

Gracilis

Semimembranosus

Quadriceps, vastus lateralis

ANATOMY OF THE BUTTOCKS

Stand with the legs slightly apart and hold a dumbbell in each hand:

- Inhale and take a big step forward, keeping the torso as straight as possible.
- When the forward thigh reaches horizontal or slightly below, use tonic extension to return to the initial position.
- Exhale at the end of the movement.

This exercise mainly works the gluteus maximus and quadriceps.

Variations: The bigger the step, the more the gluteus maximus of the forward leg is used and the iliopsoas and rectus femoris of the back leg is stretched.

A smaller step isolates the quadriceps of the forward leg.

You can perform a complete set on one side and then the other or work the legs alternately during the same set.

Comment: Because all of the weight is supported by the front leg in the lunge position and the exercise requires a good sense of balance, work with light weights to protect the knee.

KNEE INSTABILITY

When the knee is extended, the medial and lateral collateral ligaments are stretched and prevent rotation of the joint. When you are standing, the knee locks in extension, and there is no need for muscle tension to stabilize the joint.

When the knee is bent, the medial and lateral collateral ligaments are relaxed. In this position muscle tension provides the stability.

When the knee flexes and rotates, the meniscus travels forward. Then, if extension is not controlled, the meniscus may not return to its normal position fast enough and becomes pinched between the condyles, which can tear the meniscus. If a piece of the meniscus is severed when it is pinched, surgery may be necessary to remove it.

With asymmetrical exercises such as the lunge (see page 116), control the speed and the form of the movement to protect the knee.

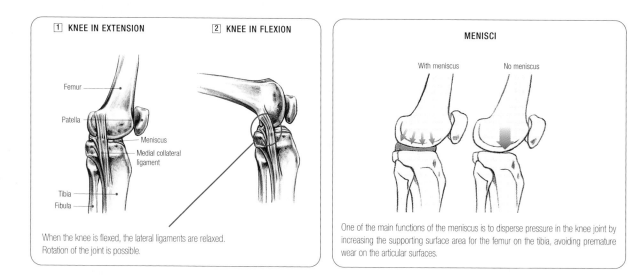

1 KNEE IN EXTENSION **2 KNEE IN FLEXION**

Femur
Patella
Meniscus
Medial collateral ligament
Tibia
Fibula

When the knee is flexed, the lateral ligaments are relaxed. Rotation of the joint is possible.

MENISCI

With meniscus   No meniscus

One of the main functions of the meniscus is to disperse pressure in the knee joint by increasing the supporting surface area for the femur on the tibia, avoiding premature wear on the articular surfaces.

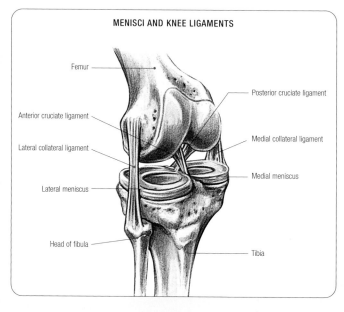

MENISCI AND KNEE LIGAMENTS

Femur
Posterior cruciate ligament
Anterior cruciate ligament
Medial collateral ligament
Lateral collateral ligament
Medial meniscus
Lateral meniscus
Head of fibula
Tibia

CABLE BACK KICKS 3

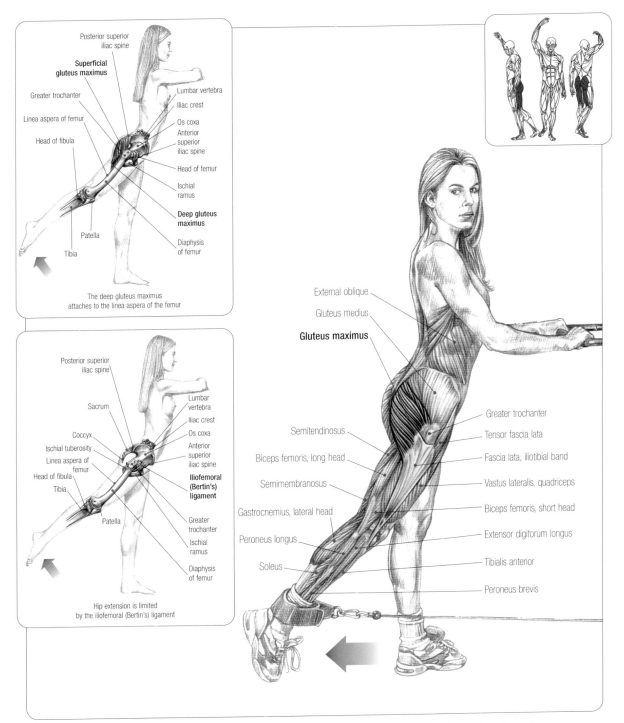

Posterior superior iliac spine

Superficial gluteus maximus

Greater trochanter

Linea aspera of femur

Head of fibula

Lumbar vertebra

Iliac crest

Os coxa

Anterior superior iliac spine

Head of femur

Ischial ramus

Deep gluteus maximus

Patella

Tibia

Diaphysis of femur

The deep gluteus maximus attaches to the linea aspera of the femur

Posterior superior iliac spine

Sacrum

Coccyx

Ischial tuberosity

Linea aspera of femur

Head of fibula

Tibia

Patella

Lumbar vertebra

Iliac crest

Os coxa

Anterior superior iliac spine

Iliofemoral (Bertin's) ligament

Greater trochanter

Ischial ramus

Diaphysis of femur

Hip extension is limited by the iliofemoral (Bertin's) ligament

External oblique

Gluteus medius

Gluteus maximus

Semitendinosus

Biceps femoris, long head

Semimembranosus

Gastrocnemius, lateral head

Peroneus longus

Soleus

Greater trochanter

Tensor fascia lata

Fascia lata, iliotibial band

Vastus lateralis, quadriceps

Biceps femoris, short head

Extensor digitorum longus

Tibialis anterior

Peroneus brevis

Stand on one leg facing the machine, the other leg attached to the ankle strap of the low pulley, and the pelvis tilted forward. Grasp the handle:

- Extend the hip and pull the leg back.
- Hip extension is limited by the tension of the iliofemoral (Bertin's) ligament.

This exercise mainly works the gluteus maximus and, to a lesser extent, the hamstrings (except the short head of biceps femoris).

It helps develop the profile of the hips while firming the gluteal region.

4 MACHINE HIP EXTENSIONS

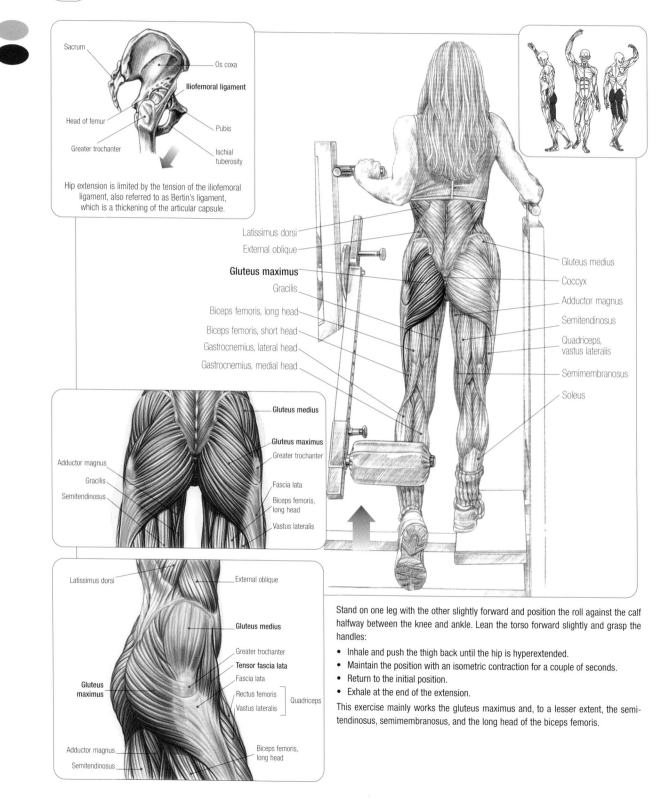

Sacrum

Os coxa

Iliofemoral ligament

Head of femur

Pubis

Greater trochanter

Ischial tuberosity

Hip extension is limited by the tension of the iliofemoral ligament, also referred to as Bertin's ligament, which is a thickening of the articular capsule.

Latissimus dorsi
External oblique
Gluteus maximus
Gracilis
Biceps femoris, long head
Biceps femoris, short head
Gastrocnemius, lateral head
Gastrocnemius, medial head

Gluteus medius
Coccyx
Adductor magnus
Semitendinosus
Quadriceps, vastus lateralis
Semimembranosus
Soleus

Gluteus medius
Gluteus maximus
Greater trochanter
Fascia lata
Biceps femoris, long head
Vastus lateralis

Adductor magnus
Gracilis
Semitendinosus

Latissimus dorsi
External oblique

Gluteus medius

Greater trochanter
Tensor fascia lata
Fascia lata
Rectus femoris
Vastus lateralis
Quadriceps

Gluteus maximus

Adductor magnus
Semitendinosus

Biceps femoris, long head

Stand on one leg with the other slightly forward and position the roll against the calf halfway between the knee and ankle. Lean the torso forward slightly and grasp the handles:

- Inhale and push the thigh back until the hip is hyperextended.
- Maintain the position with an isometric contraction for a couple of seconds.
- Return to the initial position.
- Exhale at the end of the extension.

This exercise mainly works the gluteus maximus and, to a lesser extent, the semitendinosus, semimembranosus, and the long head of the biceps femoris.

FLOOR HIP EXTENSIONS 5

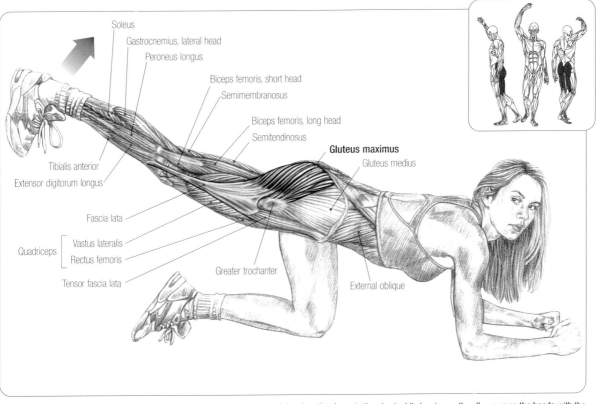

Soleus
Gastrocnemius, lateral head
Peroneus longus
Biceps femoris, short head
Semimembranosus
Biceps femoris, long head
Semitendinosus
Gluteus maximus
Gluteus medius
Tibialis anterior
Extensor digitorum longus
Fascia lata
Quadriceps
Vastus lateralis
Rectus femoris
Tensor fascia lata
Greater trochanter
External oblique

THE MOVEMENT

Kneel on one leg and bring the other knee to the chest while leaning on the elbows or on the hands with the arms extended:

• Extend the bent leg back with complete hip extension.

With the leg extended, this exercise uses the hamstrings and gluteus maximus. With the knee bent, only the gluteus maximus is used and less intensely.

This exercise can be performed with higher or lower amplitude during the last part of the extension. You can maintain an isometric contraction for a couple of seconds at the end of the movement.

To increase the intensity, use ankle weights.

Its ease of execution and its effectiveness has made this exercise popular, and it is frequently used in group classes.

BEGIN

END

VARIATION ON A BENCH

VARIATION WITH BENT KNEE

6 BRIDGING

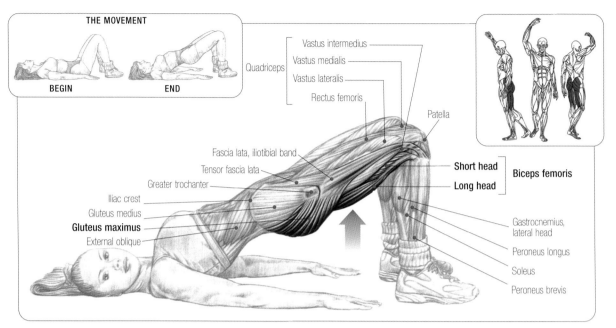

THE MOVEMENT

BEGIN   END

Vastus intermedius
Vastus medialis
Vastus lateralis
Quadriceps
Rectus femoris
Patella
Fascia lata, iliotibial band
Short head
Tensor fascia lata
Long head — Biceps femoris
Greater trochanter
Iliac crest
Gluteus medius
Gluteus maximus
External oblique
Gastrocnemius, lateral head
Peroneus longus
Soleus
Peroneus brevis

Lie on the back, with hands flat on the ground, arms alongside the body, and knees bent:

• Inhale and lift the buttocks off the ground, pushing down through the feet.
• Maintain the position for a couple of seconds and lower the pelvis without touching the buttocks on the ground.
• Exhale and begin again.

This exercise mainly works the hamstrings and gluteus maximus.

Perform this exercise in long sets, making sure to contract the muscles at the top of the lift, when the pelvis is off the ground.

Comment: Because it is easy and effective, bridging has become part of most group exercise classes.

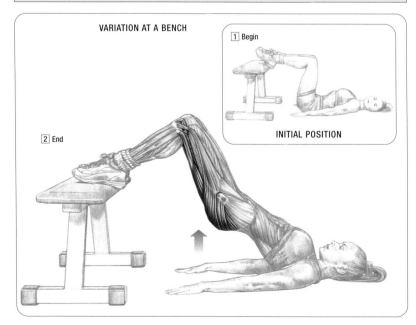

VARIATION AT A BENCH

1 Begin

INITIAL POSITION

2 End

Variation 1:

To perform bridging with the feet raised, lie on the back, with hands flat at the sides, arms alongside the body, thighs vertical, and feet resting on a bench:

• Inhale and raise the pelvis off the ground; maintain the position for two seconds and lower without touching the buttocks to the ground.
• Exhale and begin again.

This exercise works the gluteus maximus and especially the hamstrings. The hamstrings are used more in this exercise than when bridging from the ground. Execute this exercise slowly, and focus on the muscle contraction.

Sets of 10 to 15 repetitions provide the best results. Another variation is to perform bridging with the calves resting on the bench. This isolates the hamstrings even more intensely and also requires strong work from the gastrocnemius.

Variation 2:

Limit the range of the movement by not lowering the pelvis as far and create a burn.

Comment: Bridging is actually extending the hips.

CABLE HIP ABDUCTIONS 7

GLUTEAL INSERTIONS AT THE OS COXA

Gluteus medius

Gluteus maximus

Gluteus minimus

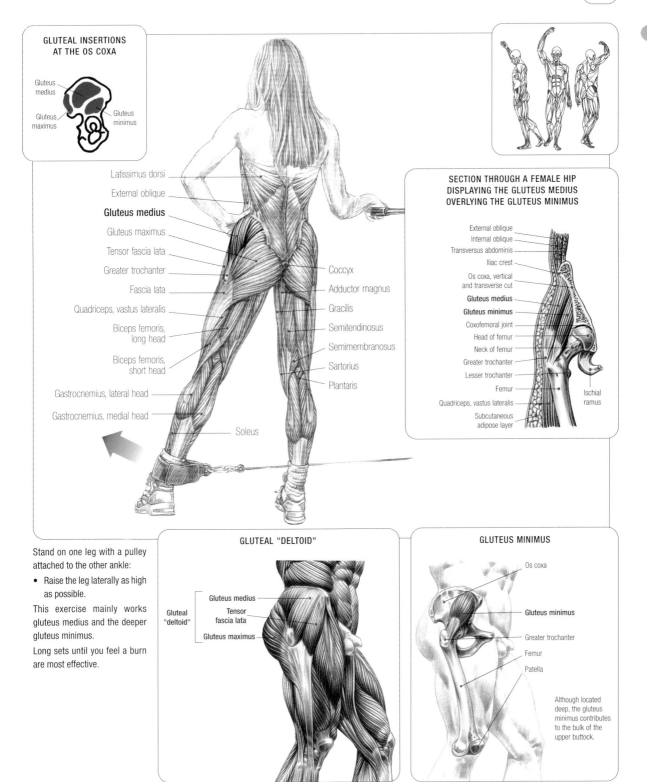

Latissimus dorsi

External oblique

Gluteus medius

Gluteus maximus

Tensor fascia lata

Greater trochanter

Fascia lata

Quadriceps, vastus lateralis

Biceps femoris, long head

Biceps femoris, short head

Gastrocnemius, lateral head

Gastrocnemius, medial head

Soleus

Coccyx

Adductor magnus

Gracilis

Semitendinosus

Semimembranosus

Sartorius

Plantaris

SECTION THROUGH A FEMALE HIP DISPLAYING THE GLUTEUS MEDIUS OVERLYING THE GLUTEUS MINIMUS

External oblique

Internal oblique

Transversus abdominis

Iliac crest

Os coxa, vertical and transverse cut

Gluteus medius

Gluteus minimus

Coxofemoral joint

Head of femur

Neck of femur

Greater trochanter

Lesser trochanter

Femur

Quadriceps, vastus lateralis

Subcutaneous adipose layer

Ischial ramus

Stand on one leg with a pulley attached to the other ankle:

• Raise the leg laterally as high as possible.

This exercise mainly works gluteus medius and the deeper gluteus minimus.

Long sets until you feel a burn are most effective.

GLUTEAL "DELTOID"

Gluteal "deltoid"

Gluteus medius

Tensor fascia lata

Gluteus maximus

GLUTEUS MINIMUS

Os coxa

Gluteus minimus

Greater trochanter

Femur

Patella

Although located deep, the gluteus minimus contributes to the bulk of the upper buttock.

INDIVIDUAL VARIATIONS IN HIP MOBILITY

Regardless of individual muscle elasticity and ligamentous tension, it is mainly the shape of the bones of the coxofemoral joint that is responsible for hip mobility. The configuration of the bone is most important in hip abduction.

Example

- When the neck of the femur is almost horizontal (coxa vara) and associated with a well-developed superior rim of the acetabulum covering the head of the femur, abduction movements are limited.
- When the neck of the femur is close to vertical (coxa valga) and associated with an undeveloped superior acetabular rim, abduction movements are facilitated.

Therefore, it is useless to try to raise the leg high laterally if your hip joint is not made for it.

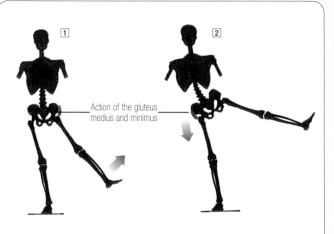

Action of the gluteus medius and minimus

1 Abduction of the hip (limited by the neck of the femur butting against the acetabulum)

2 Forced abduction of the hip (tilting the pelvis onto the head of the opposite femur)

ATTENTION

If hip abduction is forced, the neck of the femur will butt up against the rim of the acetabulum, and the pelvis will tilt onto the head of the opposite femur to compensate for lateral extension of the leg. When some people perform sets of forced abductions, over time microtrauma may occur, which develops excessive growth of the superior rim of the acetabulum, limiting the mobility of the hip and risking painful inflammation.

VARIATIONS IN OSSEOUS HIP STRUCTURE

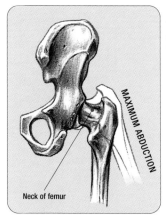

MAXIMUM ABDUCTION

Neck of femur

An almost horizontal neck of the femur is referred to as a **coxa vara**. It limits abduction movements because it butts up against the rim of the acetabulum sooner.

MAXIMUM ABDUCTION

Neck of femur

An almost vertical neck of the femur is referred to as **coxa valga**. It allows greater abduction movements.

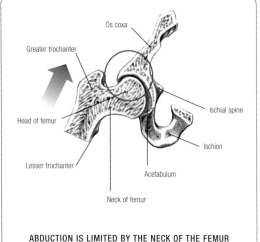

Os coxa

Greater trochanter

Head of femur

Lesser trochanter

Ischial spine

Ischion

Acetabulum

Neck of femur

ABDUCTION IS LIMITED BY THE NECK OF THE FEMUR BUTTING UP AGAINST THE RIM OF THE ACETABULUM.

STANDING MACHINE HIP ABDUCTIONS 8

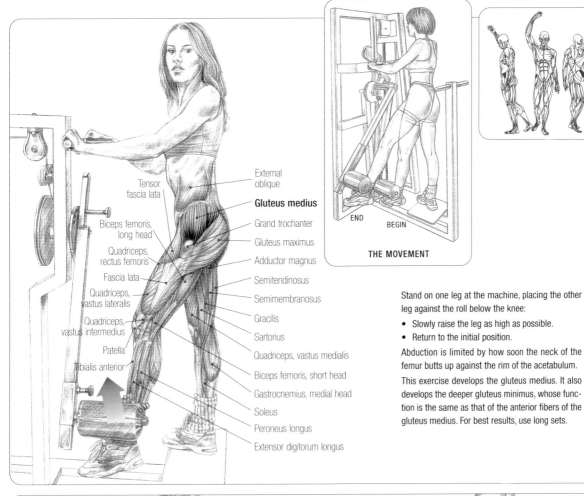

THE MOVEMENT
- END
- BEGIN

Tensor fascia lata
External oblique
Gluteus medius
Grand trochanter
Biceps femoris, long head
Gluteus maximus
Quadriceps, rectus femoris
Adductor magnus
Fascia lata
Semitendinosus
Quadriceps, vastus lateralis
Semimembranosus
Quadriceps, vastus intermedius
Gracilis
Patella
Sartorius
Tibialis anterior
Quadriceps, vastus medialis
Biceps femoris, short head
Gastrocnemius, medial head
Soleus
Peroneus longus
Extensor digitorum longus

Stand on one leg at the machine, placing the other leg against the roll below the knee:
- Slowly raise the leg as high as possible.
- Return to the initial position.

Abduction is limited by how soon the neck of the femur butts up against the rim of the acetabulum.

This exercise develops the gluteus medius. It also develops the deeper gluteus minimus, whose function is the same as that of the anterior fibers of the gluteus medius. For best results, use long sets.

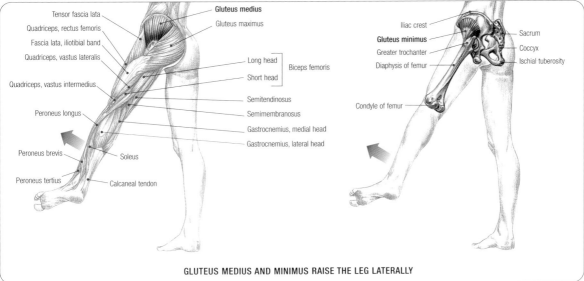

GLUTEUS MEDIUS AND MINIMUS RAISE THE LEG LATERALLY

9 FLOOR HIP ABDUCTIONS

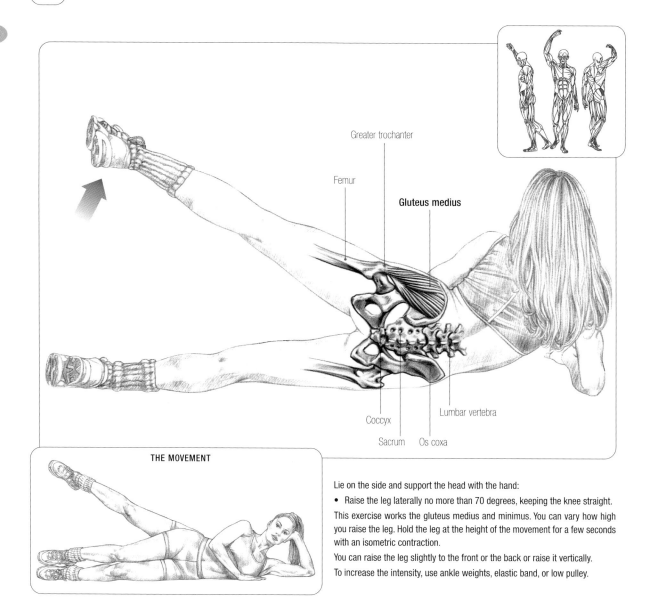

Greater trochanter

Femur

Gluteus medius

Coccyx

Sacrum

Os coxa

Lumbar vertebra

THE MOVEMENT

Lie on the side and support the head with the hand:

• Raise the leg laterally no more than 70 degrees, keeping the knee straight.

This exercise works the gluteus medius and minimus. You can vary how high you raise the leg. Hold the leg at the height of the movement for a few seconds with an isometric contraction.

You can raise the leg slightly to the front or the back or raise it vertically.

To increase the intensity, use ankle weights, elastic band, or low pulley.

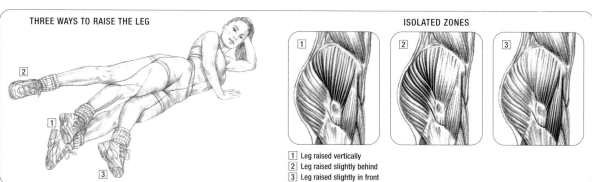

THREE WAYS TO RAISE THE LEG

ISOLATED ZONES

1 Leg raised vertically
2 Leg raised slightly behind
3 Leg raised slightly in front

SEATED MACHINE HIP ABDUCTIONS (10)

END

BEGIN

THE MOVEMENT

External oblique
Rectus abdominis
Gluteus medius
Tensor fascia lata
Greater trochanter
Quadriceps, rectus femoris
Quadriceps, vastus lateralis
Fascia lata, iliotibial band
Gluteus maximus

Sit at the machine:

- Spread the legs as wide as possible.
- Return to the initial position with a controlled movement.

The more angled the backrest, the more the gluteus medius is isolated. The more vertical the backrest, the more the gluteus maximus is worked.

Ideally, lean forward or back to change the angle of the torso during a set.

Example: Perform 10 repetitions with the torso resting against the backrest and 10 repetitions with the torso leaning forward.

This exercise sculpts and firms the top of the hip, which makes the waistline look narrower.

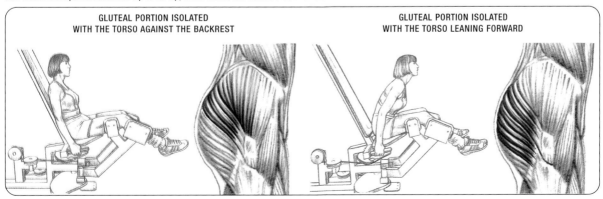

GLUTEAL PORTION ISOLATED
WITH THE TORSO AGAINST THE BACKREST

GLUTEAL PORTION ISOLATED
WITH THE TORSO LEANING FORWARD

7
ABDOMEN

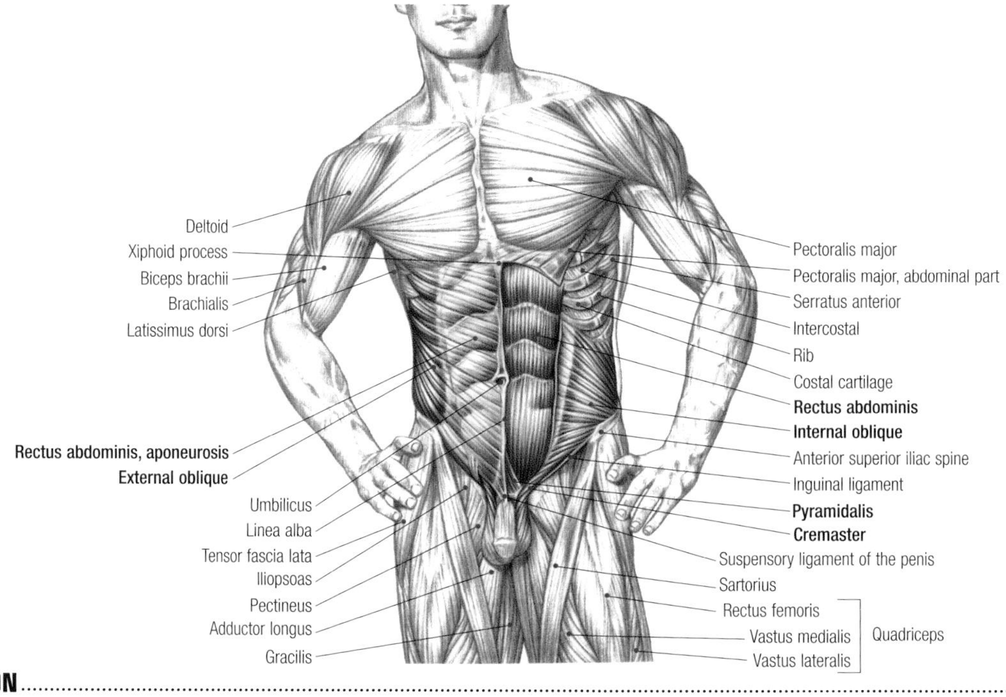

Deltoid
Xiphoid process
Biceps brachii
Brachialis
Latissimus dorsi

Pectoralis major
Pectoralis major, abdominal part
Serratus anterior
Intercostal
Rib
Costal cartilage
Rectus abdominis
Internal oblique
Anterior superior iliac spine
Inguinal ligament
Pyramidalis
Cremaster
Suspensory ligament of the penis
Sartorius
Rectus femoris
Vastus medialis
Vastus lateralis

Quadriceps

Rectus abdominis, aponeurosis
External oblique
Umbilicus
Linea alba
Tensor fascia lata
Iliopsoas
Pectineus
Adductor longus
Gracilis

ATTENTION!

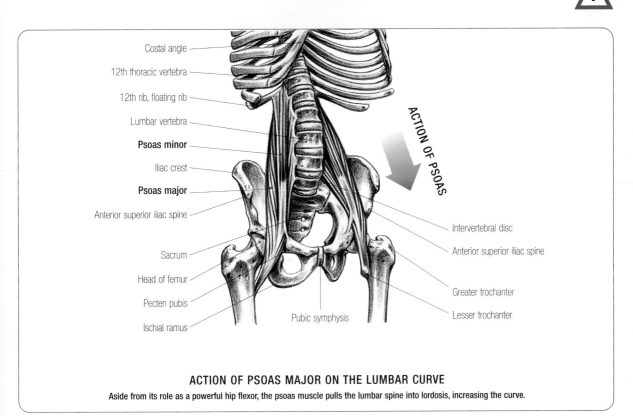

Costal angle
12th thoracic vertebra
12th rib, floating rib
Lumbar vertebra
Psoas minor
Iliac crest
Psoas major
Anterior superior iliac spine
Sacrum
Head of femur
Pecten pubis
Ischial ramus

ACTION OF PSOAS

Intervertebral disc
Anterior superior iliac spine
Greater trochanter
Lesser trochanter
Pubic symphysis

ACTION OF PSOAS MAJOR ON THE LUMBAR CURVE

Aside from its role as a powerful hip flexor, the psoas muscle pulls the lumbar spine into lordosis, increasing the curve.

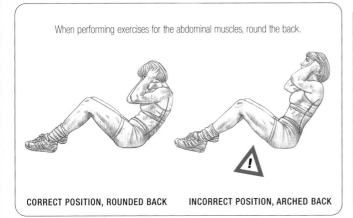

When performing exercises for the abdominal muscles, round the back.

CORRECT POSITION, ROUNDED BACK   **INCORRECT POSITION, ARCHED BACK**

As with most movements involving the abdominal core, leg raises either on the ground or at an incline bench should never be performed with an arched back.

INCORRECT POSITION, BACK ARCHED

Unlike other weightlifting movements, exercises for the abdominal core and especially those for the rectus abdominis absolutely must be worked with a rounded back (rolling up the spine).

When performing exercises that roll the spine up off the floor, as in crunches, you hold the spine differently than when performing squats, deadlifts, or other standing movements.

If during exercises with additional weights, such as squats, deadlifts, or good mornings, the vertebral column is not arched at the lumbar spine, vertical pressure combined with rounding the back pushes the nucleus pulposus of the intervertebral disc posteriorly, which can compress the nerves and cause sciatica or a herniated disc.

On the other hand, when performing specific exercises for the abdomen, if the back is not rounded with intense contraction of the rectus abdominis and the internal and external obliques, the powerful psoas hip flexors will increase the lumbar curve, forcing the intervertebral discs forward.

This causes increased pressure at the posterior lumbar vertebral articulations, which can cause low back pain or, more seriously, articular compression or shearing.

ABDOMEN

1 CRUNCHES*

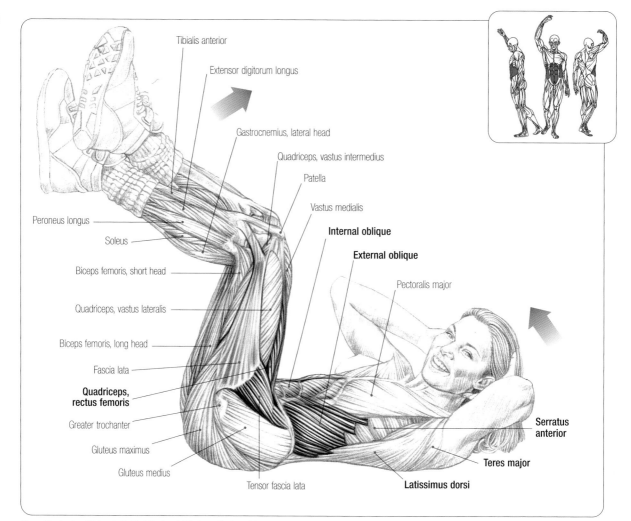

Tibialis anterior
Extensor digitorum longus
Gastrocnemius, lateral head
Quadriceps, vastus intermedius
Patella
Vastus medialis
Internal oblique
External oblique
Pectoralis major
Peroneus longus
Soleus
Biceps femoris, short head
Quadriceps, vastus lateralis
Biceps femoris, long head
Fascia lata
Quadriceps, rectus femoris
Greater trochanter
Gluteus maximus
Gluteus medius
Tensor fascia lata
Latissimus dorsi
Teres major
Serratus anterior

Lie on the back, with hands behind the head, thighs vertical, and knees bent:

• Inhale and raise the shoulders off the ground, bringing the knees and head toward each other by crunching, which means rounding the back and rolling the spine up.
• Exhale at the end of the movement.

This exercise mainly uses the rectus abdominis.

To work the obliques more intensely, bring the right elbow to the left knee, then the left elbow to the right knee alternately with each crunch.

* Perform a crunch by rounding the back and rolling the spine up, bringing the pubis and sternum toward each through voluntary contraction.

1 Begin   2 End

THE MOVEMENT

VARIATION
SEATED CRUNCH ON A BENCH

SIT-UPS 2

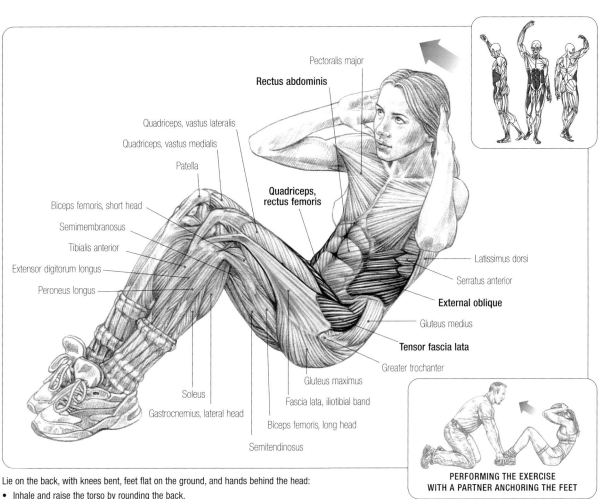

Pectoralis major

Rectus abdominis

Quadriceps, vastus lateralis

Quadriceps, vastus medialis

Patella

Biceps femoris, short head

Semimembranosus

Tibialis anterior

Extensor digitorum longus

Peroneus longus

Quadriceps, rectus femoris

Latissimus dorsi

Serratus anterior

External oblique

Gluteus medius

Tensor fascia lata

Greater trochanter

Gluteus maximus

Fascia lata, iliotibial band

Biceps femoris, long head

Semitendinosus

Soleus

Gastrocnemius, lateral head

Lie on the back, with knees bent, feet flat on the ground, and hands behind the head:

- Inhale and raise the torso by rounding the back.
- Exhale at the end of the movement.
- Return to the initial position without touching the ground.

Continue until a burn develops in the abdominal muscles.

This exercise works the hip flexors as well as the obliques, but it mainly acts on the rectus abdominis.

Variations:

1. Having a partner hold the feet makes the exercise easier.

2. Extending the arms forward makes the exercise easier for beginners.

3. Working on an incline bench makes the exercise more intense.

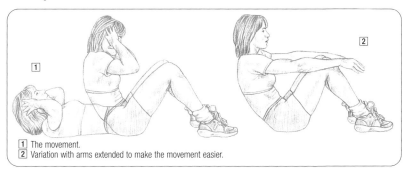

1 The movement.
2 Variation with arms extended to make the movement easier.

PERFORMING THE EXERCISE WITH A PARTNER ANCHORING THE FEET

VARIATION ON AN INCLINE BENCH
The greater the angle, the greater the effort.

Comment: Because, in general, a woman's torso is not as bulky proportionate to the legs as in men, performing sit-ups without lifting the feet off the ground is easier for women than for men.

ABDOMEN

3 GYM LADDER SIT-UPS

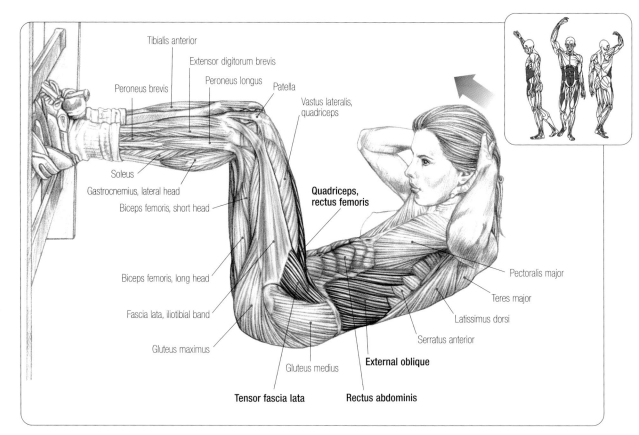

Lie faceup on the ground and position the feet between two bars in the ladder, with the thighs vertical, and hands behind the head:
- Inhale and raise the torso as high as possible, rounding the spine.
- Exhale at the end of the movement.

This exercise works the rectus abdominis and, to a lesser degree, the external oblique.

Position the feet lower on the ladder so that the pelvis can rock more and better contract the flexor muscles of the hip (iliopsoas, rectus femoris, and tensor fascia lata) when lowering the torso.

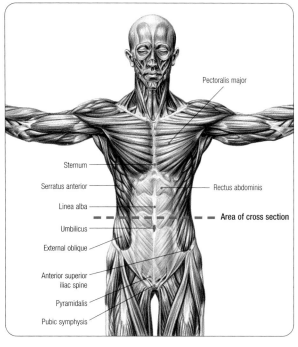

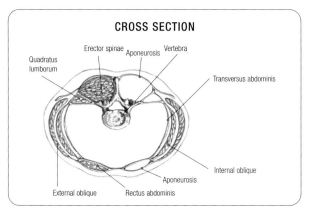

CALVES OVER BENCH SIT-UPS $\boxed{4}$

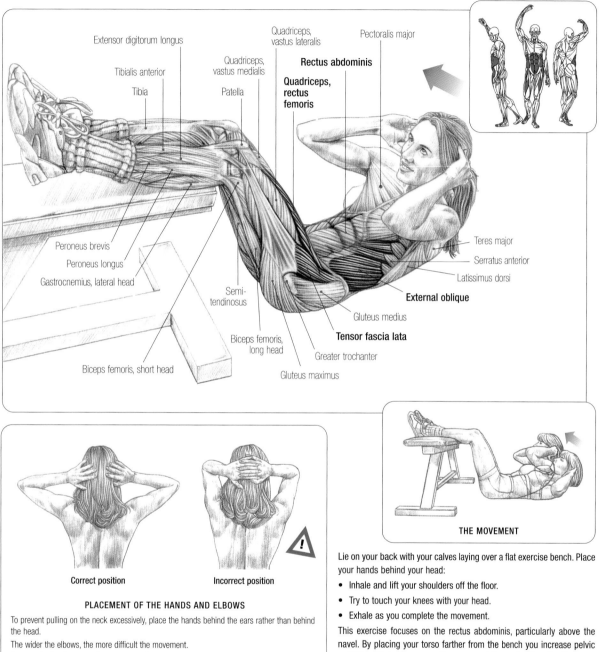

Extensor digitorum longus
Tibialis anterior
Tibia
Quadriceps, vastus medialis
Patella
Quadriceps, vastus lateralis
Rectus abdominis
Quadriceps, rectus femoris
Pectoralis major
Teres major
Serratus anterior
Latissimus dorsi
External oblique
Gluteus medius
Tensor fascia lata
Greater trochanter
Gluteus maximus
Biceps femoris, long head
Semi-tendinosus
Biceps femoris, short head
Gastrocnemius, lateral head
Peroneus longus
Peroneus brevis

Correct position

Incorrect position

PLACEMENT OF THE HANDS AND ELBOWS

To prevent pulling on the neck excessively, place the hands behind the ears rather than behind the head.
The wider the elbows, the more difficult the movement.
Conversely, the closer together and more forward the elbows, the easier the execution.

THE MOVEMENT

Lie on your back with your calves laying over a flat exercise bench. Place your hands behind your head:

- Inhale and lift your shoulders off the floor.
- Try to touch your knees with your head.
- Exhale as you complete the movement.

This exercise focuses on the rectus abdominis, particularly above the navel. By placing your torso farther from the bench you increase pelvic mobility, which allows your torso upward by contracting the iliopsoas, tensor fasciae latae, and rectus femoris in order to flex the hips.

5 INCLINE BENCH SIT-UPS

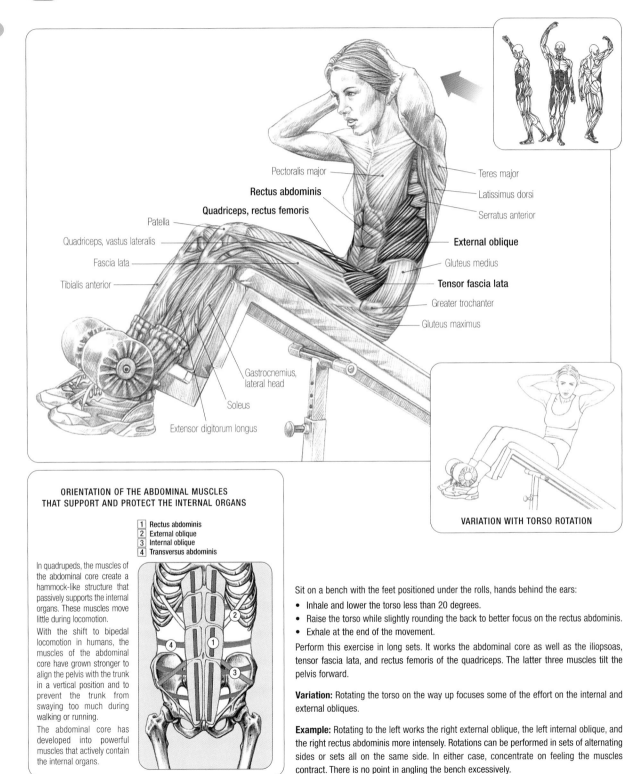

Pectoralis major

Rectus abdominis

Quadriceps, rectus femoris

Patella

Quadriceps, vastus lateralis

Fascia lata

Tibialis anterior

Teres major

Latissimus dorsi

Serratus anterior

External oblique

Gluteus medius

Tensor fascia lata

Greater trochanter

Gluteus maximus

Gastrocnemius, lateral head

Soleus

Extensor digitorum longus

VARIATION WITH TORSO ROTATION

ORIENTATION OF THE ABDOMINAL MUSCLES THAT SUPPORT AND PROTECT THE INTERNAL ORGANS

1 Rectus abdominis
2 External oblique
3 Internal oblique
4 Transversus abdominis

In quadrupeds, the muscles of the abdominal core create a hammock-like structure that passively supports the internal organs. These muscles move little during locomotion.

With the shift to bipedal locomotion in humans, the muscles of the abdominal core have grown stronger to align the pelvis with the trunk in a vertical position and to prevent the trunk from swaying too much during walking or running.

The abdominal core has developed into powerful muscles that actively contain the internal organs.

Sit on a bench with the feet positioned under the rolls, hands behind the ears:

- Inhale and lower the torso less than 20 degrees.
- Raise the torso while slightly rounding the back to better focus on the rectus abdominis.
- Exhale at the end of the movement.

Perform this exercise in long sets. It works the abdominal core as well as the iliopsoas, tensor fascia lata, and rectus femoris of the quadriceps. The latter three muscles tilt the pelvis forward.

Variation: Rotating the torso on the way up focuses some of the effort on the internal and external obliques.

Example: Rotating to the left works the right external oblique, the left internal oblique, and the right rectus abdominis more intensely. Rotations can be performed in sets of alternating sides or sets all on the same side. In either case, concentrate on feeling the muscles contract. There is no point in angling the bench excessively.

SUSPENDED BENCH SIT-UPS 6

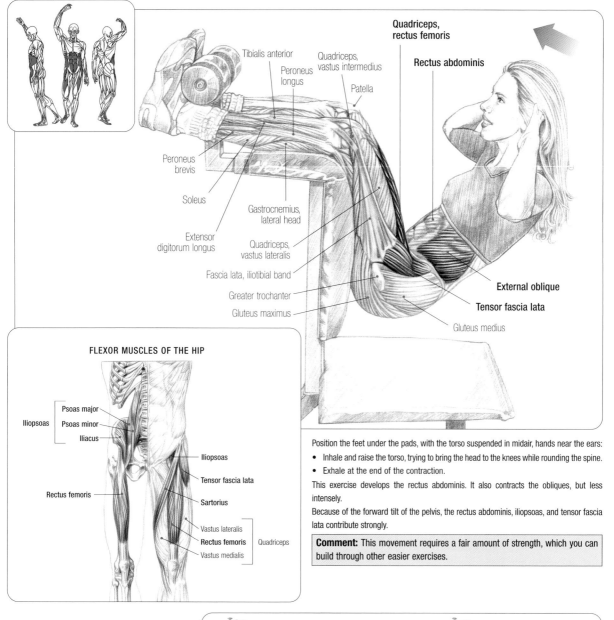

Quadriceps, rectus femoris

Rectus abdominis

Tibialis anterior

Peroneus longus

Quadriceps, vastus intermedius

Patella

Peroneus brevis

Soleus

Gastrocnemius, lateral head

Extensor digitorum longus

Quadriceps, vastus lateralis

Fascia lata, iliotibial band

Greater trochanter

Gluteus maximus

External oblique

Tensor fascia lata

Gluteus medius

FLEXOR MUSCLES OF THE HIP

Iliopsoas

Psoas major

Psoas minor

Iliacus

Iliopsoas

Tensor fascia lata

Rectus femoris

Sartorius

Vastus lateralis

Rectus femoris

Quadriceps

Vastus medialis

Position the feet under the pads, with the torso suspended in midair, hands near the ears:

- Inhale and raise the torso, trying to bring the head to the knees while rounding the spine.
- Exhale at the end of the contraction.

This exercise develops the rectus abdominis. It also contracts the obliques, but less intensely.

Because of the forward tilt of the pelvis, the rectus abdominis, iliopsoas, and tensor fascia lata contribute strongly.

Comment: This movement requires a fair amount of strength, which you can build through other easier exercises.

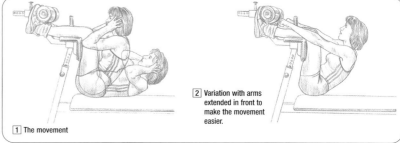

1 The movement

2 Variation with arms extended in front to make the movement easier.

7 HIGH-PULLEY CRUNCHES

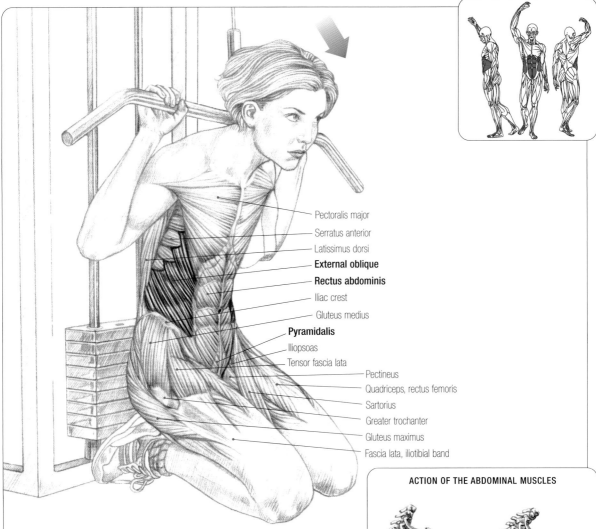

- Pectoralis major
- Serratus anterior
- Latissimus dorsi
- **External oblique**
- **Rectus abdominis**
- Iliac crest
- Gluteus medius
- **Pyramidalis**
- Iliopsoas
- Tensor fascia lata
- Pectineus
- Quadriceps, rectus femoris
- Sartorius
- Greater trochanter
- Gluteus maximus
- Fascia lata, iliotibial band

Kneel in front of the machine, holding the handle behind the neck:

- Inhale.
- Exhale and roll the spine as you lower the sternum toward the pubis.

This movement is never performed with heavy weights. Concentrate on feeling the muscles contract, mainly the rectus abdominis, in order to focus the work on the abdominal core.

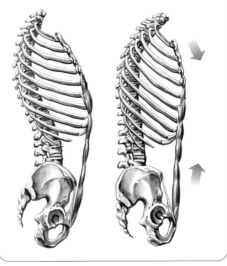

ACTION OF THE ABDOMINAL MUSCLES

MACHINE CRUNCHES 8

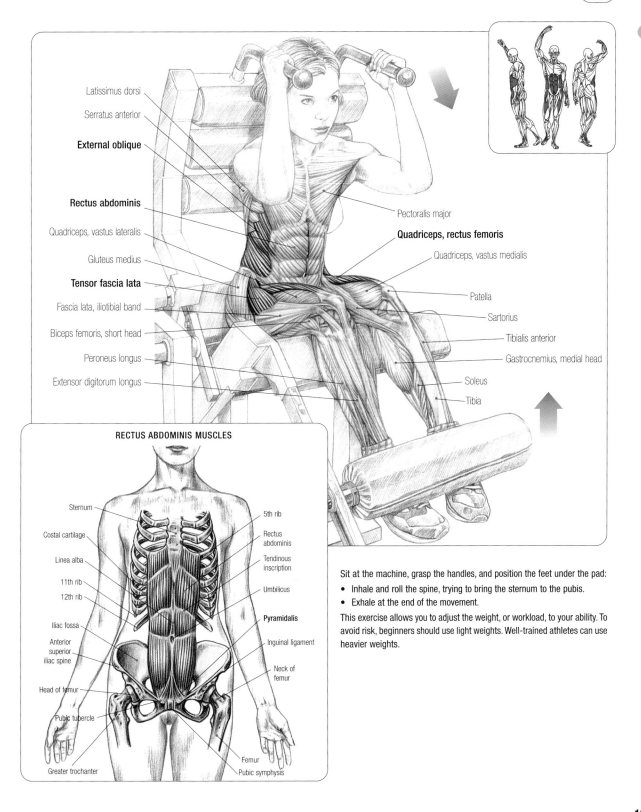

Latissimus dorsi

Serratus anterior

External oblique

Rectus abdominis

Quadriceps, vastus lateralis

Gluteus medius

Tensor fascia lata

Fascia lata, iliotibial band

Biceps femoris, short head

Peroneus longus

Extensor digitorum longus

Pectoralis major

Quadriceps, rectus femoris

Quadriceps, vastus medialis

Patella

Sartorius

Tibialis anterior

Gastrocnemius, medial head

Soleus

Tibia

RECTUS ABDOMINIS MUSCLES

Sternum

Costal cartilage

Linea alba

11th rib

12th rib

Iliac fossa

Anterior superior iliac spine

Head of femur

Pubic tubercle

Greater trochanter

5th rib

Rectus abdominis

Tendinous inscription

Umbilicus

Pyramidalis

Inguinal ligament

Neck of femur

Femur

Pubic symphysis

Sit at the machine, grasp the handles, and position the feet under the pad:

- Inhale and roll the spine, trying to bring the sternum to the pubis.
- Exhale at the end of the movement.

This exercise allows you to adjust the weight, or workload, to your ability. To avoid risk, beginners should use light weights. Well-trained athletes can use heavier weights.

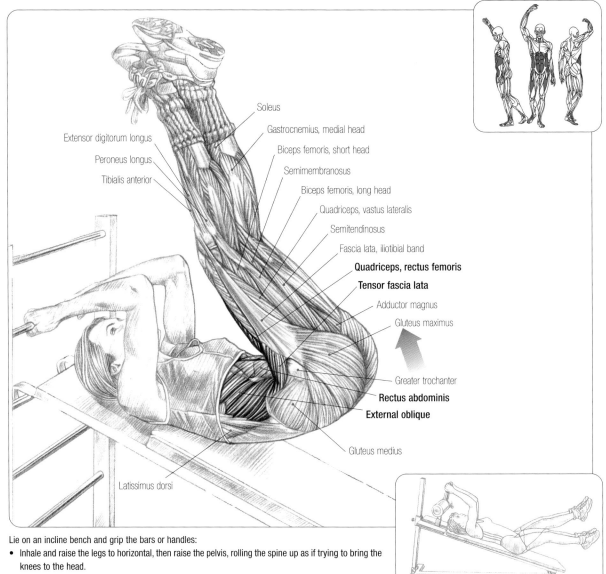

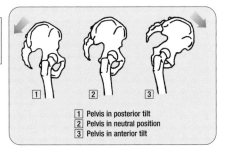

9 INCLINE LEG RAISES

Soleus
Gastrocnemius, medial head
Biceps femoris, short head
Semimembranosus
Biceps femoris, long head
Quadriceps, vastus lateralis
Semitendinosus
Fascia lata, iliotibial band
Quadriceps, rectus femoris
Tensor fascia lata
Adductor magnus
Gluteus maximus
Greater trochanter
Rectus abdominis
External oblique
Gluteus medius

Extensor digitorum longus
Peroneus longus
Tibialis anterior
Latissimus dorsi

VARIATION
Performing leg flutters

Lie on an incline bench and grip the bars or handles:
- Inhale and raise the legs to horizontal, then raise the pelvis, rolling the spine up as if trying to bring the knees to the head.

This exercise first works the iliopsoas, tensor fascia lata, and rectus femoris of the quadriceps when raising the legs. Then it works the abdominal core and contracts mainly the infraumbilical portion of the rectus abdominis when raising the pelvis and rolling up the spine.

Comment: This is an excellent exercise if you have trouble feeling the work on the lower abdominal muscles. Given the difficulty of the exercise, beginners should start with the bench only slightly inclined.

1 Pelvis in posterior tilt
2 Pelvis in neutral position
3 Pelvis in anterior tilt

LEG RAISES 10

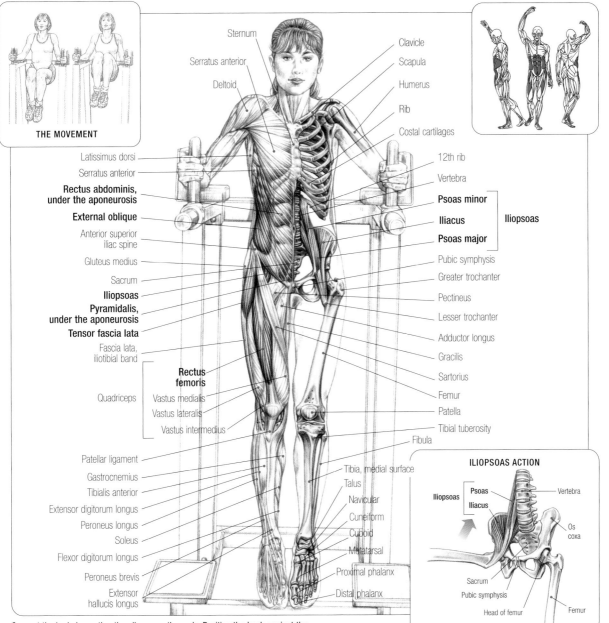

THE MOVEMENT

Sternum
Serratus anterior
Deltoid
Clavicle
Scapula
Humerus
Rib
Costal cartilages

Latissimus dorsi
Serratus anterior
**Rectus abdominis,
under the aponeurosis**
External oblique
Anterior superior
iliac spine
Gluteus medius
Sacrum
Iliopsoas
**Pyramidalis,
under the aponeurosis**
Tensor fascia lata
Fascia lata,
iliotibial band
Quadriceps
**Rectus
femoris**
Vastus medialis
Vastus lateralis
Vastus intermedius

12th rib
Vertebra
Psoas minor
Iliacus   Iliopsoas
Psoas major
Pubic symphysis
Greater trochanter
Pectineus
Lesser trochanter
Adductor longus
Gracilis
Sartorius
Femur
Patella
Tibial tuberosity
Fibula

Patellar ligament
Gastrocnemius
Tibialis anterior
Extensor digitorum longus
Peroneus longus
Soleus
Flexor digitorum longus
Peroneus brevis
Extensor
hallucis longus

Tibia, medial surface
Talus
Navicular
Cuneiform
Cuboid
Metatarsal
Proximal phalanx
Distal phalanx

ILIOPSOAS ACTION

Iliopsoas
Psoas
Iliacus
Vertebra
Os
coxa
Sacrum
Pubic symphysis
Head of femur
Femur

Support the body by resting the elbows on the pads. Position the back against the
back support:

• Inhale and raise the knees to the chest, rounding the back in order to contract the abdominal core.

• Exhale at the end of the movement.

This exercise works the hip flexors, mainly the iliopsoas, and the obliques. It intensely works the lower part of the rectus abdominis.

Variations:

1 To target the lower abdominal muscles, perform small flutters with the legs when rolling up the spine.

2 To make the exercise more intense, extend the legs horizontally. However, this requires flexible hamstrings.

3 Hold the knees to the chest for a few seconds with an isometric contraction.

11 HANGING LEG RAISES

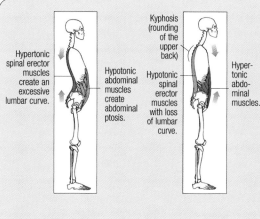

VARIATION
Alternately raising the legs to the left and then to the right side uses the internal and external obliques more intensely.

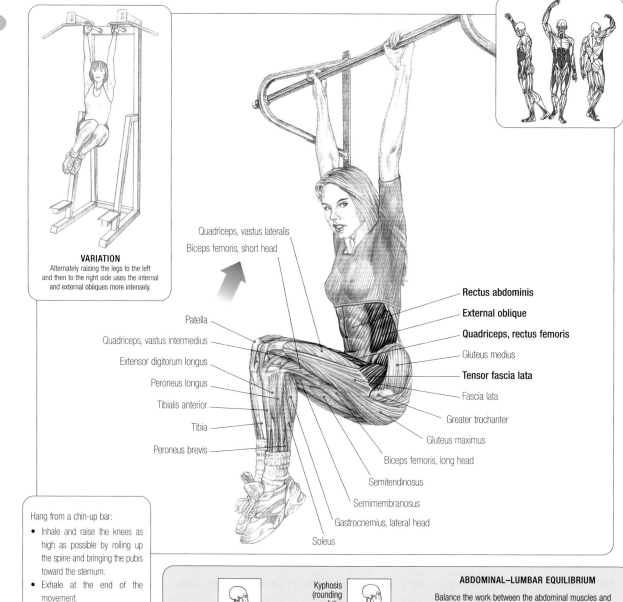

Quadriceps, vastus lateralis

Biceps femoris, short head

Patella

Quadriceps, vastus intermedius

Extensor digitorum longus

Peroneus longus

Tibialis anterior

Tibia

Peroneus brevis

Rectus abdominis

External oblique

Quadriceps, rectus femoris

Gluteus medius

Tensor fascia lata

Fascia lata

Greater trochanter

Gluteus maximus

Biceps femoris, long head

Semitendinosus

Semimembranosus

Gastrocnemius, lateral head

Soleus

Hang from a chin-up bar:

- Inhale and raise the knees as high as possible by rolling up the spine and bringing the pubis toward the sternum.
- Exhale at the end of the movement.

This exercise uses the iliopsoas, rectus femoris, and tensor fascia lata when you raise the legs and the rectus abdominis and, to a lesser degree, the internal and external obliques when you bring the pubis toward the sternum.

Small leg flutters without lowering the knees below horizontal focus the effort on the abdominal core.

Hypertonic spinal erector muscles create an excessive lumbar curve.

Hypotonic abdominal muscles create abdominal ptosis.

Kyphosis (rounding of the upper back)

Hypotonic spinal erector muscles with loss of lumbar curve.

Hypertonic abdominal muscles.

ABDOMINAL–LUMBAR EQUILIBRIUM

Balance the work between the abdominal muscles and the erector muscles of the spine.

Hypotonicity or hypertonicity of either of these muscle groups can lead to poor posture, which over time can cause injury.

Example

Hypertonicity of the lower part of the erector muscles of the spine (lumbosacral mass) associated with hypotonicity of the abdominal muscles leads to hyperlordosis with abdominal ptosis (sagging).

If addressed in time with exercises to strengthen the abdominal core, this postural fault can sometimes be corrected.

Conversely, hypertonic abdominal muscles associated with slack erector muscles, especially in the upper part (spinalis thoracis, longissimus thoracis, iliocostalis thoracis) leads to kyphosis (rounding of the upper back) with loss of the lumbar curve. This postural fault can be corrected with exercises to strengthen the erector muscles of the spine.

BROOMSTICK TWISTS 12

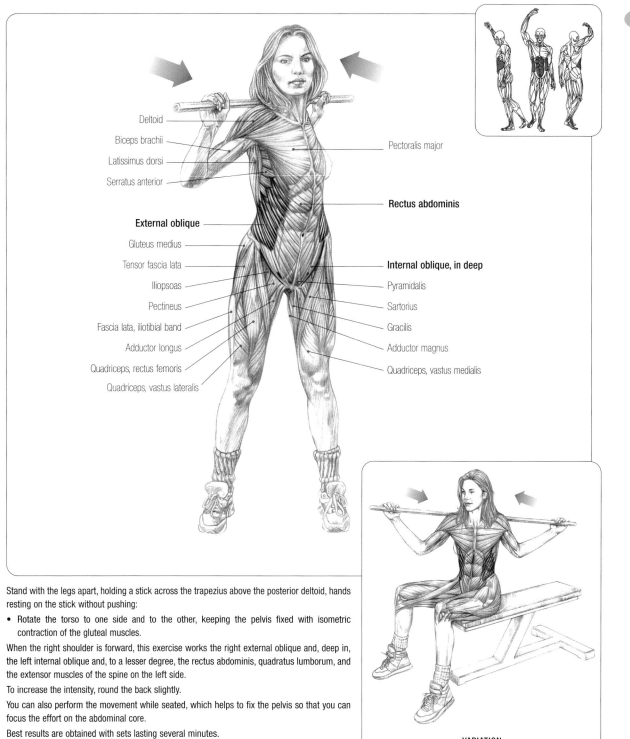

Deltoid

Biceps brachii

Latissimus dorsi

Serratus anterior

Pectoralis major

Rectus abdominis

External oblique

Gluteus medius

Tensor fascia lata

Iliopsoas

Pectineus

Fascia lata, iliotibial band

Adductor longus

Quadriceps, rectus femoris

Quadriceps, vastus lateralis

Internal oblique, in deep

Pyramidalis

Sartorius

Gracilis

Adductor magnus

Quadriceps, vastus medialis

Stand with the legs apart, holding a stick across the trapezius above the posterior deltoid, hands resting on the stick without pushing:

- Rotate the torso to one side and to the other, keeping the pelvis fixed with isometric contraction of the gluteal muscles.

When the right shoulder is forward, this exercise works the right external oblique and, deep in, the left internal oblique and, to a lesser degree, the rectus abdominis, quadratus lumborum, and the extensor muscles of the spine on the left side.

To increase the intensity, round the back slightly.

You can also perform the movement while seated, which helps to fix the pelvis so that you can focus the effort on the abdominal core.

Best results are obtained with sets lasting several minutes.

VARIATION
Seated on a bench.

13 DUMBBELL SIDE BENDS

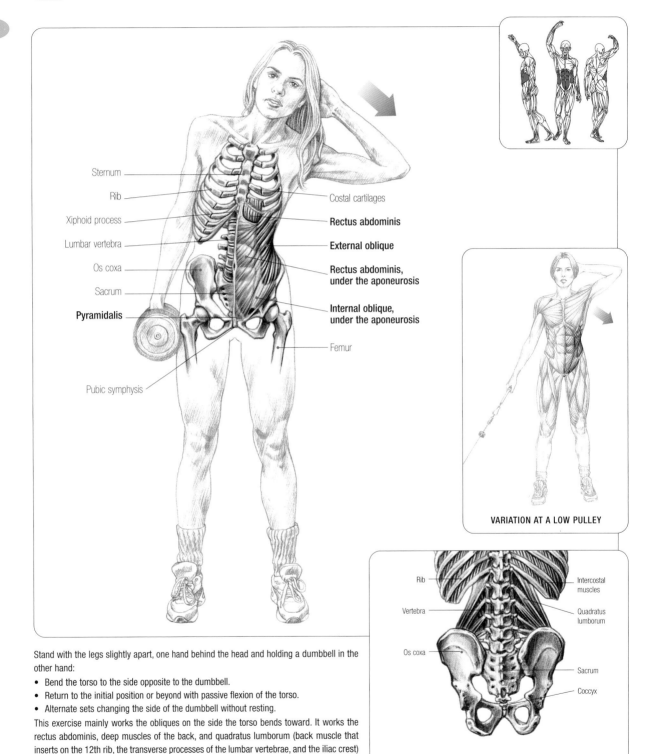

Sternum

Rib

Xiphoid process

Lumbar vertebra

Os coxa

Sacrum

Pyramidalis

Pubic symphysis

Costal cartilages

Rectus abdominis

External oblique

Rectus abdominis, under the aponeurosis

Internal oblique, under the aponeurosis

Femur

VARIATION AT A LOW PULLEY

Rib

Vertebra

Os coxa

Intercostal muscles

Quadratus lumborum

Sacrum

Coccyx

QUADRATUS LUMBORUM MUSCLE

Stand with the legs slightly apart, one hand behind the head and holding a dumbbell in the other hand:

- Bend the torso to the side opposite to the dumbbell.
- Return to the initial position or beyond with passive flexion of the torso.
- Alternate sets changing the side of the dumbbell without resting.

This exercise mainly works the obliques on the side the torso bends toward. It works the rectus abdominis, deep muscles of the back, and quadratus lumborum (back muscle that inserts on the 12th rib, the transverse processes of the lumbar vertebrae, and the iliac crest) less intensely

ROMAN CHAIR SIDE BENDS 14

This exercise is performed on a bench originally designed for lumbar extensions.

Lie on your side with the hip on the bench, torso in the air, hands near the ears or on the chest, and feet positioned under the rolls:

- Raise the side of the body toward the ceiling.

This exercise mainly works the obliques and rectus abdominis on the side that is bending, but the opposite obliques and rectus abdominis are also used in isometric contraction to prevent the torso from lowering below horizontal.

> **Comment:** The quadratus lumborum muscle is always used when bending the torso toward the side.

Pectoralis major
Serratus anterior
Rectus abdominis
External oblique
Internal oblique, under the aponeurosis
Tensor fascia lata
Adductor longus
Quadriceps, rectus femoris
Quadriceps, vastus medialis
Patella
Latissimus dorsi
Pyramidalis
Quadriceps, vastus lateralis
Gluteus medius
Iliopsoas
Pubic symphysis
Sartorius
Pectineus

5th rib
Rectus abdominis
External oblique
12th rib
Lumbar vertebra
Iliac crest
Os coxa
Sacrum
Acetabulum
Anterior superior iliac spine
Inguinal ligament
Pubic tubercle

EXTERNAL OBLIQUE MUSCLE OF THE ABDOMEN

Vertebra, spinous process
Sternum
Rib
Rectus abdominis
Erector spinae, under the aponeurosis
Costal cartilage
Rectus abdominis, under the aponeurosis
Iliac crest
Internal oblique
Os coxa
Sacrum
Anterior superior iliac spine
Inguinal ligament
Ischial tuberosity
Pubic tubercle

INTERNAL OBLIQUE MUSCLE OF THE ABDOMEN

15 MACHINE TRUNK ROTATIONS

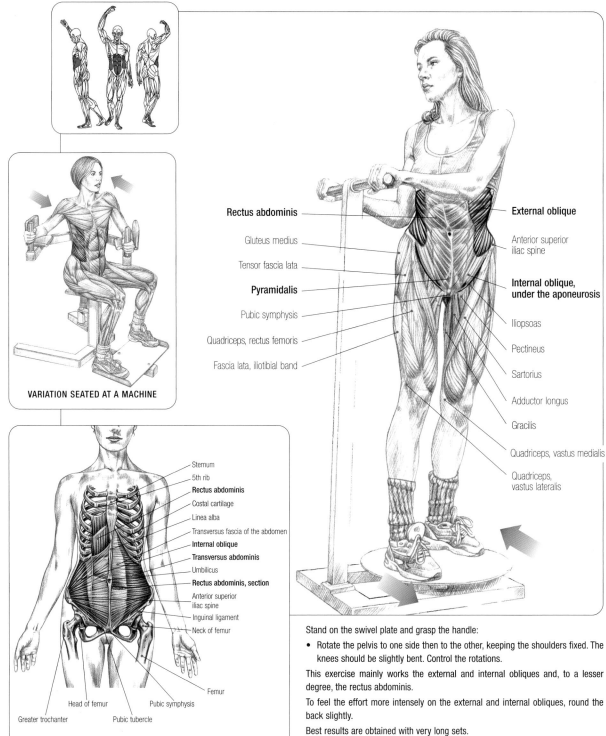

VARIATION SEATED AT A MACHINE

Rectus abdominis

Gluteus medius

Tensor fascia lata

Pyramidalis

Pubic symphysis

Quadriceps, rectus femoris

Fascia lata, iliotibial band

External oblique

Anterior superior
iliac spine

**Internal oblique,
under the aponeurosis**

Iliopsoas

Pectineus

Sartorius

Adductor longus

Gracilis

Quadriceps, vastus medialis

Quadriceps,
vastus lateralis

Sternum

5th rib

Rectus abdominis

Costal cartilage

Linea alba

Transversus fascia of the abdomen

Internal oblique

Transversus abdominis

Umbilicus

Rectus abdominis, section

Anterior superior
iliac spine

Inguinal ligament

Neck of femur

Femur

Head of femur

Pubic symphysis

Greater trochanter

Pubic tubercle

DEEP MUSCLES OF THE ABDOMEN

Stand on the swivel plate and grasp the handle:

- Rotate the pelvis to one side then to the other, keeping the shoulders fixed. The knees should be slightly bent. Control the rotations.

This exercise mainly works the external and internal obliques and, to a lesser degree, the rectus abdominis.

To feel the effort more intensely on the external and internal obliques, round the back slightly.

Best results are obtained with very long sets.